THE George Pine STORY
1891-1972

C000062788

TRENCHES TO TRAMS
THE LIFE OF A BRISTOL TOMMY

BY CLIVE BURLTON

M shed

Supported by Bristol Museums, Galleries and Archives

Dedicated to the memory of my in-laws, Ron and Audrey Pine.

It's a great shame that four of George's five children – Ron Pine, George Pine Jnr, Joan Pymm and Bill Pine have not survived to read their father's story. We hope that Ken Pine, who has been involved from the beginning with advice and support, will enjoy seeing in print the life story of George Pine, DCM.

This edition first published in the UK in June 2011 by Tangent Books
ISBN: 9781906477462

Tangent Books, Unit 5.16, Paintworks, Bristol, BS4 3EH
Phone: 0117 972 0645
Web: www.tangentbooks.co.uk
email: richard@tangentbooks.co.uk

Richard Jones: Publisher
richard@tangentbooks.co.uk
Joe Burt: Design
joe@faragherjones.com
Steve Faragher: Production
steve@faragherjones.com
Jonathan Lewis: Print Management
jonathanlewis.print@googlemail.com
Nicky Johns: Office Manager
nicky@tangentbooks.co.uk

Acknowledgements

With grateful thanks to
Members of the Pine Family for their help and support, and for providing
dozens of objects and photographs. In particular:
Ken and Shirley Pine, Eileen Pine, John and Fran Pine, Robin and Jennie
Pine – and to Alison, Tom and Holly for bearing with me over the last
decade or so.

To those, now sadly departed, who provided early help, support and
encouragement
Joan Pymm
Veronica Smith
Margaret MacMillan who painstakingly typed George's manuscript.

To the following individuals and organisations who have played their
part in enabling me to complete the George Pine Story

Roger Angerson, Julienne Belford, Gail Boyle, Alison Brown,
Richard Burley, Joe Burt, Christine Cavanagh, Matt Coles, Mike and
Wendy Cross, Peter Davey, Dominiek Dendooven, Christine Day, Stuart
Eastwood, David Emeney, Richard van Emden, Martin Everett, Steve
Faragher, Sue Giles, Graham Gordon, Simon Harding, Mac Hawkins, Rick
Hutchinson, Mike Jay, Nicky Johns, Richard Jones, John and Barbara
Lawson-Reay, Anthony Lewis, Jonathan Lewis, Margaret McGregor, Dean
Marks, Anthony Palmer, John Penny, Luke Pomeroy, Martin Powell, David
Read, Valerie Roberts, Talei Rounds, Claude Roussel, Francis de Simpel,
Maria Six, William Smith, Andy Stevens (Pastimes), Terry Storrier, George
Streatfeild, Sarah Taylor, Graham Tratt, Annick Vandenbilcke, Kenneth
Wakefield, Dr Michael Walker, Phillip Walker, Geoff Wilcock,
David Williams, John Williams

Bristol City Museum and Art Gallery
Bristol Record Office
Bristol Reference Library
Crookwell & District Historical Society, NSW, Australia
Crookwell Shire Council, NSW, Australia
Empica Limited
Faragher Jones
Fishponds Local History Society, Bristol
Glenside Hospital Museum, Bristol
In Flanders Fields Museum, Documentatiecentrum, Ypres, Belgium
King's Own Royal Border Regiment Museum, Carlisle
La Societe d'Histoire de Comines-Warneton, Belgium
Lady Forester Community Nursing Home, Much Wenlock
Little Baddow History Centre, Essex
M Shed
Trustees of Bristol Charities
The Soldiers of Gloucestershire Museum, Gloucester
South Wales Borderers Museum, Brecon
Tangent Books
The Vittoria

And, thank you to Wessex Water and The Society of Merchant Venturers

Contents

Foreword by John Pine

Think of a traditional Father Christmas; take away the beard so that you can see a beaming smile and a pair of glasses; remove the hat to reveal a slightly balding head; and replace the tunic to display a cardigan, always buttoned. Now you have a picture of how my grandfather, George Pine, appeared to me as a child.

George was not a well-educated man, few of his generation were, but he had the most incredible memory and could tell a wonderful, gripping story. He could remember 50 or 60 years ago as if it were yesterday. Later on in life George lived at an elderly persons' home in Southmead, Bristol. The whole Pine family used to visit him as often as we could, including me and my wife Fran. He would suspend his self-appointed role of organising all the residents (a legacy of his Sergeant Major training) and after a little prompting, sit down to retell some of his stories, still wearing a cardigan with buttons up the front.

We thought that these stories were so interesting that in early 1972 we asked him to write them down. What follows are the memories that George recorded. The account you can now read probably contains less than half of the details that George could remember. Fran and I were hoping to read his account and visit him to record any missing details, but he wanted to finish the whole story before we read it. Unfortunately, he never did quite finish.

George might not have had academic qualifications but he had qualities of which I am tremendously proud and which he passed on to his children. These qualities were resourcefulness, a fierce determination to always do your best, perseverance despite the difficulties and a deep loyalty to, and love of, family.

I am very grateful to my brother-in-law, who has demonstrated these same qualities in expanding on over 40,000 words of George's handwritten memories. Clive has worked tirelessly, following up every conceivable lead, filling in many gaps and expanding upon George's recollections. He has trawled through thousands of photographs and documents, delved in numerous public and private archives in the UK and abroad and visited France and Belgium, with friends and family, to follow George's story.

I recall one such visit to France. On one page in George's handwritten account he drew a map of the German and British front lines. We were astonished to find that the map was uncannily accurate with the buildings and general terrain still there some 90 years later. I am sure this was just one of the discoveries that led Clive to spend so much time in researching and producing *Trenches to Trams*. He has transformed George's handwritten pages from a family history to something much broader; touching on the First World War, Bristol Tramways & Carriage Company, Bristol in the Second World War and a slice of Bristol social history from the 19th and 20th Centuries.

The heart of George's story is that of an ordinary Bristol Tommy who showed great courage, bravery and pluck in extraordinary times. Being the modest man he was, he would wish the readers of *Trenches to Trams* to consider it as a tribute to his generation and to a remarkable group of people – his comrades and colleagues – whose stories of heroism and sacrifice may never be told.

About the Author

Born in Bristol in 1958, Clive Burlton's interest in history was inspired by Anton Bantock, MBE whilst a pupil at Bedminster Down Secondary School. Although Clive had an opportunity to further his interest in history when offered a place at Teacher Training College, Clive chose instead to pursue a career with Wessex Water whom he joined as a Business Studies Trainee in 1977.

Clive became the company's first Investor Relations Manager when the industry was privatised in 1989 and he went on to head the Human Resources function in the mid 1990s. In 2000, he decided to pursue a consultancy career and has managed projects across several disciplines and business sectors in the UK and overseas. After a successful corporate and consultancy career, Clive is now re-connecting with his interest in Bristol history.

He first read George Pine's manuscript in the 1980s and he contacted M Shed with his grandfather-in-law's manuscript in 2007 following an appeal for Bristol stories for use within the new museum. Shortly afterwards, Clive volunteered to help the Museums Service and since 2008, he has been helping to digitise, catalogue and make available for viewing the extensive Film Archive held by Bristol Record Office.

Clive is a member of the Chartered Institute of Public Relations, a member of the Friends of Bristol Museums, Galleries and Archives and a Friend of the Soldiers of Gloucestershire Museum.

Introduction

I first read George Pine's manuscript in the early 1980s when I borrowed it from my brother-in-law, John Pine. I was fascinated with the account of George's life and what his generation had endured. My grandparents also lived through the same times and my grandfathers – Stanley Barnes and Hermon Burlton – also fought in the First World War.

My interest in history stems from the teachings of Anton Bantock, MBE at Bedminster Down Secondary School, Bristol. An absolute legend, Anton had a terrific ability to enthuse his pupils and through his practical 'Looking for History' course we were encouraged to delve into subjects and find out things for ourselves.

I have always been a 'people person' and have followed this thread throughout my career where I have worked in a number of personnel management roles and headed the function at two businesses. My interest in history and what makes people tick have come together in *Trenches to Trams*.

When I read George's manuscript I promised myself that one day I would do something with it. The opportunity to make a start came in early 2000 when I was between jobs and had some time on my hands. I wanted to put something together for my father-in-law, Ron Pine, who was a lovely man. Sadly, before I could tell Ron what I was planning to do, he died. Ron had many of George's qualities and his passing made me even more determined to help tell his father's story and to do it justice.

Serendipity has played a huge part in piecing together George's life and adding depth and understanding to his words, his experiences and what was going on around him. The discovery of his 'lost' First World War Medals and of photographs of George in attics and museum cupboards were early examples of lucky finds. In 2004, the trunk that belonged to George's sister – left undisturbed and forgotten in a family wardrobe for 30 years – saw the light of day again. 'Edith's Trunk' contained over 100 items and almost all of the material that I needed to fill in the many gaps in George's recollections.

Just a few days before the publisher's deadline, I accidently came across scrapbooks that were kept by two of Bristol's former Lord Mayors as mementoes of their periods in office. They each contained more relevant photographs and documents.

Along with the chance findings that have helped to illustrate George's words, I have read many books and journals, researched War Diaries, visited dozens of archives in the UK and overseas and pored over the records of Bristol companies including the Bristol Tramways and Carriage Company.

I have carefully edited George's words so they are in chronological order and I have added Author's Notes to amplify and contextualise his experiences.

Trenches to Trams is George Pine's story. It has been an honour to help tell it.

Clive Burlton

Prelude
23rd February 1972

At the age of 80 years old I have been requested to write my memoirs. A suggestion made by a grandson at the age of 21, and me past 80. But he was so intent and brought me in the material to carry on. I trust that my grandchildren, who would sometimes listen in conversation to some little story of mine, will be interested and their children also.

It's a pity rather that I never kept a diary or memorandum that I could put all these happenings in their proper order. I could have had the help of a few records I have put away in the archives, such as my birth certificate, and army discharge papers. I will try to make it as interesting as possible for those who read these pages.

I very often wondered how I survived all these happenings. What sort of show I have made of it I leave you to judge, but when you do read it, just remember it was the head of the Pine family that has been knocked about a bit, and the Pine family still growing strong. Five children – married, five in-laws. Eleven grand children, four married, four in-laws, and four great grand children. What a proud man I should be, and the wife if she had been alive.

So I must start from the time and age when I was old enough to sit up and take notice of what was going on around me. So that would be, I should say, when I was three years old, 9th November 1894.

Now, to make a start…

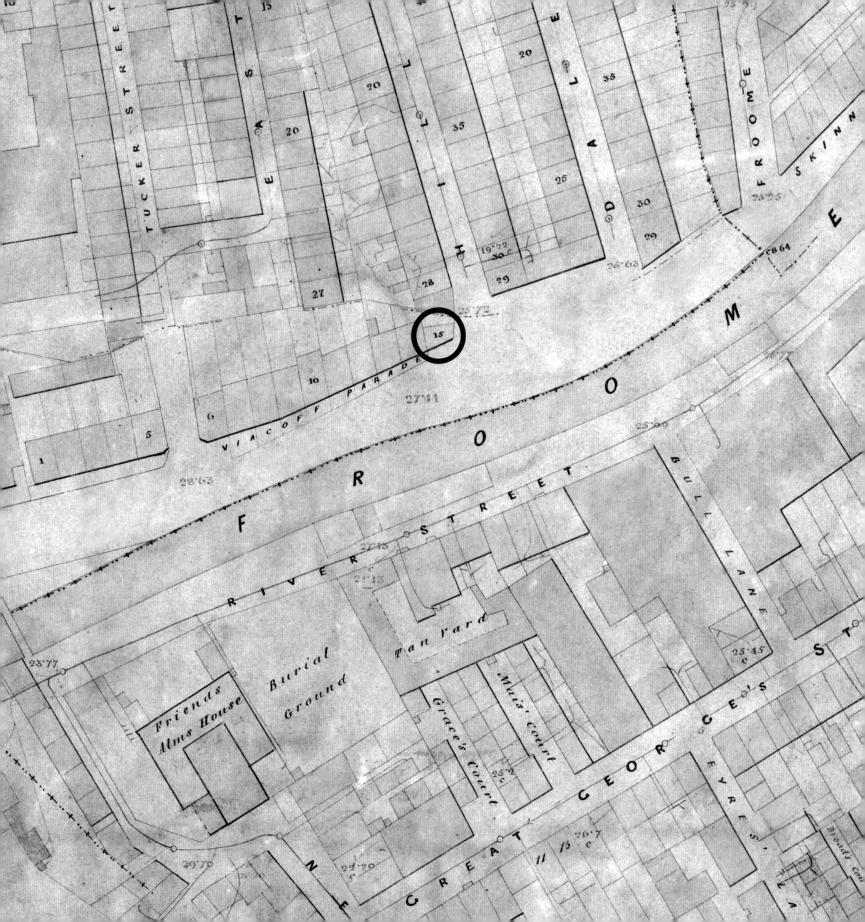

Chapter 1
Easton Hardship and Victorian School Days
1891–1905

I was born somewhere near Bristol Castle on 9th November 1891, the same day as King Edward the VII's birthday – so when the Union Jack was hoisted to commemorate his birthday it marked mine as well. I took that as an honour for me and I used to get a leg pulling.

My mother died when I was just over 12 months old – when my younger brother Tom was born. I cannot remember my mother. There were five in our family, one girl, Edith, four boys, Fred, Harry, George, Tom. Someone must have cared for my brother, Tom. I believe it was my Granny Hall, which was my mother's maiden name. When life started for us we moved to Lower Easton, Charles Street, and then to Bellevue Road. There must have been about 12 month's difference in our ages and we must have been taken care of by our relations as we never saw much of our Dad. I can remember I used to cry a lot and my sister and older brothers did sing "Cry baby Bunting, Daddy's gone a-hunting, Gone to fetch a rabbit skin, To wrap poor baby Bunting in."

My father married again. So we had a new step-mother, which I am sorry to say did not go down very well for us – especially my sister Edie. I never asked my sister about our early days and she left school at the age of 14 and went into service.

Along came the new family to make matters worse. Naturally the step-mother cared more for her children and my father was very strict. We were always in trouble and we used to get the belt for any wrong-doing. The years went on and the rest of my older brothers left school and left home. Fred went down to South Wales to work in the pits. Harry followed him, so that left me and Tom. I felt sorry

George was born at 15 Viacoff Parade, The Ropewalk, in the Parish of St Peter – shown here on the 1874 Ashmead Map of Bristol. The parade of houses was built between 1852 and 1855. Flowing parallel with Viacoff Parade was the River Frome and on the opposite bank was River Street. This stretch of the River Frome was culverted in the early 1920s. Although River Street still remains today, the house in which George was born is now the site of the Cabot Circus Shopping Centre Car Park. *(Bristol Record Office)*

A typical street scene from Grosvenor Road, St Paul's, Bristol in the early 1900s. *(Vaughan Collection at Bristol Record Office)*

for Tom, he could not rough it like me and I used to shield him when any trouble occurred. The new family was growing and my father worked at a boot and shoe factory and they did do a lot of short-time, no work. With that and a growing family the going was rough with regards to food and clothing in our school days.

We of the first family were getting to school age and a new school had just opened, Greenbank, now named Whitefield School, opened in 1896, so there was four of us ready to go there – Tom was not quite old enough.

The school has been well patronised by the Pine family for there has been one or two on the register ever since. At the present time there is one, and I am afraid in four years' time he will finish and that will be the last. So that was a record, 1896 to 1976.

School was five minutes away so that took us no time to get there and we could hear the school bell tolling. The struggle was getting poshed-up, lining up for the wash basin, then breakfast – porridge, a round of bread, marge or dripping – we used to eat that on the way to school. The cane if we were late. The step family were growing up and going to school. Seven of them, us five made twelve, so it was a house-full. We used to sleep five boys in one bedroom but we were tough. We used to get into trouble after school going to the orchards after apples and pears – get caught by the market gardener, and he was at the school next day. Six cuts with the cane. No good saying anything at home or we would get worse from my father, but take things on the whole we weren't too bad.

Perhaps I used to stop in the playground at 12 mid-day playing football and forfeit my dinner. When I got home 4pm, up to bed until your father comes home from work 7pm. Tom used to smuggle me up a slice of bread and marge, or I might come down to go to the toilet. Their mother was or might be in a few doors below, gossiping, as long as the other young-un never saw me, and when my father came home from work he was too tired to bother about me.

I had some good times in my school days, not a very good scholar, but did always seem to get a good report, and my general health was good so that I always had a good attendance record. Saturdays, no school but we were allotted different jobs to do. My job was to clean a big kitchen grate with 'Lion' grate polish. Over each side of the fire all cooking was done here. Sunday joint was on a tripod going around and around, meat dish underneath, no gas. At night a big oil lamp on the table and never had a spill, thank God. I used to make that grate come up lovely, just like a piece of black velvet. Another job was spoons, knives and forks, with scouring brick, and they were inspected when I finished.

Whilst I was in the Infants, Queen Victoria celebrated her Diamond Jubilee. We all had a day's holiday but went up to the school for a lovely tea party, a mug and a sixpence. Those tables looked lovely, plenty to eat, and we did.

Every Sunday I used to go to Sunday school and get my red star on my attendance card, and a good one meant a free ticket to Weston when the Sunday school went on their Annual Outing. We used to go by train sometimes and four-horse breaks other times. At day school I used to like the hour physical drill and section drill in the playground. I was always picked as a section commander, and would give orders to the section. I could shout loud, that's why the teacher picked me and it came in useful for me in later years.

Easter Monday we did go with the Sunday school

A typical group of Easton school children in Owen Street in the early 1900s
(Veronica Smith)

Sunday School outing at Frenchay Tea Gardens in the early 1900s
(Vaughan Collection at Bristol Record Office)

Eastville Park early 1900s *(Vaughan Collection at Bristol Record Office)*

Stapleton Road in the early 1900s. No cars here. (Vaughan Collection at Bristol Record Office)

The operation of the pit cages could be heard in Bellevue Road in the early 1900s. In 1896, eight colliery workers were killed in a gas explosion. The legendary cricketer Dr W G Grace attended to the injured. The mine was abandoned in 1911. *(Cornwell Collection at Bristol Record Office)*

hour's walk. A good soak at home were out of the question, but we looked forward to it and we were both proud when we could swim the length of the baths. Another thing we used to do, a penny to spare, hire a bike for an hour from the bicycle shop and learn to ride. In those days the means of transport were bikes, trams and trains. No motor cars then.

Bellevue Road was busy with horse-drawn traffic. Big tankers drawn by two heavy horses used to pass by every half hour going to the gas works at Eastville. They were collecting the tar that came out the coal making the coke, and other chemicals for Butlers at the Netham, over the other side the River Avon at Brislington. I believe they are now the I.C.I. at Avonmouth. Cows used to be driven to the Cattle Market at Crews Hole from the farms around Stapleton, Frenchay and around about. Save going through the main roads.

This was allowed in those days but later years forbidden. I remember playing with my brother, Tom, and we were out in the front of the house, the passage goes straight through to the pavement. He was running through the passage from me one day, right out into the road he went, got knocked down by a pony cart that was passing at the time.

Luckily he was not hurt very much, but it frightened me, and I was in trouble again. My father put a wooden gate up to stop the younger children from going out. In those days there was always something happening. Such as neighbours quarrelling or something the children had done. Or some of the fathers would have too much to drink along the Greenbank Hotel and there might be a fight. One particular family had sons that were merchant seamen. They were always in trouble when they were home. Then there was an old fellow – always tipsy – that always got out a penny farthing bicycle and tried to ride it down the street, much to the amusement of us children. And there was plenty about as most

for rambles through the fields to Frenchay Tea Gardens. Was all right if the weather was good. August and Whitsun we went to Purdown or Eastville Park. There was no lake there in those days, so no paddle boats – that was built in later days. Me and Tom used to take our towel and soap early every Sunday morning to the open air swimming bath. Good wash and a swim of course.

That was summer time. Barton Hill was the nearest enclosed baths, about half

DEEP END
DANGEROUS TO NON-SWIMMERS

OPEN AIR SWIMMING BATH, EASTVILLE PARK.

The open air pool where George and Tom swam and had a wash to avoid the overcrowding at home. (Vaughan Collection at Bristol Record Office)

families were large ones. Perhaps the Fire Brigade and Ambulance would put in an appearance – horse drawn, galloping, bells clanging, that would fetch the children out. There was a grocers shop opposite us in Bellevue Road and they used to let out the hand carts, big and small, for doing jobs. Small ones to get coal and coke.

We had a coal pit quite close to us and whilst we were in bed and the wind blowing our way we used to hear the cages drawn up and down and the trains at Stapleton Road Station.

The Welshmen came to Bristol for I learnt there was not much amusement for them at Cardiff, Swansea, Newport, etc and probably their football team was playing here at Eastville and waiting for their train to take them home, their singing was beautiful. They were the attraction for the Bristol

girls. This usually happened Saturday evenings and nights.

I was growing older, and Saturdays and summer nights I was always handy to do a job for a neighbour. 3d or 6d, take it home, give it up to keep the home going, and proud to do it too. As I grew up, Saturday mornings about 8.30am I used to go over the gas works or coke house with a hand cart and a sack for a cwt of coke to burn on the fire. It cost 6d a cwt in those days, 1p for the hire of the hand cart. I never liked those trips because we had to queue up and when the whistle went 9am one mad rush for the ticket office, get a ticket with your 6d then find out where they were serving up the coke. It was

An Elmgrove Dairy pony and cart (circa 1900) belonging to Reuben John Watkins, 123 Bannerman Road, Lower Easton. *(Vaughan Collection at Bristol Record Office)*

interesting to watch the men pull the red hot coke out of the ovens with long scrapers, damp it down with water then fill the ovens with small coal again. Get a good warm in the sheds during the winter.

I used to go over the Rovers ground, call in the sweet shop first, put on a peak cap marked Fry's, and a tray in front with packets of chocolate, watch the match and get commission on how much business I had done, take it home and put it on the table.

I always felt I was doing my bit to help for my keep. Banana boats used to come in to the Bristol Docks and a fruit shop at Eastville did always have a big supply. They did have a lot of overripe ones. Get quite a load for 6d. They never lasted long, was soon

scoffed up by so many hungry mouths, spread on a round of bread.

Me and my brother, Tom, before every Easter we used to go around getting orders for hot cross buns and rolls. I did borrow a big nice white butter basket and the wicker washing basket. Had to borrow the money and order the buns and rolls at the bakery on the Thursday evening, and leave the baskets. Up at 5.30am Good Friday morning, get the goods and away to go around the houses. It was excitement for us and the children at the houses when we called.

With a bit of luck we did get about 10/- profit. All went to buy us some clothes for it was nothing to have a big patch in the seat of our knickers. One Good Friday I ordered too many, had a lot over come breakfast time after being out since 6am. "One a penny, two a penny, Hot Cross Buns" (our cry). There was a lot of football being played Good Friday at Eastville Park, so me and Tom went out there with the buns and rolls and got rid of them in no time, and could have sold more. Anything to earn a few coppers, and those were the days. At Christmas time we used to trim ourselves up, make a coat and trousers (long) out of flour bags (white) split open and washed. Sew bells down the side of the seams and the coat sleeves, and make colour paper rosettes and sew them on and make tall hats out of cardboard. Then attach paper trimmings. About four of us boys in the road did go out with a lantern singing Christmas Carols. Finish up by knocking at the door saying, "You in there, we're out here. God knows where we shall be next year. We wish you a Merry Christmas." We used to do well when we shared out the coppers.

My father was a tenor horn player in one of the best brass bands in the West Country, named the Victoria Silver Prize Band. At that time there was two Volunteer Regiments in the city, one called the Bristol Rifles and the other the 3rd Volunteer Battalion Gloucestershire Regt.

The latter had no Band which had to be kept up by the Officers. No Government grant. Most of the men were recruited from the local firm of Mardons, so the officers got Dad's Band to come and join the Gloucesters at St Michaels Hill. This was 1904 near enough. I still have a large photo of the Band in their khaki uniform with forage caps, but they also had slouch hats turned up one side with a plume of black feathers. They were nicknamed the Mardon Cock Fowls. The Band won first prize at a band contest at Bellevue Manchester and got eleventh in the brass band contest at Crystal Palace, London, against such crack bands as The Black Dyke Mills Band, and the Besses o' th' Barn Brass Band.

They used to go to engagements - flower shows, fetes, carnivals and such like that did earn him a bit of money. He wanted me to take it up, which I did. He bought me a cheap cornet, 12/6, so I had to get on with it which needed a lot of concentration, not only the instrument but to learn to read music. I was getting on fairly well, used to go to practice twice a week, and at home. My father came home from work one night, found me out street-beating, called me in, accused me of lack of interest and took the instrument away, and that was that. His word was law. It upset me a bit but I got over it. Perhaps complaints had been made for the noise I made, but it has often entered my mind what a mistake I made in later years – when I joined the Forces.

When they turned the 3rd Volunteer Battalion into the Territorials in 1908 Dad had finished and I had joined at 16½ years old as a bugler. I will leave that for a moment…

The Pine family's soccer allegiance lay on the 'north side of the river' given their Easton roots. When George, his father and brother Harry first followed the team they were known as Eastville Rovers – their name changing to Bristol Rovers just six weeks after this 3-2 Boxing Day home defeat to Bristol St.George, played in front of a crowd of 14,897.
(Vaughan Collection at Bristol Record Office)

In doleful Memory
OF
EASTVILLE ROVERS
Who was beaten by St. George,
On MONDAY, DECEMBER 26th, 1898.
✠

When the "Eastville Rovers" gets home this evening, oh! what a change there'll be ;
Instead of a Champagne Supper some sorrowful faces you'll see.
They were all topsy turvy all through the game ;
They would much rather go to Klondyke than be beaten by the "Saints" again.
Lost for now, but not for ever.

COLSTON HALL, BRISTOL,

SATURDAY, DECEMBER 14, 1895.

Programme of AFTERNOON CONCERT by the Celebrated

BESSES=O'=TH'=BARN BAND

(Conductor - Mr. ALEXANDER OWEN).

THIS BAND IS UNDOUBTEDLY THE

CHAMPION PRIZE BAND OF GREAT BRITAIN.

AN UNPRECEDENTED RECORD

From 1884 to 1894. They have competed in 125 CONTESTS against all the Leading Bands of the United Kingdom, with the following results :—

☞ 88 First Prizes, 52 Special, and 34 other Prizes.
TOTAL VALUE OF PRIZES, £4,000.

Geo. Gordon & Son, Typ, Bristol.

Poster advertising the Besses o' th' Barn Band concert at the Colston Hall in 1895. It was the band's first time in Bristol and it played two concerts – one in the afternoon and one in the evening. The Bristol Victoria Silver Prize Band did well to compete with 'Besses' who, by 1903, were National Champions. The Band still plays today. *(The Vittoria, the only real pub on Whiteladies Road, Bristol)*

At Stapleton Road Station my father kept fowls and when a hen became broody she was put in a special pen, to sit on a dozen eggs until the chickens were hatched and when they got fat enough for the table we had chicken for Sunday dinner. Butcher shops used to keep open until late Saturday nights and likely to get a cheap joint. Our Sunday breakfast was salt fish from Newfoundland (tea fish) – we called it Toe Rag. Had to be trimmed, scraped the scales off, cut into pieces and soaked overnight, then boiled Sunday morning.

That used to be my job, watch it boil up and scum off. On my father's side we had three aunties. We used to visit them Sunday mornings, me and Tom. I can remember going to one of my uncle's funeral on a Sunday at Avonvale Cemetery. They opened the Cemetery Sundays for burials then. On the Saturday night before, me and a pal went in a boxing booth watching the boxers parading before the crowd and the bloke doing all the shouting had pairs of boxing gloves in his hand throwing to a likely one that would go in the ring for three rounds, and I, fool like, caught a pair. I never knew until my pal said you got to go in the ring. Well I did, but I never let the side down. Come Sunday, day of the funeral I had a lovely black eye (I was well in mourning).

My father also kept a garden and one of my jobs was to go out armed with bucket and shovel to collect horse dung as there was plenty of horse traffic in those days. One day he was out looking at the garden where he had a lovely strawberry patch. I heard a shout, "George!" a proper Sergeant Major Roar. I must have inherited it from him. Out I came, trembling in my boots. I had been out there before eating an orange and threw the peel on the strawberry patch. Pointed the orange peel out to me, "You did that?", "Yes, Dad".
He said don't look so frightened, he picked up the orange peel and showed me, it was full of slugs attracted from the strawberries to the orange peel. So my job was to put more orange peel on the garden. It saved him the trouble of a back aching job of picking off the slugs from the plants. A simple discovery made by an untidy act I had done, so my father told me. One up for me and we were both pleased about it.

Whenever me and Tom went out of a Sunday with Dad we had to walk tall, upright, arms swinging and no scuffing of feet, and if spoken to by people to be polite and answer properly.

The grocer shop opposite used to fetch their truck

With Every Good Wish

X'MAS · 1905

SKATING ON DUCHESS'S POND STAPLETON

PINSOCK BROS BRISTOL. S15

and carts from a shed opposite us and take them around the side window on a piece of ground off the pavement in Washington Avenue. Just before closing time I used to go over, "Take your carts in the shed Mr Moss?" Earn a big bag of broken biscuits.

All was shared. Along the Post Office they kept a big grocery business and every so often they opened a soup kitchen with cuttings from the bacon and bones from the butchers on the other corner.

I was on it when the time came with a great big jug, anything to keep out the cold winter times, and we used to get some hard ones too, more so than at the present. Plenty of snow falls, hard frosts. Roads were very difficult for the horse traffic, very often

Skating on a frozen Duchess Pond, Stapleton – Christmas 1905. *(Vaughan Collection at Bristol Record Office)*

down they would go and the heavy one had to be kept down, unharnessed and the shafts drawn back before he could get up. Always a group of children gathered, until the Police arrived. The poor horse might have both knees cut and lame. The River Frome close by flooded and the fields around the Gas Works were covered with water which froze and there was plenty of safe skating. The Rovers Ground came in for the same treatment. The Pond at Stapleton as well, a few weeks of hard frost and skating on it, but it was deep, and the Police was always there to warn the people of any danger. Of course we had to ask for permission to go out to the places but by the fire was the best place if we had a chance to get there.

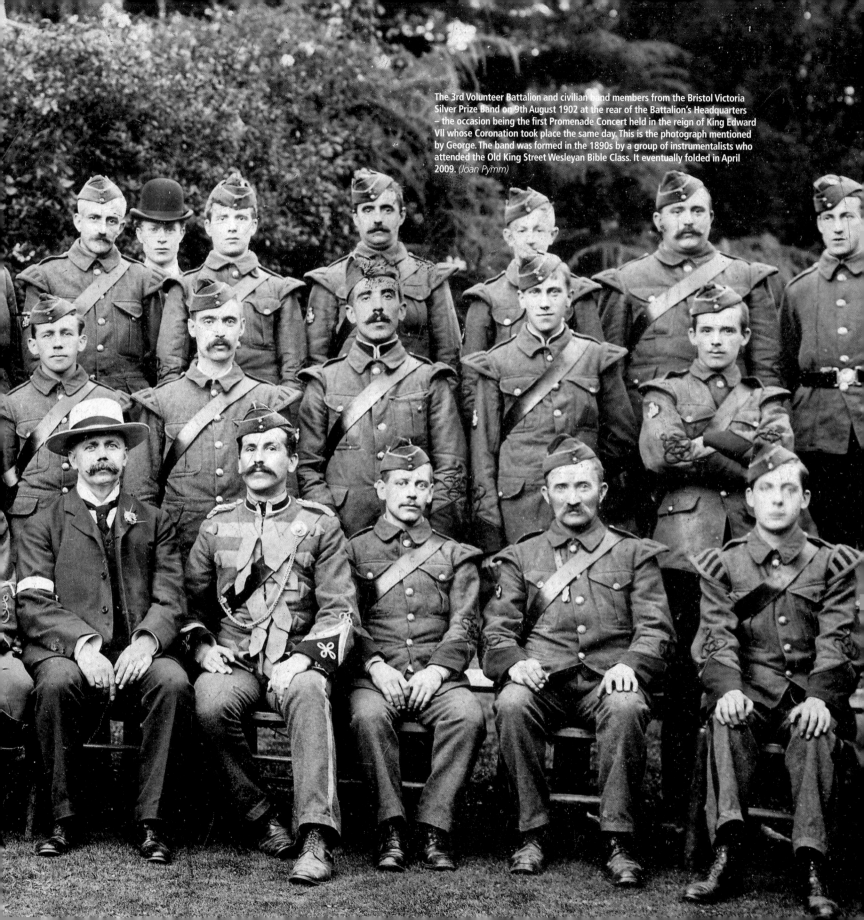

The 3rd Volunteer Battalion and civilian band members from the Bristol Victoria Silver Prize Band on 9th August 1902 at the rear of the Battalion's Headquarters – the occasion being the first Promenade Concert held in the reign of King Edward VII whose Coronation took place the same day. This is the photograph mentioned by George. The band was formed in the 1890s by a group of instrumentalists who attended the Old King Street Wesleyan Bible Class. It eventually folded in April 2009. *(Joan Pymm)*

Author's Notes

Greenbank Infants School

Greenbank Infants School opened its doors for the first time on 31st August 1896 with 261 children on the Register including Harry and George Pine. The first Head Teacher, Mrs A E Evans was initially supported by four teachers – Miss Cousins, Miss Davies, Miss Sheats and Miss Payne and three assistants – Ethel

Britton, Florence Ayers and Elsie Harvey. As George remembered, life was very tough during his schooldays and November 1896 saw the deaths of the first children at the school. Irma Isles from Class 1 and Gertrude Jeffs from Class 2 succumbed to Croup and Diphtheria respectively. In Victorian Bristol, disease was never far away, with Whooping Cough and Scarlet Fever also accounting for child deaths at the school in the 1890s. To keep the school clean its walls and floors were regularly scrubbed on Saturdays and children whose families were ill, were precluded from attending in an effort to contain infectious diseases such as Chicken Pox.

Teaching staff too were not immune from illness. Mrs Evans the first Head Teacher died in September 1898 – just two years after she opened the new school. As George recalled, the School celebrated the Diamond Jubilee of Queen Victoria on 21st June 1897 and the occasion was recorded in the school register… "A tea given to the children this afternoon in commemoration of the Queen's record reign – 357 children had tea after which Classes 1 and 2 marched in procession to the park. A holiday given for the rest of the week."

In George's first few years at the school, its progress was monitored closely by Education Inspectors. Her Majesty's Inspectors' Report for the year ending 31st July 1897 concluded:

'This new school has made a good beginning and gives promise of improvement in the future. The teaching, although not brilliant, is careful and sound and the children behave well. Under the circumstances I feel justified in recommending the highest principal grant. The backward children over seven years of age should receive some more special teaching.

The amount of Grant for 11 months - £215 16s 7d
Fixed Grant 9/-, Merit 6/-, Needlework 1/-, and
Singing 1/- Total 17/- per head'

The first day of the new school as recorded by Head Teacher Mrs Evans in 1896 – it must have been quite an occasion for staff as well as for the Pines.
(Bristol Record Office)

HM Inspector's Report for the year ending 31st July 1898 said:

'The school was seen at some disadvantage owing to the absence of the Head Teacher through illness. The teachers appeared to be working carefully, but some of the classes were too large and in some lessons the children were too crowded to work with comfort and efficiency. The highest variable grant cannot be recommended again unless considerable improvement is shown.

Amount of Grant - £273 14s 0d

Fixed Grant 17/- per head Average attendance 322'

HM Inspector's Report for the year ending 31st July 1899:

"The work has suffered from a large number of changes in the staff during the year. The teachers have evidently worked hard, and the condition of the school is on the whole satisfactory, without teaching a very high level. Under the special circumstances the higher variable grant is again recommended."

3rd Volunteer Battalion Gloucestershire Regiment

The 3rd Volunteer Battalion Gloucestershire Regiment had its origins in the days of the Boer War. The outbreak of the South African War led to an explosion in local patriotism. Many keen young Bristol men wished to enrol, although soon after the war broke out all the established units were at full strength.

In a letter that appeared in Bristol's newspapers, Ernest G Mardon, suggested that another battalion should be raised. His idea was supported by an influential committee and there was a series of meetings and concerts held on behalf of a proposed new battalion. The War Office gave its support and the formation of the 3rd Volunteer Battalion the Gloucestershire Regiment was announced on 24th July 1900.

Its uniform was quite distinct and volunteers wore a modified form of khaki with red facings, a quaint red

stock, cord breeches, leather leggings and a slouch hat adorned with plumes of feathers. A leather bandolier was also worn.

No Headquarters was provided at first, so drills were carried out at Bedminster Police Station, Queen Square and Kingsdown Baths, while lectures were given in school rooms in the area. The Headquarters in St Michael's Hill, Bristol was purchased in November 1900.

The Battalion was offered for service in South Africa, but owing to its short existence and consequent lack of training, it did not comply with the requirements of the War Office.

Slouch Hat and uniform worn by Col McClellan of the 3rd Volunteer Battalion. *(From a sketch by S Loxton. Soldiers of Gloucestershire Museum)*

3rd Volunteer Battalion and Band at the rear of its Headquarters. *(Vaughan Collection at Bristol Record Office)*

Chapter 2
Money on the Table and Teenage Employment
1905–1908

I was getting on to school leaving age, (14 years old) but my parents made an appeal to the Education Board for me to be released at 13 years old on account of family hardship. They were successful but I started work at 12 years old at a Greengrocer in Cheltenham Road – Friday nights and all day Saturday for 1s 6d – a lot in those days. Then when I left school they employed me for half-day Monday to Thursday and all day Saturday and Friday. On spare afternoons I did odd jobs or errands for a carpenter's shop. This brought my money up to six shillings a week, nearly one third of the wages my father was earning.

Most of the big factories were in the centre of the city. Fry's Chocolate Factory, Wills Tobacco, Mardons Cardboard Box Makers, Robinsons, some boot and shoe factories and clothing, all in the Centre. So it was a walk, bike, tram or a train to Temple Meads station. No motor cars in those

George looking very dapper in one of his acquired suits.
(Robin Pine)

days. My trip to the greengrocers took me half an hour, to Cheltenham Road, all for the good of the cause.

Time soon slipped by and I was away from school and Tom as well. I spoke for him at a butcher's shop who we served with greengrocery and he got a job as an errand boy delivering the joints. He got on fine, was there a good time. Harry had come back from Wales (Fred was still down there) and was in the bakery shop next to us. With me in the greengrocers and Tom in the butchers we had a week-end loaf of bread, all the veg, bar spuds, a few fruits and a piece of meat – so, we used to help the larder a bit.

The people I worked for was an old lady and her son. She was ever so kind and good hearted. Her son was the boss – a proper driver for work. They had two pony carts for order deliveries, so beside me was a man working for them, a proper rough-un. He had the other pony cart but he was a proper fiddler in making up the orders to take out.

The old lady had relatives in Cardiff and one was Chief Constable of that city. They had a son, my build; and they used to send up suits of clothes that the boy had grown out of. Drain pipe trousers were in the fashion those days. I was a proper toff.

Our boss got married and his wife was a servant in one of the big houses in Clifton, so that when she got into the ways of serving behind the counter, things began to hot up a bit. The old lady passed away, and that is when the young mistress began to show her authority and accused me of idling my time and not delivering orders. It was hard work sometimes – four baskets, perhaps 10lb potatoes in each, besides other things, and plenty of hills to climb.

I went around every Boxing Day to the customers. Touched my hat – 'compliments of the season'. I did well for three years' service. When I got in to work the boss was always at the market bringing back fresh greens or special fruit and the rest would be sent to the shop. The boss trimmed the veg window, sprouts, caulis, cabbage etc, and his mother or wife the fruit window.

I never liked Sam, (one of the horses) he very often lashed out with his hind leg when I put my foot on the front step to get in the cart. He wore no blinkers. Yet he never did it to the boss. He was just the same in his stall. I kept well clear of him. The other pony, Kitty, was very docile. Often I gave her a good clean down with the curry comb, in the

James Moffat, Greengrocer, in Paul Street, Kingsdown in about 1908. (Vaughan Collection at Bristol Record Office)

afternoon water and feed, and lay down her straw bed. But not Sam, I kept well clear of him. The stables were around the back in a lane, and if we were wanted for a special order they pulled a rope to ring a bell. We had our dinner in the loft, but tea down in the kitchen with the servant. A fellow kept a poultry farm on the land and I kept him going with cabbage leaves for the fowls. A few coppers in my pocket.

My errand boy job lasted for a couple of years and I wanted my Saturday afternoon off. So I got a job on the Midland Railway as a boy on the back of a horse-drawn trolley delivering goods to warehouses and shops from the Midland Railway station at St Phillips for 5/- a week.

They had big horses. I was proper dwarfed stood by them, when their heads did go up I was lifted off my feet. But my earnings was not so much, and that never suited me. My pal I knocked about with, he had a longer spell than me at the Midland Railway, but I left for more money.

I landed a job in a baby linen shop in Castle Street – 9am to 6pm. Wages were 6s. 6d. a week, a bit respectable, but I wanted my half day off on Saturdays to play or watch football. I met my pal Sunday afternoons or evenings and that was spent parading Castle Street or going around College Green having a bit of fun.

But I soon got another job in a saw mills and cabinet works. Started off fetching furniture for repair from private houses, helping the man behind the circular saw with the long pieces, then I learnt the fret saw. Got on well at that, but when I went for a rise, nothing doing. The mill was near my father's boot and shoe factory in Portland Square. I told him there was no chance of me improving myself at the saw mills. He got me a job in his factory as a general useful lad going from one bench to another. Keeping my eyes open when I had the chance, watching men working their machines and my chance came one day.

A typical scene close to the area where George worked. Photograph taken at Easter 1906 from the corner of Waterloo Road by St Philip's Station (Midland Railway) looking up Midland Road past the eastern side of Trinity Almshouses towards Old Market Street. Midland Railway had its goods station here and at the Upper Railway wharf, eight or nine coal merchants operated – including the one where George worked at around the time the photograph was taken. *(By kind permission of the Trustees of Bristol Charities)*

Another photograph from 1906 showing the Goods Receiving Warehouse of Midland Railway in Thomas Street, looking north towards Victoria Street. *(By kind permission of the Trustees of Bristol Charities)*

A fellow was home ill, and the machine he operated was called the Loose Nailing machine, loaned by the British United Shoe Machine Company (BUSMC) and they had to hire a specialist from them to do the work. That cost far more than having a man of their own. So I got them to get the BUSMC man to learn me and I got on well. They had a few Patents on this machine; one was the short nails changing to long nails whilst the machine was in motion. Short ones for the waist, long ones for the forepart of the soles of the boots or shoes to the uppers.

Things were going on very well at the shoe factory. I had learnt a trade as a fully fledged Boot and Shoe Machine Loose Nailing Operator and as I was reaching 16 years of age, prospects were looking brighter for my future.

Only thing was a lot of short time and I got on quite well with my machine, could pull him to pieces and put him together again if he went wrong. Being a hired one and that was the case, we were to send for the specialist, and they had to be paid. I got so competent that I was offered a job with the BUSMC but I considered that this was for later on. When working full time our hours were 8am to 1pm, dinner and then 2pm to 7pm. 8am to 12.30 Saturdays. What hours!

Corn Street and the area around Bristol Bridge (seen in the two pictures here in around 1908) were the places to visit if shopping in the city. *(Vaughan Collection at Bristol Record Office)*

Right: Believed to be a group of Bristol lads from the early 1900s receiving instruction in boot and shoe repairing. Appears to be a posed photograph that shows just how young some children were when they started in the trade. *(Bristol Record Office)*

Author's Notes

Bristol's Boot and Shoe Trade

The surge in Bristol's boot and shoe trade took place between the 1850s and 1870s when the city started to capitalise on its position as a major centre for the leather trade and tanning industry. When the earlier boot and shoe factories were established in the city, Portland Square was favoured – the large houses of the old city merchants being readily transformed into workrooms.

At its peak in the 1890s, Bristol's boot and shoe manufacturers employed around 10,000 men, women and children across 129 companies – a very significant employer in the city. The industry was concentrated in two main areas – the first in and around the parishes of St Paul and St James, where the emphasis was on lighter footwear – and the second in and around Kingswood and St George where land prices for factory construction were cheaper. Firms in these areas tended to specialise in the heavy duty part of the trade.

George's father, Charles Pine, worked in one of the 11 boot and shoe manufacturers operating from Portland Square in the early 1900s. The trade occupied over half of

King Square was also a popular location for Boot and Shoe Factories. The premises of the Bristol Pioneers Ltd, are shown here shortly after it moved its operation from Twinnell Street, Easton in the early 1900s. *(Bristol Record Office)*

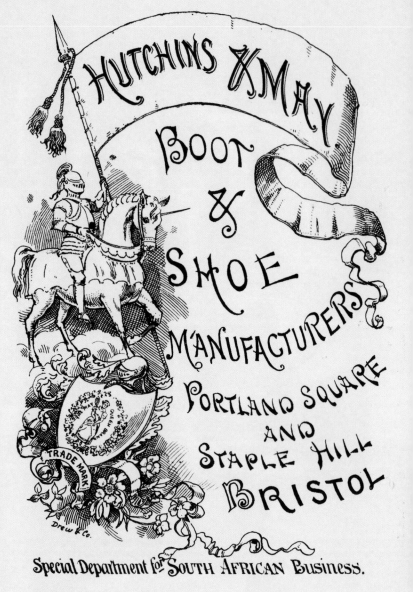

An early Hutchins and May advertisement. *(John Penny)*

the commercial properties in the Square – other trades included clothing manufacturers, a sweet manufacturer, a flour company and a tea dealer.

It is believed that Charles Pine worked at one of the two largest boot and shoe factories in Portland Square – either Hutchins & May or R W Ashley and Sons. Both companies also had factories in the Staple Hill and the Soundwell areas of the City respectively.

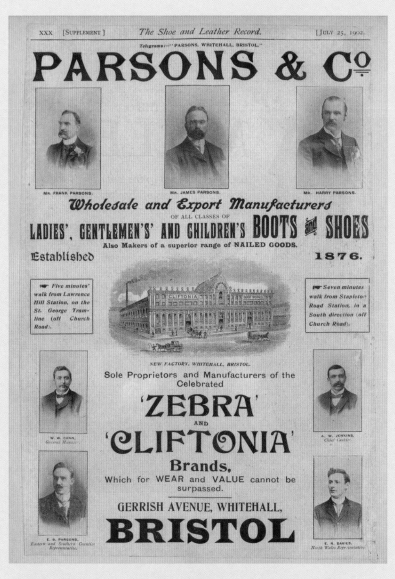

An advertorial featuring the newly constructed 'Cliftonia' Boot Works factory for Parsons and Co in Whitehall, Bristol. The business owners and senior staff are shown, including the General Manager, W W Cann, who would later become Lord Mayor of Bristol.

George learnt a trade as a 'Boot and Shoe Machine Loose Nailing Operator' while working for his father's company in Portland Square. Local companies formed the Bristol Shoe and Leather Trades Association that was affiliated to the Federated Associations of Boot and Shoe Manufacturers of Great Britain and Ireland. Minimum wage rates for men and youths were determined by the national association in agreement with the National Union of Boot and Shoe Operatives.

The local association formed the Bristol Leather Trades Athletic Association that organised sporting events such as cricket, bowls and rifle shooting for its member companies and their employees. Its President was usually a prominent member of the local Trades Association.

Programme for the Annual Dinner of the Bristol Shoe and Leather Trades Cricket and Athletic Association on 14th October 1905. Its President for the year was George Bryant Britton. *(Bristol Record Office)*

5TH. MID. DIV. DE-TRAINING FOR PERHAM DOWN CAMP

Chapter 3
The Territorial Years
1908–1914

Now, to where and when I enlisted... A lot of fellows were joining the Terries, nicknamed the Saturday Night Soldiers. So, me and my pal went up to St Michael's Hill to join the 6th Gloucestershire Regiment for four years at 16½. I put my age on as you had to be 17 years old. I saw the Regimental Sergeant Major, big fellow and a Scotsman from the Black Watch. "Well, what do you wana do laddie?" he bawled. My reply: "I want to join as a bugler, Sir."

Anyway, we were sworn in. My pal in the ranks and me a bugler. I was taken to the Band Sergeant and Drum Major. Got home, told my father what I had done. He went up in the air, "You're bringing no bugle here – if you don't give your mind to it, back it goes." I thought of my days with that cornet – it won't happen again. I was determined to show

The 1/6th Gloucesters arriving by train for the Salisbury Plain summer camp in 1910. George is somewhere in the melee. *(Soldiers of Gloucestershire Museum)*

my father that I would make good. Next night we were at the Headquarters. Drew my uniform from the Quartermaster Stores and a bugle from the Drum Major and home I went. Next Saturday afternoon I was at the Arcade music shop in the Horsefair with my pocket money.

I bought a tutor music book of bugle and trumpet calls of the British Army. The bit of music I learnt when I had the cornet came in useful. I used to study the calls and hum them until I knew them off by heart. I used to stuff the bell of the bugle with a cloth when I was at home blowing it. It was a case of keeping your lip in to the mouthpiece. I used to go up to Purdown with a pal that lived quite close, with our bugles, and we would blow to our hearts' content.

We had band practice two nights a week, Fridays and Tuesdays, when we were made full buglers and put the bugle badge up on our uniform sleeve.

We were paid 3d for practice and 6d for a parade. Church parades on Sundays, or a company officer

would take his company on a Saturday route march and a mock battle in the fields, and they would have the bugle band. We used to be paid every quarter and I was looking forward to the battalion camp in August 1908. The first time I would have been away from home for so long.

I shall never forget when I was at school, near leaving age. We had to write an essay – 'What we would like to do when we left school'. My subject was I should like to join the Army, and wear the smart uniform. When I was a young boy, I used to study the young men when they came home on furlough, dressed in their best uniform. No khaki then. Grenadiers, Coldstream Guards – Scottish Regiments in their kilts and plaid trousers, it always opened my eyes to admire them. So here I was a part-time one.

I was getting on quite well with my bugle. Used to pull the mouthpiece out and put it up to my lips to have a bit of tongue practice, and that was good for the lips as well. It was no good leaving it from one practice night to another. Otherwise as soon as you started up, your lips would swell. Result would be false notes, especially high ones. On practice night at HQ we stood in a long line according to length of service, from No. 1 to about 20. Then the Major would start, first up and down the scale slow, then quick, if not good enough, repeated. Then came the individual's playing from No. 1 bugler down the line.

The Drum Major would name a call and you would have to play it, next man a different one, so you had to memorise about thirty calls and that's where the benefit came in, keeping ones lip in. Notes would come out nice and clear. I soon got made a

Purdown where George and his pal used to blow their bugles – 'to their hearts› content'. *(Vaughan Collection at Bristol Record Office)*

Crowds start to gather for the Royal visitors. George was lining the route here at Temple Meads and then in Whiteladies Road during his first engagement as a Territorial. *(Vaughan Collection at Bristol Record Office)*

Postcard of the Royal Visit. *(Vaughan Collection Bristol Record Office)*

The Band leading a parade at the rear of the 6th Battalion RHQ. (*Andy Stevens, Pastimes, Bristol*)

Full Drummer. The band was allowed ten minutes for a smoke, then out on the square, marching, counter marching, and playing the march tunes. We had a big drummer from a regular Battalion. He would swing the sticks and was at his best after having a few pints of beer.

My first big parade was a month after I had joined the Terries. We only had khaki, and it was when King Edward VII and Queen Alexandra came to Bristol to open the Royal Edward Dock at Avonmouth, July 9th, 1908. We had to line the route, first at Temple Meads main road. After the procession had gone we marched to Whiteladies Road and lined the route there on their way up Blackboy Hill, Upper Belgrave Road and on to Avonmouth.

Well, my first camp, August 1908 at Salisbury Plain. The camp was for two weeks but my firm could only let me have one. Go early Sunday morning from Temple Meads station to Ludgershall. Weather was fine, thank God. I got detailed as Guard Bugler when it was my Company's turn to do guard duty on the gate of the camp, mount at Retreat, and finish 24 hours later.

What the Bugler had to memorise was the most urgent calls, fire alarm, and alarm for troops and, of course, guard salute for the General once a day for the CO, Officer Commanding. Sentry would shout "turn out the Guard" so that we had to be fully dressed during the day and, of course, there was the

George (standing on the far left), proudly clutching his bugle on this, possibly his first camp. *(Andy Stevens, Pastimes, Bristol)*

Orderly Bugler detailed for every day. His duty would start at Reveille to Lights Out at 10.30pm.

Well, I got over that lot as Guard Bugler and the whole Guard had a day off when they came off duty. Being my first year I was not detailed for Orderly Bugler for you were on the go all the time outside the RSM's office. "Bugler" sound Orderly Sergeants at the double, give the mouthpiece a warm up then Regimental Call, Orderly Sergeants, at the double, three calls had to be played. The Regimental Call always so as anyone could tell whose Bugler was sounding it. If you were on a brigade camp four Battalions. More for Divisional. All Regiments had different Regimental Calls. I got on alright with my first week's camp and was sorry when it was over and back to work Monday morning. Battalion orders were posted in the local papers and we had a month's rest then started again.

When anyone passed away in the Regiment they were given a full military funeral. Gun carriage was loaned from the Artillery, Whiteladies Road, Firing Party, and three volleys of blanks over the grave, Reveille and the Last Post was sounded by the Buglers, with the roll of muffled drums.

The Band and Drums had an engagement at the Bridewell Fire Station, Horsefair. A fireman lost his life at a big fire in a cabinet works in Redcross Street that lasted for some time.

Police and Firemen were in the Parade from Bridewell to Greenbank Cemetery. On the way, a slow march in prominent places, then break into quick-step for a time. Then we played them back to Bridewell again, a quick step all the way, 120 to the minute. When we got back to Bridewell there were

refreshments for us. A mate of mine advised me to have a small Guinness as I said I felt hungry. So I had one and chanced it for it was the first intoxicant I had ever tasted and it filled me up. So you see, apart from going to camp we had other items to fill in.

Me and my pal stuck together for a few years and he was in the Gloucesters with me but in the ranks. He hung on to his job at the Midland Railway and we were looking forward to our next camp which was at Swanage – what a lovely place. We did a torchlight tattoo on the sea front and we also went over to Weymouth and Bournemouth.

Now back to Civvy street… All the step-family were growing up. Mable left school, worked at the tailoring, Dora to Wills Tobacco Factory then Gladys, two boys, two girls at school. We had moved from Bellevue Road back to Charles Street, No. 16. Their mother had a serious illness and I am sorry to say

During the wake of Albert Smith at Bridewell Fire Station in April 1909, George tasted Guinness for the first time in the company of many of these firemen. The photograph is of a happier occasion two years later when the Station was decorated to commemorate the Coronation of King George V on 22nd June 1911. *(Bristol Record Office)*

passed away. Edie came back home from service and offered to help Dad with the home. But I am afraid it never worked with the elder step-sister and away she went again. Me and Harry was sorry to see her go for everything was laid on for us, and we were always pulling up the girls on how they treated her – like a stranger in the house instead of one of the family.

We moved across the road to No. 19 Charles Street. Mable left work and looked after the home, a suggestion of her own, but she got fed up and wanted Dora to take it on, but she refused. There was a quarrel and Dora packed up and went to live in Barton Hill with her friend at work, Lil Watkins. She was about 16 years old then. My father let her go for

Mr S J Stone, Factory Manager at J H Woodington and George's boss. *(Bristol Record Office)*

he was fed up with them. Albert went to work at Wills, and Reg on the buildings, so that left Joy and Ethel near leaving school age.

I was getting restless about my job – a lot of short time. This was about 1910. I got to learn the factories at St George and Kingswood were very busy, so during a lay off from work I told my father I was going to see what I could do. The firm was J H Woodington at Air Balloon Hill, St George. Dad knew the Foreman there in the Rounding Department where I worked. Told him I was a specialist on the loose nailing machine. I was in luck, "Just what we want" he said, "When can you start? I said "Tomorrow". So I was there, 6.30am start instead of 8am, finish 5pm Mondays, 5.30pm rest of the week, and 12.30 Saturdays, and a rise in wages by 10/-. A big factory all on one level, all departments divided off by wire netting with the office up high, glass around. The staff could look all around and machines were Gimsons. When I came in contact with him and he learnt what I could do on their machines he wanted me to come over to them. But I was under contract for my firm, a two years' agreement.

My new boss knew he had a good one and made sure of me for the old firm was after me to come back, offering more money. I got my father to get them to write a note to me to that effect. When I received it I showed it to the Foreman, he took it to the office. Couple of days after the Manager called

me in his office: "Pine, I hear your old firm want you back. I want you to stay. Do you want to go?"

"No sir."

"Right, I have drawn up an agreement, a contract for two years so that we shall be sure of your services during that time with a rise in wages. Read it and if you are agreeable, I want you to sign it."

I did. I had a copy, signed and sealed. For two years I was established with regards employment and I never regretted it. I was happy, it was a changed world for me, for before getting that job it was up and down to go in the regular army, and I was past 18 years old. I had plenty of time after getting home from work to get poshed up, tea and ready for whatever was on. Evenings which I never had at the other factory. To improve my standard of education I went to the Merchant Venturers' Technical College (MVTC) Night School twice a week to learn how to use other machines.

I paid 2/6 and the firm 2/6 per week and I picked up quite a lot. I never let the grass grow under my feet. I was strong and healthy. Mondays, practice blowing on Purdown, Tuesdays band practice, Wednesdays MVTC, Thursday's ditto, Fridays band practice. Saturdays I played friendly games for the Drums Football on Durdham Downs. When we never had one, over and watched the Rovers. Sunday mornings baths, Sunday afternoons out parading Castle Street or College Green – having a lot of fun with the girls, but nothing serious.

Now, back to the Terries… The next camp was at Salisbury Plain (Ludgershall August 1910), a Divisional one, 4th Battalion Warwicks, 2nd Battalion Worcesters, 2nd Battalion Gloucesters, Engineers, RHMC, and RHSC. What a crowd, like a small city, and our Colonel was Sir Charles Hobhouse MP. He had a big chestnut hunter. His private groom came with us to look after the horse, but not when on manoeuvres – us Buglers had that job.

Whilst we were at Ludgershall, I believe it was at the time of the Doctor Crippen affair with Miss Ethel Le Neave making a getaway to America. I remember the boys in the paper vans all the way from London did arrive about 6am; out jumped the boys with the London papers from Fleet Street shouting 'Crippen' and 'Read all about it'. Those were the days I enjoyed.

It was not very long after we were issued with our best dress. The band and drums were fitted out first. Scarlet tunics trimmed with small white crowns on the sleeves around the collar. Epaulets in the shoulder plaited green, dress cord worn on the right breast, two green tassels and a cord going down under the arm and up the back to the collar. I looked quite smart in the dress.

The whole Regiment was fitted out later on and this was worn on ceremonial parades, such as Church Parades or big inspections. The Parades were always inserted in the local papers, this more or less for recruiting purposes and it worked.

I had already attended two camps and there was a third at Salisbury Plain. It was getting on to the year 1912 and if I wanted to re-engage I had to sign-up for another four years. As I was enjoying it this I did. We used to go to weekend camps Whitsun, Sat, Sun, Mon, to Lansdown near Box and Bath. These were optional, please ourselves whether we went. Just give our name in a week before.

The next Royal visit we had to turn out to was King George V and Queen Mary, June 28, 1912 to open the new building at the Bristol Royal Infirmary. We were in scarlet uniform then, and other ranks were lined up Park Street to Queens Road, they had a stop at the Museum and Art Gallery. Band and drums were stationed in a side turning at the top of Park Street. The Band played the National Anthem when they passed.

Now I think I had better go back to Civvy Street for a time… Tom had left the butchering and had

THE TERRITORIAL. On Parade.

PERHAM CAMP, LUDGERSHALL.

There was clearly some kudos in being a Territorial as depicted by this 1909 postcard. *(Author's own collection)*

Tented village at the 1910 Salisbury Camp. *(Soldiers of Gloucestershire Museum)*

joined the Border Regiment, Westmorland and Cumberland. They had a cap badge that was very beautiful, a big Maltese cross with all their battle honours on it. After twelve months he joined the Battalion cookhouse as a butcher. Whilst carrying a shoulder of beef in through a door, hit the top of it, down went Tom, meat on top of him and a broken

WHAT! AGAIN ALREADY

PHOTOCHROM COPYRIGHT   CAMP SILHOUETTE No 7

From this camp postcard, it appears that George and his fellow buglers were not always fully appreciated when sounding the Reveille. *(Author's own collection)*

leg. So he was in Army Hospital for some time.

Harry had left the bakers and gone to Packers Chocolate Factory at Greenbank. Before going to Packers, Harry had joined the Gloucesters Special Reserve, called the Militia and did six months training at Horfield Barracks. I used to go to see him whilst he was there and he had to be ready in case of emergency, for call back to the Regiment which happened in the 1914 war with Germany.

We formed a Workman's Club around our district. We had bagatelle tables, one large and one small one. The large one was used for league matches in the Workman's League. My father, my brother, Harry and myself, we played such teams as Mardon's, Fry's and Robinsons.

The team consisted of six men, three played on the home table, and three on the away table. Dad, Harry and me were always the ones to go away so that if we won at home we had to wait for the away three to come home to know the results of the game for the total score. We also ran a football team and entered the Suburban League on Saturday afternoons.

We had quite a good side but it fell through when the season finished. I had a set of shirts on my hands, as I was secretary of the club. They came in useful later on with the firm I worked for. We had a piece of wasteground outside the factory. 12.30-1.30 break, the young-uns got out there with a ball, half dozen a side. Plenty of support from the fellow workers until the whistle went.

The Suburban League ran a six-a-side tourney at Longwell Green every Easter for clubs not in any league and I formed a team at the firm, J H Woodington & Co. That's where the football shirts came in handy. Started playing at 9am and I think we finished about 6pm, for we had to meet six teams before we reached the final of the knock-out. The scores were three points for a goal, one for a corner. I was playing on the right wing. Three forwards, one half back, one back and one goalkeeper. We started off by winning the first round by one point, a corner forced by me; the goalie put a shot around the post. We must have got our second wind for there was no stopping us in the rest of the rounds. The only drawback was the waiting about between rounds and we had a couple of byes in between.

Anyway we won the final, a cup and six medals. The cup was placed in the big office window in the centre of the factory for a twelve month, and then returned. We celebrated at the Rodney, St George. I gave my football medal to Gerald but it was fun and as they say, a good sportsman, a good worker.

Our team used to play at Eastville Park. Greenbank United, most of the fellows were members of the Workman's Club. I asked my father to come out and watch us one day, Saturday afternoon. Rovers were playing away. So he came out and watched us.

He was a very good judge of a footballer so when we were sat down to tea I said to him "What did you think of it Dad?" His reply was, "If you want my opinion of the game, on the whole it was good, but

ROYAL VISIT TO BRISTOL JUNE 28th 1912.
PROCESSION PASSING ART GALLERY.

As the Royal Procession passed the City Museum and Art Gallery, George and the band were in a side road opposite (probably Berkeley Square) and played the National Anthem.
(Vaughan Collection at Bristol Record Office)

you, George, was a very dirty player." I nearly choked myself with a mouthful of cake. Sit back, George, told off good and proper. But the following season Dad, Harry and me spent every Saturday the first team were playing home, over the Rovers Ground. Sixpence in the Ground, threepence in the Small Enclosure at the halfway line by the Gas Works side. Harry one side of Dad, me the other. Presently Harry's arm would come around and touch my back. That was a sign to watch Dad, first his right leg then his left doing imaginary passes, and one of us would get a good shoulder charge. We used to watch him more than the game. We had a very good amateur team called Bellevue Athletic. They went right through every

division in the Suburban League. Run by a Mr Morgan who kept a General Store in Bellevue Road. He belonged to the Morgan family of footballers; they could raise a team of their own for charity purposes.

So that's how it went Saturday afternoons.

Packer's had a good football team – the pick of the Bristol and District, and they had a lovely ground at the factory. Old Georgians play on there now and the county cricket matches are played there also. Before the ground was enlarged a lane went up through to Whitehall. I used to go through there

George (left) with family friend PC Bill Lugg (middle) and Tom Pine around 1911. Like his sister, Tom Pine had left home by 1911 and was lodging at the Army Recruitment Office in Colston Avenue, Bristol. Still working as a Butcher's Assistant, it appears he too had had enough of living at home and like his brother Fred wished to pursue an Army Career. It was from his temporary address that Tom enlisted with the Border Regiment in Carlisle in 1912. *(Robin Pine)*

was no wireless or television. The first form of music we had apart from Dad's tenor horn and my bugle, was a phonograph. Edison Swan, worked by a spring that had to be wound up.

The records were made of wax, a cylinder type; you had to be careful how you got them out their box, as to touch the surface would damage them. You had to put your fingers inside them, tip the cardboard box a bit, get them out and slip them on the cylinder, switch on and adjust the sound box with a new needle attached to an arm when it was fully revolving to the record very careful and out will come the music.

His Masters Voice, picture of the dog listening still used I believe.

We used to club around for new records. Dad's was for military marches and selections. In those days rag time dancing was the rage from America and there was plenty of songs and tunes for the teenagers.

Entertainment was improved on by the Gramophone with flat disc records. Still a big trumpet for the sound to come out. Very often it would over wind and snap would go the spring. No music until a new one was got. A shop in the Arcade stocked all that sort of material, second-hand records as well.

My work was improving and progressing very well and I had learnt quite a lot going to night school at the MVTC and I was reaping the benefit of it, for my first two-year contract had finished and the boss had me in his office to sign another two-year contract.

That suited me, a rise in wages. I always gave my father my wage packet Fridays and when I put my first big one down he looked at it and said to me "You are earning more than me. From now on you will give me eleven shillings a week for your keep and you look after yourself with regards to clothing." I was just about proud of myself, as long as my father was satisfied. My responsibility rested with me and I

every morning at 6am to work at J H Woodingtons Boot Factory, 6.30am start, half hour breakfast, hour lunch; 5pm finish Mondays, 5.30pm rest of the week, 12.30pm Saturdays. What a difference to town job, 8-7pm every day, Saturdays 1pm.

The 4th Gloucesters had a new Headquarters built in Old Market Street. Very often there were military band concerts there from the Regular Army. Me and Dad always used to go to them. In those days there

The New Headquarters, Fourth Battalion Gloucester Regiment.
Old Market Street, Bristol. COPYRIGHT. BURGESS & CO., BRISTOL.

The new Headquarters of the 4th Battalion Gloucestershire Regiment.
(Vaughan Collection at Bristol Record Office)

just knew how to grasp it, for I had been brought up the hard way, and knew what to do to make life a success. I was a freelance and could please myself.

I never went in to anything serious with the ladies, though I admit I was popular with them – that came later. And what more did I want? Happy at work, at my pastime or recreation, tailor-made suits – suits I had never wore before – and, above all, enjoying good health, thank God. What more could I wish for?

Now I will go back to the Terries again… As I stated I had re-engaged for four years, which would expire in June 1916. I had my first Stripe 1912 – Lance Corporal Drummer and was given the numbered one bugle of a new set we had. I had also signed on for service overseas and anyone that did that was given a Silver Imperial Service Badge.

Our next camp was at Conway, North Wales

– what a time we Drummers had. There was a bus service running to Llandudno. Four of us had a pass out until 10pm. In our scarlet uniform. Missed the last bus back to Camp, had to walk four miles, lost our way, had to climb up sign posts to get our bearing, got back near camp. Then we knew it was no good going in the gate where the sentry was on duty, so we had to make a detour and come in at the back of the camp. It was dark then and luck was with us, we all four managed to get to our tents without getting pulled up by the Provost Sergeant. We had to undress in the dark in the tent as lights were at 10.15pm, or the Provost Sergeant would spot it and that would have finished the show and we would have been up

Lt Col H C Woodcock at camp in around 1913. He took command of the 6th Battalion when Col Hobhouse stood down in 1911. (*Andy Stevens, Pastimes, Bristol*)

for orderly room next morning. We had a pal in the tailor shop tent to look over our uniform next day and put a crease in the trousers and sleeves of the tunic, and that was that, and no one was none the wiser, thank God. But I often think of it, and me a Lance Corporal. Had visions of being drummed out and disgraced. But we were a fine lot in the Drums and stuck together well. We were sorry when that camp was over. I noticed at Conway there was a sort of miniature suspension bridge over a small river like ours in Bristol but not so high up. It was a long ride up country to Chester, I believe, then into Wales, and what wonderful scenery.

George, seen here sat down in the centre holding his bugle. One of the last Camp photographs before the start of the First World War. (*Robin Pine*)

The Battalion had a competition for the best marching team. There were eight companies, A–H Company and the Drums entered. There was a cash prize £5. We all had a given route to go, referees at different points unknown to us. This was about 1913. We put up a good show and won a prize.

There was one more camp at Salisbury Plain, then things were warming up in the gossip of Germany waging war with us. This was early 1914 and we learnt that our next camp would be at Minehead, August 2nd, on a Sunday away from Bristol. So, until then we just had to read, mark and inwardly digest people's opinion of the outcome of it all and wait and see, but be prepared…

Author's Notes

6th Battalion Gloucestershire Regiment

On 1st April 1908, following reforms proposed by Lord Haldane, the Territorial and Reserve Forces Act came into effect. The purpose of the reforms was to bring the regular army and the auxiliary forces into proper relation to each other – having in mind the work they would have to do in time of war. As a result of the reforms, the 3rd Volunteer Battalion became the 6th Battalion Gloucestershire Regiment (Territorial Force) – nicknamed 'Mardon's Own' in recognition of its volunteer roots. At the time, the new structure for Territorial and Reserve Forces brought much criticism.

Many volunteers did not like the new regime and so would not continue to serve, while others, who were not so critical or sceptical of the Territorial Force, re-engaged under the new conditions. The general effect however, was that strengths of the local units decreased significantly.

RSM Farquharson (standing) and Captain R.E. Rising on his horse at a Territorial Camp. The RSM looks a formidable character!
(Soldiers of Gloucestershire Museum)

It was this backdrop and a spirited recruitment campaign in Bristol that prompted George and his friend to enlist at St Michael's Hill on 4th June 1908. The 'big fellow' that George met on joining was Regimental Sergeant Major Farquharson, formerly of the Black Watch, who had joined the 3rd Volunteer Battalion on its formation in 1900. By all accounts he was a forceful character but he was also very popular with the new Territorial recruits.

Redcross Street Fire – 7th April 1909

At 3.37am on 7th April 1909 a call was received from an alarm box in Old Market Street and a fire was found at the premises of William Brice & Co, Cabinet Makers in Redcross Street.

The fire was so strong that the brigade could do no more than prevent it from spreading to adjoining property. The blaze was brought under control after nearly two hours and some Firemen returned to the Central Fire Station at 5.45am.

At about 6am while two firemen were still at work inside the damaged building, there was a sudden fall of the roof and upper floors and Firemen Ernest Lear and Albert Smith were buried in the debris. Other Firemen on the scene assisted by members of the St John Ambulance Brigade immediately started digging to reach the trapped men. Fireman Lear was rescued after five minutes and apart from shock and bruises was unhurt. But Fireman Smith was buried deeper and 20 minutes later was brought out dead.

Albert Smith left a widow and two small children and he was buried with full honours. The coffin bearing his helmet and belt was carried on a fire engine drawn by four horses. A large contingent from the Bristol Police force, together with George and his fellow Territorial band members marched in the funeral procession.

J H Woodington and the Merchant Venturers' Technical College

In around 1910, George left the Boot and Shoe Factory where his father worked in Portland Square and joined J H Woodington, Boot Manufacturer at Hillside Road, St. George. Joseph Woodington built the St George site in 1905 and the company also had a factory in Clevedon and a Leather Works at St. Phillips, Bristol.

Having left school early at 13, George wished to better himself by learning further boot and shoe skills at college as well as on the job. The Merchant Venturers' Technical College (MVTC) operated its Boot and Shoe

School from its workshops in Rosemary Street, Bristol. The principal college building in Unity Street was largely destroyed by fire in October 1906. It re-opened in time for the 1908-09 college year.

George first attended the MVTC's Workshops in around 1910-11, shortly after joining his new company. Joseph Woodington helped George with his fees by contributing half of the 5/- per week charge for the two night classes.

The local Boot and Shoe trade supported classes at the MVTC in many ways including an annual grant collected directly from manufacturers; the supply of materials for the practical classes and occasionally, the loan of specialist equipment for the students to practice on. Bristol Education Committee also provided an annual grant and any periodic shortfall was usually found from the Merchant Venturers' funds.

The MVTC appointed the Instructors and the support staff were provided by the British United Shoe Machine Company (BUSMC) whose Bristol base was in Wilder Street. Each class contained between 12 and 15 students. Instructors were paid 3/6- for each session that ran from 8pm-9.30pm. During a typical term, the Boot and Shoe School ran practical workshops on four evenings per week:

Tuesday – Machine Lasting and Machine Finishing
Wednesday – Elementary Clicking and Pattern Cutting
Thursday – Blake Sewing, Standard Screwing, Loose Nailing and Stitching
Friday – Advanced Clicking and Pattern Cutting

George attended the Wednesday and Thursday night sessions and would have practised on some wonderfully-named machines loaned by the BUSMC – Smith Heel Trimmer, Square Base Edge Trimmer, Swift Heel Scourer, Duo Bottom Scourer, Regal Edge Setter, Universal Heel Finisher, Swan Top Ironer, Column Brush Shaft, Chainstitch Welter, Welt Beater, Welt Channel Groover, Welt Splitter and a Blake Sole Sewer. The latter machine, which sewed the bottom to the upper, was capable of

The Merchant Venturers' Technical College Workshops in Rosemary Street, Bristol where George attended Boot and Shoe School classes. Rosemary Street was in the Broadmead area, close to Quaker's Friars. *(By kind permission of the Trustees of Bristol Charities)*

sewing around 94 pairs of shoes an hour. As well as Loose Nailing (or 'riveting') that George was already familiar with, he would have picked up 'Clicking' at the evening classes.

Clicking involved the cutting out of leather to the correct shape using metal patterns. The click of the knife against the edge of the pattern gave rise to the name. This was a skilled job because 'Clickers' not only had to get as many uppers out of a skin as possible but also had to place them in the best position to align the strongest part of the skin with the section that would get the most wear.

Owing to the skill levels, the pay for a 'Clicker' tended to be determined by an Arbitration Board. In 1910, the minimum wage for a 'Clicker' in Bristol was 30/- per week.

Joseph Henry Woodington, founder and owner of J H Woodington, Boot Manufacturer. Woodington and his managers at the St George and Clevedon sites were active members of the Bristol Shoe and Leather Trades Association in the early 1900s. *(Bristol Record Office)*

Chapter 4
The Calm Before the Storm
1914–1915

Things weren't looking rosy at 19 Charles Street, for it meant four of us first family would be involved in war. Fred (South Wales Borderers in China), Tom (Border Regiment in India), Harry (Special Reserve Gloucesters), and me (Terries Gloucesters). I could see my father was very worried about us because it was a pull from one family. But there was plenty of families hit the same as ours. At the factory where I worked there were only two of us who had to go when general mobilisation was ordered. The other was in the Navy, Sailor Thomas, we called him.

We were given the news at the Headquarters that we must expect to go to war and it was getting on time for our next camp which, was at Minehead on 2nd August 1914.

We got back to Headquarters at St Michael's Hill about mid-day (on Monday 3rd August 1914) and we were kept there until about 6pm. Had the cooks on the go for a brew up, then we were told we were on active service. We should be back at Barracks for a week to be fitted up with the equipment we should want for active service. Finished or dismissed at 6pm. Report 9am next morning. It was a proper do, this getting fitted out – 120 rounds of live ammunition.

We in the Band and Drums missed that lot until we went abroad in 1915. Then, Bandsmen acted as stretcher bearers and Drummers as runners or messengers. On the Tuesday morning my Company Quartermaster Sergeant was after me. "Pine, if you want to keep that stripe and get paid for it, you will have to rejoin the rank." I said "Carry on, three pence a day is OK with me." I told the Drum Major what had happened. He said they won't break up the Band until

The 6th Battalion marching down St Michael's Hill on 10th August 1914. George Pine (circled) is marching just behind his band . This photo was donated to the Soldiers of Gloucestershire Museum in 1998 by a lady from Bower Ashton in Bristol whose husband is also in the frame – one of the young lads in the foreground. *(Soldiers of Gloucestershire Museum)*

The mobilisation scene at the back of the 6th Battalion's Headquarters on St Michael's Hill during the first week of August 1914. *(Vaughan Collection at Bristol Record Office)*

we go abroad. As the week went on we learnt we were moving to Swindon on the Monday. Then there were eight Companies to the Battalion, A to H. But before leaving Bristol we were reduced to four, A, B, C, D. Mine was 'B' Company – commanded by Captain Protheroe, a high-class photographer. He had a studio in Whiteladies Road. Lieutenant Colonel Woodcock commanded the Battalion. We were about 600 strong then, including transport, signallers and pioneers.

All the week we were being fitted up with boots, field dressings and lectures of how to carry on active service, the hazards we should meet when out in company, of careless talk, information to the enemy. The country was full of spies. Everything was commandeered by the War Department, such as horses, wagons, trains, factories for munitions and boots, clothing, food, the aeroplane factory at Filton and Patchway that had been started by Sir George White a few years earlier was enlarged and employing men all over the country to Bristol. Planes were only in their infancy.

Men were enlisting in the Services and the women were taking their places in the factories and fields. While we were at the Depot we Buglers were detailed to sound the different calls for the troops on the parade ground – all for a shilling a day, what a come down. We were allowed ration money in Bristol but when we moved out, embarked for Swindon, that was finished. We left Bristol on the following Monday morning marching from St Michael's Hill to Temple Meads station.

We had a good send off. At the bottom of the incline opposite was a clothing factory (Todds) and a young lady was waving her white handkerchief with other girls. She was to become Mrs G W Pine later on. So, we were on the move and the freelance but a memory, for now it was strict discipline and liable to be called on any minute for some sort of duty.

We arrived at Swindon and billeted in private houses with people. The billeting party had gone on before. Asked how many they could take and that was that. The new town was just beginning to be built then. The people were paid for putting us up and we were there a fortnight. Then, on our way on a long easy stage trek to the east coast at Essex, where the Germans were likely to land, should there be a landing or invasion in this part of our country. So as not to block the roads we moved off a company at a day interval, stopping a day or two then on the move again until we reached Chelmsford. It took us a fortnight to get the Battalion together again. Then it was soldiering in earnest.

So, at nearly 23 years of age, I was saying to myself, goodbye to a few years of pleasure and joy as a freelance, and wondering what was in store for me. Going back to my childhood days of watching the big circuses come to the Rovers Ground, Lord George Sanger's, Bostock's and Wombwell's, Bertram Mills, Buffalo Bill's Wild West Show and Bill Cody – they were all memories of the past that would come up now and again.

As far back as 1912 people were getting uneasy, for Germany were sending their Zeppelin over England, violating this country's international rules. Warnings were sent to Germany but the trips were increased in 1913 and that put the idea into people's heads of this country being invaded and spies working in Germany found they were practising

OWING TO THE WAR

Welcome to all

WE HAVE BEEN COMPELLED TO TAKE IN LODGERS.

Thousands of people across the country – like the Cockerton's in Little Baddow – were asked to take in lodgers as depicted in this cartoon postcard sent from Essex during the war. (*Author's own collection*)

with them to bomb a target. Churchill was Lord of the Admiralty and got to work on our defences with planes, anti aircraft guns and warships. But what started the war was, as far as I know, some foreign monarch being assassinated and the Kaiser

Gloucestershire Regiment soldiers and troops from other regiments look reasonably merry in this Christmas Day pose taken in Little Baddow in 1914. *(Christine Day, Little Baddow History Centre)*

St Mary's Church, Little Baddow – from a postcard sent in September 1914 by Pte Joe Blacker to his sister Iris in Whitehall, Bristol. Following his Christmas Day 1914 'disgrace', this is where George went steady and attended Church with Mr and Mrs Cockerton. *(Author's own collection)*

overrunning Europe with the help of his son, Little Willie 6'4". Relations with Germany were broken off and we were at war, August 4th 1914. My brother Harry was off to France with the Expeditionary Force. Fred had already had a bash at the Germans in China and had routed them at a port they held called Tsingtao. Tom was in India. I will tell you more about them later on. And myself on the East Coast, our destination, until March 1915. Then off to France.

But I must tell you of our stay at a

country village called Little Baddow, just six miles from the town of Chelmsford – 6th Gloucesters were stationed there – we had to guard the East Coast. We were first billeted in some new cottages but we had a scrounge around and three of us were allotted to an old couple and they were very good people.

He worked for a big gentleman that owned a big farm – Tofts farm, had a lot of ground there – plenty of rabbits about. The old lady knew how to make the different wines and we certainly sampled them. They fed us good grub and they were satisfied with the cash the Billeting Officer paid out weekly. Their cottage was just off the main country road and there was an inn close by, the General's Arms. We soon got pally with the locals there and we had some good evenings. We were with our company, now the Drummers. There was three in B company and we used to take it in turns to sound the Reveille.

My lips had got hard to the mouthpiece. Just a warm up and I could play off the Long Reveille as easy as anything and the tone nice and sweet. I used to get a leg pull from the villagers, "Had some of Mrs Cockerton's wine before you started off?" I used to play him twice, bottom of the hill and to the top of the hill. Meet some of the folks going to work on the farm, or to catch the bus to town. Our duties were to do with the Drum Major. It would be practice for a couple of hours then a football match. Afternoons off, every other day Battalion marches and manoeuvres and lectures, and we were always waiting for the mail to arrive. My firm got my address from home and I did get a parcel from them every so often. Collection from the workmates, that was a good gesture to us in the forces, and they came in useful for I was making an allowance to my father.

Winter was coming on, Christmas 1914 too, and spent at Little Baddow. But I am sorry to say I made a fool of myself and was in disgrace. All off duty as soon as the Generals Arms opened, we were in there.

Drinks were free for us Tommies and what a time, all men, rarely see a woman in this room we used, singing all the songs of the day, me and a pal on the harmonicas. I was stacked out, beat to the world, ashamed to go back to the old people to Christmas Dinner. I was too helpless so slept it off in the pub and poshed myself up later in the day and faced the music. They were OK with me, but I was sorry I disappointed them at Christmas Dinner but I went steady after. Sunday mornings when we were off duty I used to go to church with the old couple.

During my stay there I learnt that my brothers Fred and Tom were back in England, South Wales Borderers at Rugby and Border Regiment at Coventry. Their Battalions were attached to the 29th Division and they were there to be fitted out with new equipment for Gallipoli against the Turks. Fred I had not seen for about seven years and Tom four

years. I mentioned it to the Drum Major about a leave. He in turn turned it over to my Company Sergeant Major then Company Commander. Finally, I had an appointment with Colonel Woodcock. I stated what I wanted and what for. His reply was you will see your brothers plenty soon enough in France (Dismissed).

This was about mid-week and their leave was getting short. I applied for a weekend pass from the Drum Major. I was determined to see them if I could, with a bit of luck. So, with pass to Chelmsford, weekend Friday after duty until Sunday midnight, arrived Chelmsford, train to Victoria, then to Bristol from Paddington. Arrived Saturday midnight. Luck was with me, no stopping by Red Caps (Military Police). I managed to see Fred for one day, but Tom had gone back to his unit. He started his leave earlier

Just up the road in Danbury, soldiers from the other Bristol Territorial unit – the 4th Gloucesters – are sharing a beer with the locals outside the Cricketers Arms. (Author's own collection)

George, shortly before he went overseas in 1915. *(Robin Pine)*

Violet Winterson – George's fiancée. *(Robin Pine)*

and I never saw him, worse luck. I will tell you about him later.

My weekend was up so I returned to Little Baddow, but I knew my luck would not turn for the good. All went well until I was just leaving the station at Chelmsford and a Red Cap asked me for my pass, 12 midnight. He said "It's now Monday morning 8am." I told him I caught a slow bus and train, being Sunday, and here I am. He made a note, gave me back my pass, then I was out as quick as possible. A bus was waiting for Danbury that saved me a six mile walk too

and it was only down the hill to Little Baddow. On the way down I ran into the Drum Major. He greeted me with "OK George, I know where you've been. On parade for practice 9.30am." What a relief!

Next thing I did was to have dental treatment. This was at the Army's expense. All my back teeth were gone, and the dentist wanted to pull the lot out but I would not allow it for it would stop my blowing

the bugle. Just one at the front and all the back ones, this was after Christmas. Then we had a scare leaving for France end of March 1915. Had to have my new teeth in before my gums were really set. So that later on they were no good to me. They were wrapped up in my tunic pocket more than in my mouth.

As it was time for us to go overseas people were beginning to get upset. Those that had not signed were separated from us going. Most of the Band and a few of the Drummers stayed behind and they were then forming the Second 6th Battalion. One of my pals that stopped behind joined the Band and learnt music and an instrument and did himself a good turn. But the war lasted a lot longer than we bargained for. I wanted to be like my three brothers, Harry in France, Fred and Tom in Gallipoli against the Turks.

I came home on leave before going abroad and became engaged to the young lady that waved her handkerchief to me from the factory window. So I had my first lesson of keeping her supplied with letters and news. They were not censored until we went abroad. Then they were, and had to be kept unsealed to be censored by the officers. We were issued with green envelopes and field cards. Green envelopes were not censored. Field cards had information phrases and what never applied, you scratched out, 'I am not well', 'Am in hospital', 'Wounded', 'Haven't heard from home', 'Coming home', and 'Send parcel'.

51

Author's Notes

Minehead and Back Again

Just three weeks before war was declared, Lt Col Woodcock wrote to Bristol employers seeking their support for the release of employees who were in the Territorial Forces. He was keen for maximum attendance at the annual training camp at Minehead that was due to run from 2nd to 16th August 1914. It was as if he knew what was around the corner.

At the same time the local papers were also reporting concern at the reducing number of Bristol-based troops and the 6th Battalion in particular was shown to be short by 319 ordinary ranks and four officers.

At 9.30am on Sunday 2nd August, the 6th Battalion left Bristol for Minehead. The 4th Battalion and the South Midland Engineers had left a little earlier in the morning. Fuelled by a War Office communiqué about military 'precautionary' movements, the departure for camp was accompanied by 'wars and rumours of wars'. As the Battalion was making its way to camp, German troops were entering Poland, France and Luxembourg. Later in the day, Belgium refused Germany's demand to allow passage across its territory.

When the 6th Battalion arrived at North Hill Camp, Minehead, several unusual occurrences became apparent. The local police had asked why they were all instructed to be still on duty, and the station master came to the Camp to say that for the first time in his service he had been telephoned from London and told to remain on duty all night. During the night a telegram was received ordering the Battalion to return home the next day – in fact all Territorial units across the country had been ordered to end their annual summer training camps and to return to their stations.

At the early morning muster parade on Monday 3rd August, Lt Col Woodcock addressed the men, telling them that they would strike camp and return to Bristol that day. Tension spread through the ranks, and the silence which followed his address showed that the announcement came as quite a surprise. On the way home at various stations, particularly at Taunton, it was evident from the numbers of people on the platforms that the Reservists were being recalled to their Regiments. As George remembered, the men were dismissed to their homes during the afternoon when they returned to St Michael's Hill.

Later in the day, Germany declared war on France and completed preparations for the invasion of Belgium. The following day, German troops crossed into Belgium and at 4pm on 4th August 1914, the British Government ordered the mobilisation of the Army. Two hours later, Lt Col Woodcock received a Telegram from the War Office

The first telegram of the War with the mobilise instruction. The telegram is believed to have been kept as a souvenir by Col Woodcock and was found in a scrapbook at the Soldiers of the Gloucestershire Museum. (*Soldiers of Gloucestershire Museum*)

No sooner had the 4th and 6th Battalions arrived in Minehead, they were 'striking camp' and heading back to Bristol. (*Vaughan Collection at Bristol Record Office*)

containing the word, 'Mobilise'. The country, the 6th Battalion and George were at war.

War Preparations

Having taken command of the 6th Battalion three years earlier, Lt Col Woodcock was well placed to oversee war preparations and to generate support from within the Bristol community. He was regarded as one of Bristol's most prominent citizens and had many civic and business associations with the City. In particular, he was a stockbroker by profession, a Member of the Bristol Stock Exchange and a director of several companies. Among his civic duties, he represented St Michael's Ward on the City Council, served on several committees and was President of the Society of Bristolians in London.

Preparations in Bristol began in earnest and there was an immediate appeal for recruits to bring the 6th Battalion up to war strength. In the three days following the return from Minehead, 220 new recruits had been enrolled, medically examined, fully equipped and posted to companies within the Battalion. In addition, a further 100 men had been rejected for service on medical and other grounds.

Many Bristol businesses also sent recruits from their workforce. The Imperial Tobacco Company sent five staff; The British American Tobacco Company sent several clerical workers and the Bristol branch of the Wilts and Dorset Bank telephoned to reserve four places for their employees. Even a previous member of the 6th Battalion who had lived in New Zealand for five years, turned up at St Michael's Hill and was 'fortunate' enough to secure one of the remaining vacancies in his old Battalion. By the end of a frantic week of activity the 6th Battalion was getting close to war strength and on Saturday 8th August, the 'colours' were presented to the Lord Mayor for safekeeping at a ceremony at the Council House in Corn Street. On Sunday 9th August, the day before the Battalion left Bristol, Colonel Woodcock announced that a Committee was being formed to

provide assistance to any members who might have to return through any unfortunate circumstances, or to any of their dependants who may require help during the absence of the Battalion on service.

On Monday 10th August the 6th Battalion left Bristol to make their way to their appointed war station. The occasion of their departure was reported in full in the *Bristol Times and Mirror*…

"The departure of the Territorials yesterday was favoured with sunshine and a heartfelt send off from the thousands who lined up the route from headquarters to the entraining platform, in the vicinity of the Bedminster passenger station. A crowd began to assemble outside the 6th quarters at St. Michael's Hill early in the afternoon, and waited with exemplary patience for more than an hour. Just after half-past four the gates swung open and the bands emerged, followed by Lt Col Woodcock (officer commanding) and Captain Wilson (adjutant); both, of course being mounted, and behind them came the former's splendid battalion in full service kit.

"The mothers, wives, sisters, and sweethearts were much in evidence, and great were their efforts to prevent tears from breaking through the smiles they bravely bore upon their faces. The terraced walk on one side of St. Michael's Hill was a capital elevated stand from which to watch the corps pass. The steepness of the thoroughfare was all against marching in comfort, but the battalion

A postcard issued as part of the 6th Battalion's campaign for recruits.
(Vaughan Collection at Bristol Record Office)

Before leaving Bristol the 6th Battalion deposited the King's and the Regiment's Colours with the Lord Mayor for safekeeping at this ceremony at the Council House, Corn Street on Saturday 8th August 1914. *(Vaughan Collection at Bristol Record Office)*

swung down the declivity stepping as one man, and that, too, without the assistance of the bands.

"Cameras were busy and many a picture was snapped. One amateur, the cadet of a local wealthy family, had taken up a splendid position and doubtless secured some additions to his collection of Territorial plates which he has made since mobilisation. Down the hill and round into Colston Street marched the Battalion, and on reaching the latter the bugles struck up. The crowd kept growing as if by magic; the stirring strains of the band affected the accompanying crowds, and they kept step, men and women, with the boys in khaki. There is nothing like a good band to take the slouch even out of those who do the looking on.

"Colonel Woodcock has enrolled upwards of 300 recruits since the regiment responded to the King's Proclamation: but the bearing of the column did not disclose this – it might have been composed exclusively of three-year men and upwards. Passing the Colston Hall, the guard on duty at that building came smartly to the present, to which the 6th responded with "eyes right." There was a concourse of spectators in the neighbourhood of St. Augustine's Bridge, several tramcars being loaded. One of these conveyances,

chartered by the members of the Bristol Stock Exchange, gave a rousing round of sustained Cheers, producing Union Jacks and waving them vigorously. This demonstration was in compliment to Colonel Woodcock, who in private life was one of their number.

"The crowds behaved in a quiet way which has characterised the city from the first. Everywhere, handkerchiefs were waved but there was nothing approaching noise, but the glistening eyes of those on either side of Baldwin Street and Victoria Street showed how hearts were beating with hope for the Empire's cause.

"In Victoria Street the brass band thundered forth the French National Hymn, the Marseillaise and what a grand marching tune it makes! From here Bath Bridge was taken, and down the left bank of the New Cut to the entraining station at Bedminster. Reaching this, the crowd was kept back by the police. The arrangements of the entraining officer were excellent and the battalion took their seats expeditiously and without confusion; indeed, no regiment of the line could have done better. Two trains were necessary, and quite early, the 6th were steaming out to the appointed rendezvous.

"Colonel Woodcock has offered his regiment to the War Council for Foreign Service, 80 per cent of his men having enthusiastically volunteered therefor…"

Essex bound

As the 6th Battalion set off for Essex, so did dozens of other regiments from around the country. There was real concern that any German invasion would first threaten the East Coast and there were over 20 regiments stationed in the Chelmsford area alone.

Exactly a month after hurriedly returning from their Minehead Camp, Bristol's Territorial Battalions were becoming acquainted with their new surroundings. The September 1914 edition of the monthly magazine, 'The Bristolian and Clifton Social World' ran a story on the 'Mystery of Bristol Territorials' and asked the question…

'Where are the men of the 4th and 6th Gloucesters and other local forces?' The article sought to allay local concerns about the whereabouts of loved ones and the site of postcards and letters with postmarks removed and addresses obliterated. There was genuine anxiety that the enemy was in 'our very midst' and hence the need for strict censorship to keep secret the whereabouts of the troops. However, it wasn't long before Bristol families knew precisely where their loved ones were based with many postcards home avoiding the censor.

The 4th Gloucesters were based in Danbury, whilst George and the 6th Gloucesters were in Little Baddow. George was fortunate to secure a relatively comfortable billet with Margaret and George Cockerton in their cottage. Members of the 6th were billeted in all sorts of places across the village. Even the school was used to sleep 26 soldiers for four days in early September 1914. The Regiment paid £2.16.6 for the privilege and the soldiers left before school assembled in the morning.

A youngster at the time, in 1977, village resident Roy Warsop recalled the impact on his family…

"After supper, with us younger children in bed by 8.30, my father answered a knock on the front door and was confronted by two military men. 'We want to billet some men in your house. How many can you take?' Father made a swift calculation. 'About six,' he said. Less than half an hour later there was a tramp of marching feet, a call to halt, a pile of arms on our lawn, and they started to come into the house – over 50 of them that night, just sleeping where they could.

"They had had a long march. My father's house was a largish villa type. There were two attics where we slept in the summer time and where my father had a small billiard table. There were four bedrooms, a bathroom on the first floor, sitting room, dining room, kitchen and large scullery with a mangle and water supply, both hot and cold. Underneath the kitchen was a large cellar which could hold five tons of coal. There were also two workshops, one just newly built – these were

Extract from the Bristolian and Clifton Social World in September 1914. *(Bristol Record Office)*

also occupied by troops – C Company, 6th Gloucesters Territorial Battalion.

"The next day things were straightened out a bit. My eldest brother had enlisted in the Navy so there were six of us Warsops – mother, father, three boys and a 17-year-old sister. We were allowed three bedrooms, kitchen and scullery.

"For seven months this went on, at one time there were over 80 men on the premises but a lot of the rougher types were weeded out, and my sister suffered no discourtesy of any kind during the time they were there, although at the start she had lost some small articles of jewellery – nothing valuable. Latrines and a cookhouse were also built near the workshops. Most of the men were employees of W D & H O Wills, the famous cigarette makers of Gold Flake, Three Castles, and the very cheap Woodbines. The firm used to send the troops thousands of cigarettes.

"The troops were courteous to us all, allowed us boys to look at their rifles and fix bayonets on them and at Christmas time gave us presents. About the end of March 1915 they went away to France – most of them never to return."

On 31st March 1915 many children went to see the troops leave for the Front and as the troops departed the Chairman of Little Baddow Parish Council sent this message to the *Bristol Times and Mirror*:

"To the Commanding Officer, 6th Battalion Gloucestershire Regiment:

"Dear Sir, I am writing to convey the good wishes of the inhabitants of Little Baddow to the 6th Gloucesters on their departure for the Front. The stay of the battalion here has created many pleasant friendships, which it may be hoped will not cease when the present troubles are over.

"The conduct of the men has been excellent and everyone speaks well of them. We all realise the difficult conditions as to housing under which they have laboured; even under normal conditions the village is badly housed, and provision has had to be made for two and a half times the usual population.

"The cheerfulness of the men under these difficult conditions has been apparent to all, and we only wish that we could have done more for them than we have been able to do, for the sacrifices they have made and are making for us are far more than we can ever repay. We wish you all a hearty God-speed and pray for a successful and victorious campaign and a triumphant and speedy return."

(Signed) A E BRISCOE, Chairman, Little Baddow Parish Council, The Hoppet, Little Baddow, Essex

As the 6th Battalion was preparing to leave for France, recruitment continued in earnest back in Bristol and there was no let up in the campaign to encourage more men to join up. *(Soldiers of Gloucestershire Museum)*

6TH BATT. GLOUCESTER REGT.
HEAD QUARTERS:
ST. MICHAEL'S HILL, BRISTOL.

— THE —

GALLANT SIXTH

Follow the Gloster Boys and Fill the Gaps in the Fighting Line of

THE SIXTH AT THE FRONT

Every Man must do his bit, or he will be ashamed to meet the Gloster Boys when they return.

Back in Bristol

As soon as George and the rest of the 6th Battalion left for Essex, recruiting continued apace back at St Michael's Hill not only to keep the Battalion up to war strength, but to form a second Battalion.

The number of volunteers, reservists and former NCOs coming forward was such that by 9th September 1914, over 600 men had joined up and the Second 6th Battalion came into existence shortly afterwards. It went across to France for the first time on 23rd May 1916.

In addition to the recruiting work being carried out by the 6th Battalion at St Michael's Hill, and the 4th Battalion at Old Market, the formation of a special Bristol Battalion of the Gloucestershire Regiment as a contribution to the 'Kitchener Army' was announced on 4th September 1914.

Within two weeks of the announcement, nearly 500 men had completed application forms and enrolled for the new Battalion at the Colston Hall which became its temporary headquarters. Two weeks later, and the 12th Battalion – or 'Bristol's Own' as it became known – was at full strength with an initial establishment of 1,100 men. The Battalion soon outlived its temporary home and on 19th September 1914, the War Office confirmed that it had purchased the site of the Bristol International Exhibition which was located on the banks of the River Avon at Ashton Meadows – opposite and adjacent to the bonded warehouses. The Exhibition opened on 28th May 1914 and was due to run until 10th October 1914. However, the war intervened and with the number of visitors lower than anticipated and the organisers experiencing financial difficulties, the site was destined to close early. Its acquisition as a military barracks was timely and the various temporary wooden structures were substantially strengthened and adapted by the Royal Engineers and the Army Service Corps. 'Bristol's Own' made the site its home from around the middle of October 1914.

The Battalion spent the next eight months preparing to join the fray on the Western Front – route marching, musketry and bayonet practice, physical drills, night operations, sham fights in Ashton Park and trench digging on Brandon Hill were among the various exercises carried out.

12 Glo. Rg Bristol own 5.Co No 510

To help raise money for the new Battalion, a Regimental Fund was established and Portishead-born songwriter Fred Weatherly wrote the rousing *'Bravo Bristol'* with the music provided by the legendary composer Ivor Novello. Fred Weatherly went on to write the iconic Irish anthem *'Danny Boy'* and *'Roses Are Shining in Picardy'* one of the most evocative songs of the First World War. Both Weatherly and Novello gave the entire proceeds from the sale of *'Bravo Bristol'* to the Regimental Fund.

Fundraising carried on in earnest too for the families of soldiers in the Territorial Battalions who might suffer hardship with their breadwinners away on military service. During the autumn of 1915 and from his Essex base, Colonel Woodcock wrote a letter to the *Bristol Times and Mirror* on behalf of the 6th Battalion, thanking Bristolians for their generosity in supporting

A group of 'Bristol's Own', standing on the site of the Bristol International Exhibition in 1914. Behind on the left is 'B' Bond – home to the excellent Bristol Record Office. The author's grandfather – Stanley Barnes is stood in the front, fourth left. *(Soldiers of Gloucestershire Museum)*

the Battalion Relief Fund. Some 66 people had subscribed £149.12.11 towards the Fund. In addition, Annie Woodcock (Col. Woodcock's wife) and Nan Mardon who represented the Ladies Committee of the 6th Battalion War Fund also appealed through the press for socks and warm flannel shirts to help the troops ward off the cold winter on the East Coast. Very quickly, more than 800 shirts in addition to socks and other warm clothing had been donated and dispatched to the troops in Essex.

Chapter 5
To the Trenches and a Baptism of Fire
April to December 1915

Well, as I say the day came, March 31st 1915, so we had spent seven months in Essex. Not too bad, but the rough was to come and we landed at Boulogne on April 1st – what fools? Had a destroyer escort over. Sea was very rough. Soon as we were clear of the docks and on the way to the rest camp the French kiddies were on us… "Souvenir, Anglais soldats, tres bon, la guerre finis tout suite – Allemagne no bon…" and that's how it went on for a time. We were soon getting used to them and we got to our billets at last. I was now carrying a rifle, bayonet and 120 rounds of ammunition. Bugle was packed away. Band and Drums were finished, and I was in command of a section of 10 men. Four sections to a Platoon – mine was No. 6 Platoon, four Platoons to a company – mine B Company.

German trench at Ploegsteert Wood. (*In Flanders Fields Museum, Ypres, Belgium. Kurt Zehmisch Collection*)

We had a new Commanding Officer join us not long after arriving in France. Colonel Micklem, a regular from the Rifle Brigade, he was turned out at Sandhurst in peace time. A proper soldier – he knew how to treat his men. We were on the move all the time getting nearer the front line as the Germans were moving fast. I learnt that the Zeppelins had been dropping their bombs over London.

We and Jerry had plenty of observation balloons up and what planes that were roaming the skies were doing the same but they soon became a strong weapon of war and outshone the cavalry – horses were no good then. Cavalry men were put in line regiments.

Germans were halted almost near the coast, then Von Kluck's army that got so near, turned back and it was a mystery what made him do it. It was the rapid fire of the Old Contemptible's that shook him. He said every man had a machine gun. We got near the front line at Pont de Nieppe and went in the line with

A tethered German observation balloon during the early part of the war. *(In Flanders Fields Museum, Ypres, Belgium. Kurt Zehmisch Collection)*

the Rifle Brigade Regulars at Ploegsteert. We called it Plug Street. Then, finally, we took over ourselves, and that's where we had our first baptism of rifle fire and field guns. So we were in it on our own.

Trenches were made up of breastworks, could not dig down very far or we would strike water. So sandbags had to be used and filled with earth. Whilst we were out the line resting I had to go around with an Officer searching people's houses for pro-Germans. For complaints were made of being sniped at whilst moving up to the front line. The Officer could speak French but I never trusted them myself, but there it was, they never wanted to move. We never moved about there during daylight because we were under observation and it was asking for it.

We held the line there for a time (six weeks) then moved to the right to Hebuterne, those were breastworks too. To get to those trenches we had to go through a ruined village and across a road. Just before entering the trenches there was a big monastery, and there was just the four walls standing but the cellars were all right.

We used to get fresh drinking water from there by working a hand pump, take a couple of clean petrol cans. We could only do this by day and at the end

of the trench on to the road was exposed to enemy snipers, baiting with telescopic rifles, so we had to be careful. I took a man with me one day. I dashed around first, in the shelter of the high brick walls, told him to come after me after a five minute lapse. I went on down the cellar, filled my two cans, and came up; found him sat down holding his head. A sniper had got him. His head sort of went up to a point. I looked at his wound, right on the tip top of his head, a small groove. I dressed it for him from our field dressing we carried on us – small packet of bandages, gauze and iodine – and got him back to the trench and down the base he went and back to Blighty. A letter a friend had from him said that his wound paralysed him down one side of his body, yet to me it looked a mere nothing. Steel helmets had not been thought of. Then we had a change of equipment and rifles. Webbing with small pouches each side for ammunition, haversack, entrenching tool and handle and the rifle was a short Enfield.

Then the Germans started to use gas. If the wind was favourable before an attack they would send over dense clouds of gas. Our troops were useless, they had respirators. We had them issued in a small satchel. This was not much protection and they improved on it to a hood. We looked like the Ku Klux Klan when we had them on – eye-pieces and a mouthpiece to breathe out, which would close on intake.

A klaxon horn would warn us of an approach of gas, it was terrible. Germans had to wear them as well but theirs were treated with the chemicals to counteract it, we soon learnt that. Then came along a good respirator that was carried on the chest at all times in the trenches, easy to slip on, and they were tested every so often and a new one issued if found defective. This happened when we were out the front line for a rest. Sometimes the wind would change and the Germans would have a taste of their own

German trench and soldiers at Ploegsteert Wood.
(La Societe d'Histoire de Comines-Warneton)

medicine. Our artillery used to paste them, but the trouble was we never had the guns or ammunition to use. Our officers might send a message over Morse code 'being heavily shelled, please retaliate', about one salvo and finish. Then at home in England Lloyd George got on the Government as Minister of Munitions and what a difference, several new weapons were invented. The Lewis gun was a good one. Something like a machine gun but lighter. Cartridges were loaded in a drum instead of a belt. Gunner No. 1 firing, No. 2 ready to take off the empty drum, clip on a new one, no trouble if the ammo and the gun was kept clean.

Our rifles were our best pals, and it was up to us to look after them, if not it might mean our life. Things used to come subconscious to us as to our alertness, such as a lot of noise going on over the other side, driving in stakes, mending the barbed wire about six yards in front of the trench. So we would do the same, as the bombardment of trenches would smash them up, that of course happened at night. It was OK in daylight fog if it was thick enough to screen us from Jerry. Men would be detailed for working party out over the top. Stakes, rolls of barbed wire, and plenty of it, well spread out. For if that was well done, we felt more secure from surprise attacks from German patrols with a few grenades. We used to do the same with about a half dozen men. The Germans might be about 150 or 200 yards away. What we had to watch was the star shells – fired from

Sgt Jack House of the 4th Gloucesters models the 'Ku Klux Klan' outfit that George described. *(Soldiers of Gloucestershire Museum)*

Verey Light pistols. They would go up like a sky rocket then burst into a bright light and we had to keep still. The German ones were far better than ours; they would hang about in the sky for five minutes. Ours, after bursting, would start falling again.

Now and again a raid on the enemy trench, a few bombs and a quick return. Our Battalion was the first to make a big raid on the enemy trenches. It was practised for a few weeks out on rest and done when we got back in the line. It was a success and Jerry was

taken by surprise so that when he tried to hit back he fell into so many booby traps and the communication trenches were blocked with Germans trying to drive us out. Oh Boy! They had a real good pasting. Next day our spotter planes reported many German ambulances on the move in that section, back and forward. That was our first real action, and only on a small scale. That was trench warfare and it carried on through the winter of 1915.

The Battalion was starting to send men home on leave, but it was only for six days, and two of them were took up with travelling. We were issued with fur jackets and I looked like an Eskimo. We had caps that pulled down at the back and strapped over the ears and under the chin. I was away, six-day leave to UK, Blighty – Le Havre to Southampton with everything I possessed. Four hours outside Southampton (fog). Eventually I got home, 19 Charles Street. Got more of a welcome from the people in the Street than at home, and it was my birthday, November 9th, 24 years of age. The first thing I did was to go to the baths and have a good bath, change of clothes and a good posh. Dad was home when I got back and we had a good tuck in.

There was two of my pals in Charles Street home at the same time – one from the 4th Gloucesters and one from the REME.

Evenings I spent with my young lady. Daytimes, we pals went touring the town, meeting friends in the Services. Drop in to have a chat and a drink. Call in the factory where the young lady worked and bring her home, and the four days were soon gone.

Before I left the boot factory I bought a little puppy – gave a shilling for him. He was quite a pet at home and grew into a fox terrier. I had to leave him in the care of Dad and my brother Harry. I noticed there was no dog at home. My father told me that he had to have it destroyed. People over a high wall at the top of the garden made a complaint to the

Police that the dog was disturbing their sleep at nights. Police came to our house and gave my father a warning, any further trouble and the people would take out a summons against him. He took the dog down the Home and had him destroyed. I was wild and a war on too. I told them a few bombs, not barks would please them perhaps.

We had Harry's pigeon house up the top of the garden and I had my photo took stood by it with Harry's photo in uniform stuck near the wire. I was in my full kit, rifle and all, and Dad sent one out to Harry.

Harry had some valuable homing birds, quite a few men kept them around Easton. They would hold competitions. Put some birds in a special basket; take them to the railway station with instructions to liberate them and at what time from stations up country. All this was done, and then the owners of the birds would be watching for their return. First that was clocked in was the winner. Of course there was a side stake on it. The pigeon house had to be left behind by Harry for Dad to look after.

Wore my civvie suit for a time whilst my uniform was being de-lined and cleaned. Had I been pulled up by MPs I had a good excuse.

So it was back to France again – Folkestone to Boulogne and in the cattle trucks somewhere near Hebuterne, and a little bit of snow to make matters worse, wondering what Christmas 1915 would bring us. If we had the Anglo Saxons opposite us they were quiet in this trench warfare, but the Prussian Guards or Bavarians were letting us know they were about. Sniping all day and patrols at night. During daytime one sentry per bay would be on duty at the parapet, taking a look through the periscope, and down again, then change to another place for a sniper might be looking for him to put it up again – and my God they could hit them too, smash would go the glass – or we would have a sniper's front plate fixed in the trench,

George (centre) and his pals from the 4th Gloucesters (left) and the Royal Engineers in Bristol on leave in November 1915. *(Ken Pine)*

George in full military kit standing in front of his brother's pigeon house. The photograph of Harry can just be seen by the chicken wire. *(Robin Pine)*

camouflaged so that Jerry could not find it with his field glasses. He would wait to see the slit go back to have a pot at him and we had to be careful. Many were killed or wounded this way.

At night during sundown and coming daybreak the next morning, every man was on the alert. That was when the most trouble was likely to start. At stand down when it was daylight we had a rum issue that

5th Gloucesters front line trench at Hebuterne. Testing a French periscope rifle and spotting the results. *(Soldiers of Gloucestershire Museum)*

warmed us up for a time. Being a Section Commander I had to draw my section rum and issue it to the men. Run to about two spoonfuls per man, some refused it and that made more for others. I remember once I had too much and it upset me. The smell of it used to make me shudder. It was the real McCoy but I still had a job of dishing it out to the men, and the weather got worse. Plenty of rain and snow, flooding the trenches. We were up to our knees in it and they issued us with waders up to our thighs. Had to make sumps in the bottom of the trench and cover them with sump boards and bail them out, throwing the water over the top. Most of us cut the bottoms of our overcoats off, for they were always dragging in it.

We were always glad when it was time to be relieved for four days a few miles back from the line. Most of our time was spent on scraping the mud off our clothes and puttees, on our rifles and ammo and foot inspection by the ambulance men. Perhaps pay day maybe a shop would be hanging on near our billets and sold the goods the Tommy wanted, and when the fag issue came along they were a Godsend, and a letter from home, or one from home with some in. Our fag issue used to come up with the rations.

A Sergeant of the 4th Gloucesters wearing a knitted woollen cap, shaving in a trench. *(Soldiers of Gloucestershire Museum)*

A. Watched Pot never? Boils. RGB 1915

A field cooker on the go in the trenches from a 1915 sketch by Henry Buckle. *(Soldiers of Gloucestershire Museum)*

Our rations used to consist of hard tack biscuits and a small tin of bully beef. We would go mad over a tin of Fray Bentos. Those were the best – Maconochies and a piece of bread if we were lucky. Out of the line we had the field cookers going and we used to get a good brew up of tea. Perhaps bacon, porridge, and everything would be OK so long as Jerry spotter planes never saw the smoke coming out the cooker, then the light guns would send over a few shells to try to put a stop to it.

I remember they had a direct hit. Put the cooks, cooker and grub – a nice stew was doing doughboys – all out of action. So it was hard tack biscuits and bully. My new false teeth, agony – nothing to make the biscuits soft. As I said, now and again one or the other of us had a parcel from home. Eatables, cakes, mostly biscuits, fags and chocolates, and we always shared them around. That helped to fill our tummies.

And here we were spending our first Christmas away from the old country (Blighty) 1915, on active service in Flanders, and wondering what sort of time we should get from Jerry. But I am pleased to say it was very quiet with regards hostilities. Greetings were exchanged across No Man's Land and plenty of music over there, so I take it the next changeover had been made, and we had the Anglo Saxons opposite us. It was a good change and rest for us and it lasted for a day or so. We had an extra issue of fags but the cold was terrible and our feet – had to rub plenty of whale oil in them to prevent frostbite.

Author's Notes

British Cemetery at Ploegsteert Wood. *(In Flanders Fields Museum, Ypres, Belgium)*

Ploegsteert Sector

The 1/6th Gloucesters were part of the 48th (South Midland Territorial) Division that was in existence prior to the War. In peacetime, many of the Territorial Camps that George attended were massive 'divisional' ones. When it crossed to France in April 1915, the Division was made up of three Infantry Brigades; each with four infantry battalions…

143rd (Warwickshire) Brigade
1/5th Royal Warwicks, 1/6th Royal Warwicks, 1/7th Royal Warwicks, 1/8th Royal Warwicks

144th (Gloucester and Worcester) Brigade
1/4th Gloucesters, 1/6th Gloucesters, 1/7th Worcesters, 1/8th Worcesters

145th (South Midland) Brigade
1/5th Gloucesters, 1/4th Oxford & Bucks Light Infantry, 1/1st Bucks, 1/4th Royal Berks

The 1/6th Gloucesters was organised into four companies (A, B, C and D) of around 640 men in total. Each company had 160 men and was divided into four Platoons of 40 men. Each Platoon was divided into four Sections of 10 men. At the start of the War, George was a Section Commander in No. 6 Platoon of B Company.

By the time George and the 1/6th Gloucesters had reached Ploegsteert Wood in April 1915 to relieve the regular soldiers from the Rifle Brigade, the trench-lines in the sector had settled down following the battles of late 1914 and early 1915 that halted the German advance towards the French coast. By spring 1915, deadlock had been reached along the whole of the Western Front

and as the area was regarded as a relatively safe spot in which to serve, the trenches in and around Ploegsteert Wood were often used to blood the new Territorial Battalions in the art of trench warfare.

That said, in the six weeks that George and the 1/6th Gloucesters were in the Ploegsteert Sector, 23 members of the Battalion were killed and 73 were wounded – so, not that safe.

The Home Front

Back home, 'Bristol's Own' left the City at the end of June 1915 and following brigade and divisional training in Yorkshire, the Battalion moved to Codford, on Salisbury Plain in August 1915 where it stayed until it crossed to France on 21st November 1915.

Away from military preparations, a branch of the Women's Relief Corps was formed in Bristol. With its headquarters in London, the Corps had already established several centres across Great Britain and Ireland. Consisting of an organised body of women, its aim was to undertake civil and semi-military work, thus enabling more men to go to the front – and for every woman to be of use to her country in its hour of need.

Those joining in civil work were expected to undertake the duties of men and to surrender them to the men on their return from the War. The helpers who preferred semi-military work underwent training in drill, route-marching, signalling, first-aid and other duties; also in the use of arms, so that when trained they may release men from such work as the guarding of railways and public buildings, do home patrol and picket work, etc and as a last resort, defend themselves and their fellow women from barbarity. Semi-military helpers wore a simple, inexpensive uniform and the allowable age range was from 16 to 50. The watchword of the Corps was 'United we Stand'.

The publication, *'Bristol and the War'* on 1st July 1915, made the following appeal to the women of Bristol… "Now is the time for all the women in Bristol to come forward in a body in response to the call: 'Every woman wanted.' To our brave men at the Front, it will act as a tremendous stimulus to know what the women at home are doing. Apart from the discipline and developing the character, the women who join this Relief Corps are making themselves of greater value to the State. Let July; therefore, prove a record month for recruits, who will be welcomed every Wednesday evening at 7.30 at the Barton YMCA. The enrolment fee is one shilling, with a yearly subscription of the same amount. The number of members in the Bristol branch is now running into hundreds, and when not in uniform wear a distinguishing badge on the left arm of a khaki band, with the letter 'H' (for Helper) in red on it. Full particulars can be obtained at the YMCA".

In the 1915-16 college year, the MVTC established a course for women in conjunction with the local Boot and Shoe Manufacturers Association. The course aimed to train women to take the places of boot and shoe operatives like George who had joined the Army. There were 49 applicants and 24 were selected for attendance at the classes. Of these, 18 qualified for certificates through satisfactory performance and punctual attendance.

However, the remuneration offered proved insufficient to attract a suitable supply of women and the classes were discontinued.

In the same year, the MVTC also offered classes for women in connection with the West of England Commercial Reserve. The idea was to prepare educated women to take the place of male clerks in offices during the period of the war. Many of the women who attended were the daughter's of 'leading Bristol citizens', including the daughter of the then Master of the Society of Merchant Venturers. There were 93 applicants for the course but many had not received a sufficiently good education. Of the 47 selected for attendance, 41 gained a certificate at the end of the four-week course and of these, 32 found employment in Bristol offices.

Attendees on the MVTC's Munitions Classes rose from 58 people in 1914-15 to 479 by the end of the 1915-16 year.

Gommecourt Wood raid

Although not involved himself, George was proud of the surprise attack that C Company made on the night of 25/26th November 1915. The raid on German trenches and shelters took place in the Hebuterne area and in the South East corner of Gommecourt Wood. The aim of the raid was to cause loss to the enemy, reducing his morale and obtaining information as to the enemy's trenches and to secure prisoners.

The raid was highly successful and achieved its objectives. The event was notable because it was proudly reported as the first such attacking raid on German trenches planned and carried out by British troops – the Canadians had carried out a similar raid a few days before. The achievement received much acclaim with congratulatory messages coming from Divisional, Corps and Army Commanders as well as Lord French himself. For this episode and other good work in the field, the Battalion was mentioned in dispatches – one of the first Territorial Units to receive this distinction.

Chapter 6
Best Day in France, Best Day in Bristol, but a Blighty end
1916

The months were moving on and we were drawn out of this line for the big Battle of Vimy Ridge. Day back we were in a derelict village resting and waiting for reinforcements. There was an estaminet cafe across the road we used to go in and have a drink and a game of cards.

I was going back to the billet when I spotted a horsedrawn mess wagon used for Officers' goods and, on the side was 1st Battalion Gloster Regiment, my first thoughts were of Harry. I stopped the driver, asked him if his unit was about. He said not a mile away. I told him to get in touch with Harry Pine and tell him where to find his brother, George. And next day Harry was there with a couple of dozen mates from the 1st Battalion. That was a day that day. The best one I ever had in France and we were sorry when it broke up, for them to return to their unit. A bit of

George and Violet with George's father, Charles Pine and Violet's mother, Clara Winterson. *(Robin Pine)*

luck for me, spotting that Officers' Mess cart.

It was time for us to go to Vimy Ridge. Our whole Brigade – Cornwalls, Devons, Gloucesters, Argyles – in support of the Canadians, moved up at night. Halted parallel with the long ridge. Devons and Cornwalls were over and driving Jerry back, we were ready if those were held up. All along the ridge was great long shafts dug and boarded up, each big enough to hold a company of troops. Our troops did well, drove Jerry back behind Loos, a big town with coal pits that was the other side of the ridge. One long plain in front of us – we had to do the mopping up. We never stayed there very long and was on the move again to another part of the line, it was near enough March/ April 1916.

We had a little snow to cheer us up and I was thinking of June – I shall be time expired (after eight years service) and any man that re-engaged was offered a month's leave in Blighty and £15 as well. So that set me thinking, for Conscription was in force

Bread wagon about to take supplies to the 6th Gloucestershire Regiment. *(Soldiers of Gloucestershire Museum)*

and a man that came home and finished had about three months before they were down on him again. So I thought it over and decided to re-engage. I wrote home, told my Dad and the young lady what I had done. Naturally they liked the idea of the long leave, but not the going back to France again.

I said just now we were on the move again near the Somme. I got promoted to Full Corporal with pay before going to Vimy. On active service with some casualties of no return, promotion was quick for those that had tact and good leadership – one the men had confidence in. This was quickly noticed by the Platoon Officer. It was no time before I had my third stripe and a Full Sergeant too with pay – so my wages were going up.

I must mention that we had one at home that was proud of her four brothers. She wrote to us all, that was our sister, Edith, the eldest of our first family.

It was coming up to June 1916 and I was looking forward to my month's furlough. We were moved over to the Somme. Trenches that had been dug by the French, long communication trenches leading up to the front line, which ran through three copses named, Mark, Luke and John. They had tall trees in them, a mark for German artillery. Trenches of the enemy were less than 200 yards away and our trenches ran along parallel with the copses. No protection from blow backs of shrapnel. It was very lively here and there was talk of a big offensive pending. Well, the good news came at last. I was warned to get ready for my month's leave, wrote home and told them in a green envelope to expect me. I arrived OK, but while I was waiting for this, when I had time to relax my thoughts were – 'should I have the misfortune to be maimed for life, who should I have to look to?' We were engaged, me and Violet. I should have to put the question to her and her widowed mother. There was only them two at 89 Bellevue Road. Her mother had about five sisters, four of them married with families. Her mother was a cleaner at WD&HO Wills and Violet worked at the tailoring.

So, home I got and what a month. The first thing my young lady greeted me with was Aunt Annie has been married to a Canadian at the Registry Office, St Peter's Church. Just the information I wanted. Find out the proceedings and we will get on with it straight away. Violet saw her mother and my father, and both agreeable, so to get busy. First I wrote to the Army Pay Office and drew out my credit which covered everything, and the day was fixed for the 10th June 1916.

It soon got around to relatives, friends and neighbours. We got busy with invitations and other things in preparation for the Great Day. A car was ordered for the bride, and her uncle gave her away and was the witness. We walked there so I had to meet him at the Dolphin Hotel outside, 11am time of wedding. I left home, poshed-up with my swagger cane under my arm. I had previously visited the Headquarters at St Michael's Hill and got a complete new uniform, a tip for the quartermaster, he wished me luck. The car that picked up Violet arrived a bit early so he took her and her escort for a ride around first in the opposite way to town. Neighbours were mystified, wondering what was happening. Anyway I met her uncle outside the Dolphin and we had to go

in to get my courage up, and when we got to St Peter's everyone was waiting. I should think all Todd's Factory girls were waiting for her. Confetti in the face – but when that hit, it never hurt. Back to Bellevue Road, No. 89 which was to become my home until June 1966.

We had the reception at No. 89 and everything was laid on. Champion! The wife had five uncles and they did their share to make her day a good one. The photographer was ordered for about 3pm. When he came they found me fast asleep up on the bed. I was

George and his new wife Violet in front of the apple blossom tree in the garden of 89 Bellevue Road, Easton on their wedding day. (Ken Pine)

GOOD LUCK AND SAFE RETURN

George with William Radford – Violet's uncle who gave her away at the wedding. A very poignant strap line to the photograph. Another copy of the photograph was found in the private collection of Andy Stevens of Pastimes in Bristol. He acquired the photograph as George's cap was one of the best examples of a 'cor blimey' hat that he had seen. Apparently the cap attracted its nickname following the reaction to it when the CO saw it worn by his men for the first time – 'Cor blimey, we're not wearing these hats are we?' *(Ken Pine)*

blotto. Had to have a good douse in cold water, the crowd was waiting for me out in the back garden and it was a lovely summers day, and there was a lovely orange blossom tree out in full bloom, he was a picture, and me?

Anyway we got the photographing over and another tuck in. Them uncles and wives could mop it up, and the party went on until about 10pm, then the clearing up. All helped and did their share and gradually drifted to their homes. So that was that. I still had near enough a fortnight home and it was going to be a big heartbreak when that came.

We were invited out quite a lot and there was never a dull moment. I learnt that Fred and Tom were in Gallipoli against the Turks, that Tom had been sent home with a wound near his right eye, and arrived home from hospital with the bullet in his neck. He could hardly open his mouth on seven days sick leave. Dad was upset about this and took him to the Infirmary. He was kept in and the bullet was extracted. Dad sent to his Depot at Carlisle a notice to say that his sick leave would start from the time he had his Discharge, then to report back to his Depot.

My sister, Edie had a letter from brother Fred out there that he saw Tom being carried down to the Hospital Ship, but what shocked my Dad was to learn in a letter from Tom that he was being sent out there again. He was never a fit man for he could not open his mouth or eat solid food properly. My Dad sent him money to buy soft food.

He never lasted long out there and he was shot in the other eye and killed. He was buried from the Hospital Ship, Dongola, at sea. My sister Edie had a letter of condolence from the Padre on board ship and Fred went through the evacuation with great losses whilst it lasted, but the withdrawal from there, so it was said, was a marvellous job with hardly any losses. So, after a rest in England, Fred's Regiment was sent to France.

The group wedding photograph with George looking a bit the worse for wear and Violet's uncle, William Radford, seemingly holding him upright!
(Robin Pine)

Finally my time was up to return to France. I learnt that the Battle of the Somme had started. Our Regiment was relieved by fresh troops for the purpose – The Yorkshire Light Infantry (The York and Lancaster Regiment) and they caught a packet from the Germans, worse luck. What happened was this. Before an attack a heavy barrage is laid down on the enemy trenches, barbed wire and back areas. They failed to move the barbed wire, so that when zero hour came Jerry was waiting for them, and it was a proper slaughter for our men for they were mowed down with machine gun fire. Jerry must have got hold of some good information of the attack, for it was a proper fortress. Attack after attack was beaten back. I learnt all this when I got back to the Regiment after my leave. I reported to the Company Sergeant Major, told him what had happened whilst I was home so that the wife had to be put on the strength of the Battalion and the allowance I made per week was transferred to her and my Pay Book altered. This was drawn by her every week at the Post Office. It was a struggle for them to carry on what with food rationing, and the black-market was a curse not encouragement for us abroad, and that's how it went on through the war.

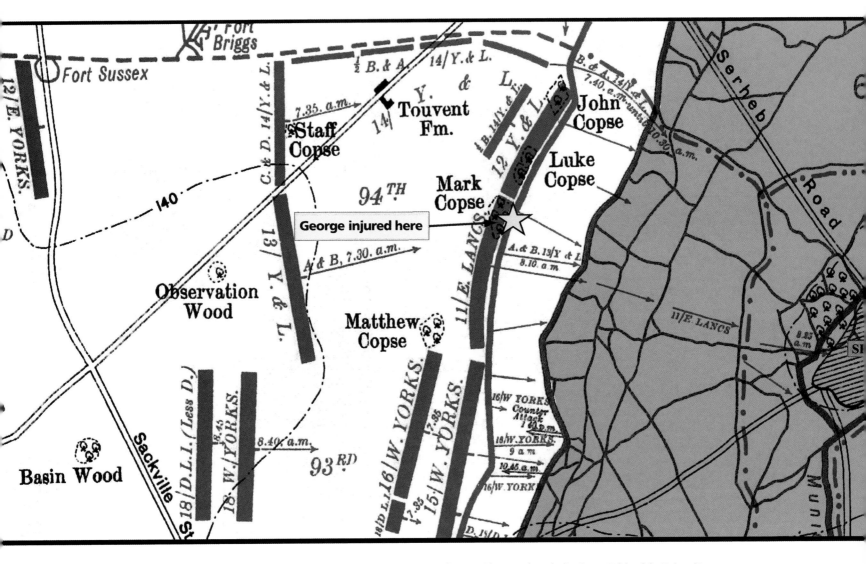

The area where the 'Accrington Pals' and the York and Lancaster Regiment lost so many men when they went over the top on 1st July 1916. The Sap in front of Mark Copse where George was injured some days later is also shown.

I had as I said rejoined my Battalion and we were getting to relieve those poor fellows, the Yorkshire Light Infantry, in the same trenches on the Somme. I shall never forget the sight of the communication trenches – a shambles. We had a job to move through them with the side trenches filled with dead bodies, and we had to move a section at a time on account of shelling. I got to the top, into the front line, saw a Tommy stood up, rifle in his hand. I said "Which way did they go, mate?" No answer, he was dead to the world. I was uncertain whether they turned left or

right. I turned right to the old position we held a few months previous and caught up with the rest of the company.

Got settled in. Our Platoon held a post by Mark Copse at the top of a Sap dug towards the Jerry. It was still intact, the men got down there during the day. Jerry used to send a Whiz Bang shell over every now and again. Explode on percussion. My Platoon Officer, myself and a messenger was stood by the entrance to the Sap and over came a Whiz Bang. We had it. Officer had the heel of his boot took off, the messenger a nasty one on the cheek and myself, my face was covered with splinter shrapnel and in the left arm, and I caught the force of the explosion across my shoulders.

It was Blighty for me and the messenger. So I was home again in Blighty at the end of July 1916, and found myself in a village called Much Wenlock in Shropshire. Lady Foresters Home for Women and Children, turned into a Voluntary Aid Detachment (VAD) Hospital for the wounded soldiers. There was about 30 of us there.

Just a couple of days in bed and I was walking about. All my bits of shrapnel were got out with tweezers. My back was the worst – a proper Charley. Had to have it massaged every day and night before returning. For those who could get out in the grounds they had a game of clock golf. Big black face marked up to 12 and the hole was about halfway from the centre and 12 O'clock. Golf balls and irons and start off at one O'clock and carry on to 12. Alternate turns. Just one turn at each until you holed, then on to 2 O'clock and so on – who reached 12 O'clock first was the winner. It passed the time away and a bowling club lent us their rink. I was there until November. During that time I spent about three months at their convalescent home at Llandudno – September, October and November. Then seven days sick leave and that long travel down to Bristol and glad of it.

As usual our time was took up in visiting people. My sick leave was up and I was instructed to report to the Fourth Reserve Battalion Gloucesters at Salisbury Plain. And, what a place – ticking down with rain, floods, mud, under canvas, but no shooting. That lasted about a fortnight and then the whole Battalion was on the way to Cheltenham, billeted in big houses.

Lady Forester Hospital, Much Wenlock.

The Lady Forester Convalescent Home, Llandudno

A couple of weeks there, then on to Hipswell Camp, Catterick, Yorkshire, just before Christmas – the well-known Military Barracks, miles of wooden huts, like a small town, and the day after we arrived we had a fall of snow – three foot in no time. Proper heavy stuff so we were busy making paths to different big huts for meals. Had a month there then was posted for draft back to France, but what a place to spend Christmas.

Lady Forester's Hospital at Much Wenlock in Shropshire where George had the shrapnel removed from his back. *(Author's own collection)*

Lady Forester's Convalescent Home at Llandudno, North Wales where George spent three months recuperating from his injuries. It must have been a far cry from the trauma of the Somme trenches. *(The J L and B A Lawson-Reay Collection)*

Author's Notes

Somme Injury at Mark Copse

Fortunately, the Gloucestershire Regiment did not go 'over the top' on the disastrous first day of the Battle of the Somme but it was soon to be heavily engaged. The 1/6th Gloucesters were brought up to the Serre Sector on the 5th July 1916 to relieve the 94th Infantry Brigade and to fill the gaps left by the 12th York and Lancaster Battalion whose numbers had been decimated on 1st July. Around 3,600 officers and men had been lost in the Serre Sector by early afternoon on 1st July.

The scene that greeted George as he tried to find his way back to his Platoon following his leave in Bristol must have been awful. Communication trenches full of bodies – what a contrast from the happy wedding snaps of a few weeks before. At 1.30am on 6th July, two platoons from George's B Company were ordered to raid the German first and second lines between Matthew and Mark Copses with a view to penetrating the enemy's defences. For identification, the raiding parties wore pieces of white bandage tied to their shoulder straps and their password if challenged was 'Old Market'.

The two Platoons were easily beaten back and in the War Diary, the Commanding Officer commented, "I do not consider that parties of the strength sent out could possibly have penetrated the German line in the face of the resistance offered."

During the raid the German defences aimed field gun shells and large 4.2 inch shells at the Gloucesters front line. It appears that it was one of these 'whiz bangs' that injured George and several others who were in the Sap in front of Mark Copse.

The shrapnel wounds that George received proved to be a blessing. As George was on his way back to England for treatment, the 1/6th Gloucesters, along with the 1/4th and 1/5th were heavily involved in the capture of Ovillers – a key village in the German line. There were over 1,000 casualties among the three Gloucestershire Territorial Battalions and during the month of July 1916, George's Battalion had lost 90 men killed and 307 injured – including George.

George was reported wounded in the Bristol Journal on 6th August 1916. He would not fight with the 6th Gloucesters again.

Much Wenlock and Llandudno

Across the country the War Council had requisitioned hospitals, wards and beds for use by the sick and wounded soldiers returning from the Front. Many hospitals were supported by the Voluntary Aid Detachment (VAD) who worked alongside local nurses and other staff appointed to care for wounded soldiers during the war. The VAD was formed in August 1909 to provide nursing and medical help in times of war. VADs worked in a variety of roles including nursing assistants, ambulance drivers, chefs, and administration assistants. The majority of VADs worked in the UK and some were posted overseas with the British Expeditionary Force in

The hospital staff who cared for George at Much Wenlock in August 1916. The four staff in the centre of the middle row are Dr Lockyer, Matron Smith, Dr Bigley and Sister Hill. (*Museum at Much Wenlock Nursing Home*)

Miss K E Elphick, Commandant and Matron of Lady Forester's Convalescent Home. She was by all accounts, just like a mother to the recuperating soldiers. *(J L and B A Lawson-Reay Collection)*

Slightly ironic tone to this cartoon postcard from Llandudno. The card included an insert showing many attractions in and around the town. *(J L and B A Lawson-Reay Collection)*

France, Belgium, Gallipoli and Mesopotamia. The British Red Cross Society trained the VAD nurses in first aid, bed making, giving a patient a blanket bath, feeding a patient and keeping a ward clean.

George spent most of August 1916 at the Lady Forester Hospital at Much Wenlock in Shropshire and a further three months at its sister Lady Forester Convalescent Home in Llandudno – both establishments were VADs for the duration of the war. At Much Wenlock there were 43 beds for use by wounded or sick soldiers and by the end of May 1918 there had been 963 military admissions.

The building is now the Much Wenlock Nursing Home and on the first floor a small museum preserves a number of objects and photographs from the First World War period. The Gift Book details the generosity of the local community who brought in extra food and provisions for the wounded. During August 1916, George would have sampled the delights of Lady Constance Gaskill's fruit, scones and cakes as well as her chutneys and jams.

The Electric and Therapeutic (X-rays) Department Book records the names of many soldiers from UK regiments together with those from Irish, Canadian and French battalions. Although George's shrapnel wounds didn't appear to warrant an X-ray, Harold Sandys Williamson's did. A Lance Corporal in the King's Royal Rifle Corps, Williamson was wounded during the Battle of Delville Wood on 15th September 1916 and spent a month undergoing treatment at Much Wenlock.

Williamson studied art at the Leeds School of Art between 1911 and 1914. The following year he attended the Royal Academy Schools in London, 1914-15 and was awarded the Turner Gold Medal. He wrote many letters to his parents during his stay at Much Wenlock and in one, he describes the diet as "very plain, much plainer than the trenches!" The hospital day started with temperatures taken at 5.30am ("even if your nose is only scratched"); a wash and shave and breakfast at 6am, which included tea, bread and butter, ham or bacon. At 9am, a drink of milk. Dressings were done between 10am and 11am followed by a doctor's round. Dinner was at 12.30pm and at 4pm was tea. Lights out at 8.00pm".

On 22 October 1916, Williamson joined George and around 40 other convalescing soldiers at Llandudno, where they both stayed until the end of November 1916. After the war, Williamson became a respected artist and from 1930-1958 was headmaster of The Chelsea School of Art. His letters home to his parents are in the Imperial War Museum in London, where one of his paintings, 'A German Attack on a wet morning in April 1918' also hangs. George never knew that he spent around six weeks in the company of a very accomplished war artist.

Chapter 7
Back to France with 'Bristol's Own'
1917

Had my seven days draft leave and had to return on an early train on the Sunday morning. Report back to Barracks, Catterick, 12 midnight. Never got there until Monday morning about 9am. Reported to the R.T.O. Temple Meads. He examined my pass, gave us the departure of train to the North, 9.30am, and I think we stopped at every station on the way, then only got as far as Sheffield or Leeds – no more until early Monday morning. Got to Ripon, change for Catterick, eventually arrived at the Barracks. What a train ride. A few weeks there, then on our way across to France.

Arrived at Rouen, one of the big reception bases, where the new troops arrive to go up to the front. I was there for three weeks hoping to be sent up to my own Regiment, the 6th Gloucesters, but the 12th Gloucesters had a bashing at Pozieres – lost a lot of

The Third Battle of Ypres (also known as the Battle of Passchendaele, 31 July-10 November 1917) had smashed the landscape around Zonnebeke, Belgium to pieces. *(In Flanders Fields Museum, Ypres, Belgium)*

men – and about 50 of us were drafted to the 12th Gloucesters, 'Bristol's Own' Battalion. I kept my rank and seniority and soon fell in OK with them. The wife's cousin was a tailor on Headquarters' Staff; he got killed out there and was buried at the big military cemetery at Rouen. Whilst there in charge of a burial party I came across his grave.

The first time I went in the trenches with my new mob was at the Brick Stacks at Festubert, and I was in charge of the listening post. All eyes were on me to see what sort of show I would put up. I overheard them talk about me. They said "He's OK". They had a lot of Bristol Police join them when they were formed and trained at the White City, Ashton Court, before going abroad. I recognised a plain clothes man at Eastville Police Station. He got killed at Nieppe Forest in front of Merville, which I will tell you more about later on.

I forgot to mention in a previous engagement when we went back to Lens for a short spell, I got

wounded a second time. Little bits of shrapnel in the face, not serious, but the injection upset me the worst. I got as far as Calais in hospital and could see the white cliffs of Dover on a clear day with field glasses. Not to my liking, so near and not so far to Blighty.

Now back to Festubert. We left there and took over a part of the line at Colincamps, previously held by the French. Deep wide trenches – you could walk three abreast, but too exposed to shell fire. We held the line there for a long while then we were brought out for a rest and our next move was in Reserve for the Third Battle of Ypres (Passchendaele). I shall never forget that, whilst we were waiting, a telegram from home came for me "Come at once. Violet very ill. Doctors Orders. It's a boy". But that was useless; there were men in the Battalion that had not had a leave for 18 months – what a hope for me.

I showed the telegram to my Company Officer and he confirmed my fears. After seeing the CO we went to Ypres with that worry on my mind, and we were not called to do battle, but took over the newly won trenches afterwards, and I was anxiously waiting for more news from home.

But what a shambles at Ypres, low laying country, all mud, no good moving about during the day, sandbags for cover. There was pill boxes here and there with the entrance the wrong way around, facing the Jerrys. Made one for the Officer and Signaller with his Morse Code, and about a 100 yards away was a big one used by the Company Headquarters. First night there I had a Lance Corporal with me. He found a small shell hole and began to make a platform in it so that we could sit down for a bit, covered with empty sandbags. He sat down but I was on the move seeing the men were all right.

A troopship arriving at a French port. *(Author's own collection)*

The ruins of Festubert. *(Author's own collection)*

A soldier outside his temporary shelter in Sanctuary Wood, Passchendaele.
(In Flanders Fields Museum, Ypres, Belgium)

Violet with George Junior.
(Robin Pine)

I went to the Company pill box and drew the Platoon rum ration at stand down just before daylight, and the men welcomed it but later I was vomiting, and I learnt that the shell hole the Lance Corporal had disturbed was where a mustard gas shell had exploded. It was a good job for me that I brought it up, and I believe I still suffer from the effects of it. The Lance Corporal who sat down was burnt terrible underneath and had to go to hospital. I was sorry to lose him. His name was Tanner of Gloucester – a wire man that climbed the poles fixing the telephone wires. Those gas shells were awful, also the tear gas shells, they both would fall with a little explosion, enough to burst them, and let out the gases.

Well, I was lucky to get my second leave from France and back again. See my strapping son, George, and this made it harder for me when it was time to return to the Battalion.

Author's Notes

With 'Bristol's Own' from 1917

George left Hipswell Camp, Catterick on around 24th January 1917 and when he returned to France he was drafted into 'Bristol's Own'. The Battalion was part of the 95th Brigade which was attached to the 5th Division. The other Battalions in the Brigade were the 1st Devons, the 1st Cornwalls and the 1st East Surreys.

Although he wished to return to the 1/6th Gloucesters, 'Bristol's Own' was seriously under strength following heavy losses during the Battle of the Somme at Longueval and Delville Wood in July 1916 that accounted for around 320 casualties; at Guillemont on 3rd September 1916 where 323 men were either killed, wounded or missing and at Morval on 25th September 1916 where there were a further 76 casualties during the capture of the village.

Inexperienced new recruits and soldiers recovered from injury were drafted into 'Bristol's Own' throughout the Autumn and Winter of 1916 and George was one of 157 to join the Battalion in two drafts in February 1917. George joined C Company and the first 'in the field' entry in his new Pay Book was on 17th February 1917.

May 1917

Although in his memoirs George was understandably reluctant to describe in detail the gory reality of war, it is a little surprising that he didn't mention the Battle for Fresnoy in early May 1917, where he was one of the fortunate survivors. Perhaps the experience was just too painful to recap.

Following a successful push by the Canadians through Arelux in late April, German positions in and around the village of Fresnoy became the scene of fierce fighting on 28th April 1917. By 3rd May 1917, Canadian forces had captured the village and handed over the won ground and new front line to 'Bristol's Own' late in the day on 4th May.

However, as the Battalion was trying to get established in its new surroundings, heavy retaliatory shelling commenced and continued throughout the evening and into the 6th and 7th of May. The bombardment was described by some as the heaviest and most sustained that 'Bristol's Own' had experienced throughout the war. In addition to the shelling which flattened the trenches, German planes were unopposed in the sky and were strafing the defenders with machine gun fire. The soldiers used shell-holes for cover and despite several requests for air support and counter-artillery fire, none was forthcoming and the Battalion took a massive battering.

In addition, communication lines were broken and heavy rain from the early hours on 8th May only exacerbated the situation and caused havoc with the functionality of rifles and Lewis Guns that became caked in slimy mud. So, when the crack troops of the 5th Bavarian Division were brought up to the front line in force, they had everything going in their favour. A Company was almost completely wiped out before the Bavarian Infantry attack and the brunt was born by B Company. The remains of George's C Company fell back with a group of Canadians and by the time the Battalion was relieved, only five Officers and 177 other ranks had survived the German onslaught. Fresnoy had fallen into German hands again at the cost to 'Bristol's Own' of 300 killed, wounded or missing.

In his War Diary report, Lt Col Rawson, the CO, referred to the battle as a disaster and attributed it to:

- Attempting to hold an impossible salient as a defensive position.
- Lack of aeroplanes.
- Lack of artillery support of any kind.
- The bad weather, with thick dust forming into mud at once and visibility being nil.

George was very lucky to have survived and as one veteran of the battle recalled… "So ended Fresnoy, where the 12th Gloucesters for the first and last time, yielded ground to the Hun"

June to September 1917

The next four months were relatively quiet with just a handful of casualties. Most of the time was spent behind the lines in camps where the infrastructure of the Battalion – so brutally damaged at Fresnoy – was undergoing repair. New and inexperienced reinforcements joined in several batches and underwent training. Working parties of men were at the disposal of company commanders to carry out maintenance work, for example to strengthen trenches and shelters. There were kit inspections, drills, lectures, a service to mark the third anniversary of the war and during September, there was even time for some fun with platoon boxing and football competitions and a performance by the 'Whizz Bangs' – the Divisional Concert Party.

Between 3rd and 13th September, George attended a Musketry Course and passed with the following positive observations from the course examiner… "A good instructor, keen, intelligent, should do well with practice".

The 'Whizz Bangs' – the Divisional Concert Party entertained 'Bristol's Own' during September 1917.
(Soldiers of Gloucestershire Museum)

On 25th September the Battalion left camp for a long march to Meteren in preparation for the 3rd Battle of Ypres – Passchendaele. During the march, George received the telegram from home telling him that his first son had been born – on 23rd September – and asking him to come home as Violet was seriously ill. There was no chance of that. The Battalion arrive at Meteren on 29th September and two days later was in the mud and grime of the Passchendaele trenches.

October 1917

Although the Battalion played a largely supporting role, between 1st and 11th October casualties were high, particularly through the effects of gas inhalation. On 2nd October alone, three officers and around 100 men were gassed and were lost to the Battalion. The Battalion continued to support the 1st Devons and the 1st East Surreys and would bring up supplies – food, water and ammunition to the front line troops. This was not an easy task as the terrain was terrible. German artillery would pepper the duck-boards and trenches day and night with shellfire and on one evening several soldiers disappeared completely while bringing rations up to the front line. As well as carrying out burial party duties, on 4th October, George's C Company was ordered to reinforce the 1st Devons and while moving to its new position was heavily shelled and suffered around 150 casualties.

On 6th October, the Battalion withdrew to Sanctuary Wood and took cover in shell holes and dug-outs. For the next few days it continued to alternate between Sanctuary Wood and provide working parties and support to the attacking Battalions.

On 11th October the Battalion withdrew from the battle and although George didn't say too much about the events, 14 officers and 345 other ranks were killed, wounded or were missing during the 11 days spent at Passchendaele.

Similar to post-Fresnoy, post-Passchendaele saw the Battalion re-grouping and re-organising to fill the

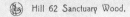

Hill 62 Sanctuary Wood.

Very little sanctuary and few trees for the troops to take cover in. *(In Flanders Fields Museum, Ypres, Belgium)*

A recruiting march for the Women's Land Army on its way to The Colston Hall, Bristol during the War – following behind a local boys band. *('Bristol and the Great War' 1920)*

gaps in its numbers. Battalion training, exercises and drills were a feature of the latter part of October as yet more drafts of new men joined. To get back to some form of normality, just a week after they had left the horrors of Passchendaele the Battalion even held a rugby match against a team from the 1st Devon and Cornwall Light Infantry – winning 23 points to nil.

December 1917

In December 1917, 'Bristol's Own' left France for Italy for probably its quietest and happiest spell of the war. The aim of the move was to shore up Italian defences against the Austrians and be on hand should Austrian/Hungarian forces attempt to cross the River Piave.

The Home Front

In the two years following the establishment of the Bristol Branch of the Women's Relief Corps, female workers across the city became a common sight. At first, in the less physically demanding jobs like serving behind shop counters or working as clerks in city offices. As the Western Daily Press reported in 1916… "For some months, local employers have been responding well to appeals to get women to work and young female

clerks are no longer a novelty. Female shop assistants are now engaged in numerous shops formerly staffed by men. It is no longer uncommon to see a young woman driving a tradesman's motor van and driving it very well."

As the war progressed and more of Bristol's men folk left for the Western Front, women filled the employment gaps and proved every bit as capable as men, even within the more physically demanding roles. Women worked across most types of occupation, including the postal service, in munitions factories, and in the hazardous Mustard Gas factory at Avonmouth where around 1,300 female workers were badly gassed during the war.

The Bristol Tramways and Carriage Company was desperately short of male conductors and it embraced the need to employ women to fill its gaps. An early 1917 edition of 'Bristol at War' enthusiastically reported on the first group of lady tram conductors to be seen on Bristol's streets… "We have pleasure in reproducing a photo-group of the first batch of the young ladies who have adapted themselves to needs produced by the War, and have relieved a considerable number of male conductors that have gone to the front. The scheme has proved a remarkable success, both as regards the efficiency reached by the 'recruits', and in the civil and obliging manner in which an often trying duty is carried out. The Tramways Company are to be congratulated upon the success of the scheme, and it proves what can be done by ending the present War by releasing plenty of young men for the Colours – to achieve an early victory. At the time of writing about 150 young ladies have been trained and passed out as efficient 'conductors'…"

Long before the Women's Land Army was formed in April 1917; women had gone to farms in the suburbs and surrounding countryside to help as hay balers, field workers, gardeners and tractor drivers. By the end of 1917, there were around 250,000 women working in agriculture across the country – including 20,000 in the Land Army itself. However, there was some reluctance to employ women as Police Constables. Although 'lady-clerks' were employed in the Administrative Department to replace men serving in the army, Bristol's Chief Constable wrote to Police Forces in other large cities to find out what plans they had to employ women as 'Police Assistants'. He thought there was no need to employ such women in Bristol and by the end of 1917 there were only 13 women in police uniform on patrol across the City. He

The author's grandmother Daisy Barnes – one of Bristol's Land Army Volunteers during the First World War. Typical of her generation, Daisy also volunteered during the Second World War – cooking food for troops from the YMCA canteen on platform 13 at Temple Meads station.
(Betty Burlton)

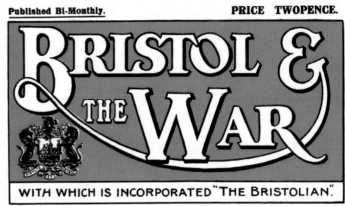

Published Bi-Monthly.   PRICE TWOPENCE.

BRISTOL & THE WAR

WITH WHICH IS INCORPORATED "THE BRISTOLIAN".

Vol. II., No. 31.   JANUARY—FEBRUARY, 1917.

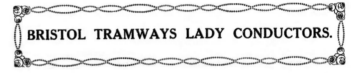

BRISTOL TRAMWAYS LADY CONDUCTORS.

The above photograph comprises the "first twenty-five" Lady Conductors on our Tram Cars. An account of their training and work is given on page 199. Over one hundred are now in course of training.

preferred to re-employ retired police constables and delay the retirement of older employees in order to cover the gaps in personnel. In addition, more than 200 Special Constables (men who were too old or not fit for military service) were taken on to help plug the gaps and release Police Constables for military service.

Bristol's first batch of 'Clippies' pose for the camera outside Horfield Depot.
(Bristol Record Office)

Chapter 8
Distinguished Conduct at 'Gloucester Farm'
1918

The Regiment was still on the move and we were sent to Italy. The Italians were our ally then but they had no fight in them and were on the point of giving up. I never saw much action there as I fell victim to trench fever.

Rheumatic? Right word for a 104 temperature. When the MD saw me, I was packed off to hospital. Got better, had a relapse, 104 temperature again and back to bed. Finally, when I was marked fit they were waiting for all 5th Division men to rejoin units as soon as possible. Going back to France again, April 1918. Jerry was making his last fling, where one never knew, but he chose the part of the line that was the weakest, held by Portuguese troops and that was that – for they were worse than the Italians, and retreated

A German map of Merville and Nieppe Forest from July 1918 showing the British trench system in red. The German advance in the Spring of 1918 was halted along this line, thanks in part, to the efforts of 'Bristol's Own'. The circled farm (known as 'Gloucester Farm') was the scene of fierce fighting on 25th/26th April 1918 that led to George being awarded the Distinguished Conduct Medal. *(In Flanders Fields Museum, Ypres, Belgium)*

miles. It was like the war starting all over again. Roads blocked with what the French civilians could carry or push in a cart, praying at the shrines, which was plentiful on the walls. The French civvies swearing at us for prolonging the war. This was what we found after four days travelling through the Alps.

April 1918

We detrained at Nieppe Forest thereabouts. The Guards Brigade was sent up to stop the German advance at Merville. There was terrible fighting there and the city was burning and our troops falling back a mile or so behind Merville near to Nieppe Forest, and that was where we found ourselves, this side of the forest, not knowing where Jerry was, how far away. No more smoking, action any minute, new surroundings, not knowing the lay of the land. We were glad when daylight came for we were in the forest out of sight of enemy aircraft and balloons. Then we moved up through it to the front line

A Royal Aircraft Factory SE5A shot down in 1918 on the German side of the line. *(In Flanders Fields Museum, Ypres, Belgium. Kurt Zehmisch Collection)*

running parallel with the forest, about 500 yards outside it. Jerry had been halted and things got quiet. We held the line outside the forest for quite a time, and at stand to at daybreak we wanted no warnings, for the clatter of the birds singing in the trees was beautiful and the skylarks, watching them soaring up in the sky in song, then finish and drop like a stone. One morning one of our planes came over to spot over Jerry lines. We could hear machine gun fire up in the sky. He was having a dog fight with a Jerry plane and had to break off. We could not hear his engine so we knew he was coming down and he was ever so low when he passed over our heads, down in the trench. We heard him land in the trees. So I took a couple of men with me to have a look around to see if the pilot was OK.

We found his plane right side up but no pilot. Had a look at the clearing at the back and we spotted him running, called out to him. He saw we were British Tommies and soon found us. I directed him to BHQ, told him he would get all the help there. He was overjoyed to find he came down in his own lines and he was off. Next day the RAF were there getting all

that was any good off the plane. I tell you our fellows had been over it before for souvenirs. My Platoon was in the reserve trench so I got my men to camouflage it with tree branches out of Jerry sight, or they would have bombed and shelled it until it was destroyed. The first thing the RAF did was to empty the petrol tank of what was left.

I often wondered what would have happened had he caught fire. It might have caught the forest and we should have been in a hot spot. I got a telling off from the Company Officer for letting my men move about on top of the trenches, though it was dusk and we had the forest behind. He was a mad-un at times, but no guts. After the warning I wanted to get to another part of the trench quick so I hopped out at the back and a revolver fired from the front line at me. I gave him the raspberry but heard no more.

The Company Officer was a student at the university at outbreak of war, was a good footballer, but never liked playing against me. He was an outside left, and me right half. I bowled him over when I had the opportunity for I always took it, playing in games like that, we were all on the same level, regardless of rank and got stuck into it. But he never liked it. We had some good games at times, but rugger was in favour of soccer chiefly, and the Gloucestershire Regiment were Army Champions at the time 1914 war commenced, and we had quite a few of them with us, both officers and men.

Now back to action again at the front line. I had lost my Platoon Officer – the other three platoons had one – so I was in charge of my Platoon. We were practising a stunt on Jerry lines to get rid of a Jerry machine gun that was causing a lot of havoc to traffic and troops moving up the cobbled road. Our aim was to get rid of him and advance about 3,000 yards driving Jerry back to straighten the line as we were getting a lot of cross fire from the enemy. We were out of the line for a while and practised what we had to do and each Platoon had a certain task. This was only a company affair; rest of the Battalion was on our right and left and behind, holding a different part of the line.

25/26th April 1918

Now I will describe how it went. We had re-enforcements join us to make up our losses. They were men that had just come out from England and I am sorry to say some of them were only in action that one day and were gone. I will describe the action as best as I can so that those that read this and are interested will learn what led up to me being awarded the DCM.

Also, on the following page I will draw a diagram of the ground we had to advance and capture and hold at all cost. Our instructions were drilled into the Platoon Commanders. I was in charge of No. 6 Platoon, No. 5, 7 and 8 had a Platoon Officer. No. 5 left position, No. 7 centre and No. 8 right position. My Platoon was to creep close to and behind No. 7 who had to get rid of the machine gun. Us Commanders had small scale maps of Gloucester Farm as we called it, so until the time came we had to drum it into our men what it was they had to do, and what was expected of them.

We all carried two extra bandoleers of ammunition and shovels and sandbags, then had to wait for the day. Our flares had been busy strafing the back areas and heavy guns as well, and when zero hour came we had to move forward behind a creeping barrage which was moving fifty yards in front of us. Most of us had done this before but I was sorry for the new men for they never had much briefing.

The Company Officer and Sergeant Major stayed behind and the instructions were as follows: a Verey light was to be fired back to our lines through the gap where the Jerry machine gun was, to let

our Captain know we had reached our objective. So, about half an hour after dark, the battle for Gloucester Farm and the 3,000 yards behind had begun. First the creeping barrage, No. 5, 7, and 8 Platoons 50 yards behind, the closer you kept to the barrage the better, for you were on top of the Germans before they could look around.

My Platoon keeping well up to No. 7 Platoon. When ours had got up to the German wire, the others were held up. I asked what was the matter – they said all officers were casualties, no leaders. This is where leadership came in as I mentioned previous.

Ordered the men to throw a few mills bombs and went forward myself, shouting "Come on, The Old Braggs forward" and there was no hesitation, we were through and put the machine gun out of action. The gunner and his mate was killed. I dropped a Jerry that was about 50 yards in front of me, got the men to clear out the two barns, and threw about a dozen bombs down the door steps leading down the cellar where the Jerries were feeding the machine gun with an endless ammunition belt. Spotted the Jerries running along the hedge under cover to the back of the house, got our Lewis gunners on them then it was clear for us to advance to 3,000 yards behind.

With a bit of luck we reached there. I got out my Verey light pistol and fired back to let the Company Officer know we had reached our objective, and I hoped it hit him true and proper for having a pop at me, as I had mentioned.

I had a runner with me and I was able to scrawl a message. "All Officers casualties, Sergeant Pine in command of Company, reached objective. Digging in, plenty of casualties send up reinforcements." Away he went down the road. He didn't care to go through the houses. He got there and got back and said "Delivered", and no more so I was glad to see him back for he had to follow me where I went. All the men were digging like hell to get a bit of cover, in

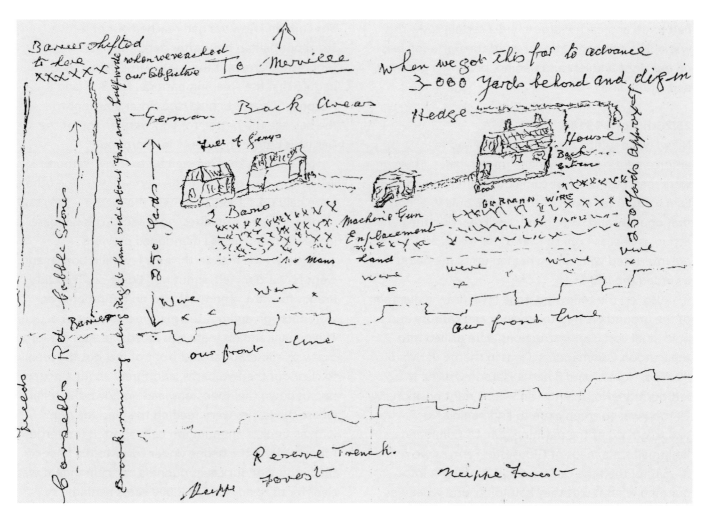

George's handwritten map of the area around Gloucester Farm (Le Vert Bois, the scene of fierce fighting on 25/26 April 1918 that led to the award of his Distinguished Conduct Medal. *(John Pine)*

groups of four, one on the look out, and getting the barbed wire out in front.

So, again it was reading from left to right, No. 5 Platoon over the other side of the cobbled road, the stream, the big long barrier had been pulled up in front of the road and it was No. 5 Platoon there – 6, 7 and 8 all mixed up stretching along the rest of the front. With your humble carrying on in charge. I went on a visit down the right of the line to see how they were getting on with their digging and one of the lookout men covering the front came back to say a couple of Jerries were approaching to find out what had happened. I told the men to wait until they

got close, creeping under cover of a hedge. Then we challenged them, they turned and bolted. I ordered the men to open fire, managed to drop one. The other got away; he must have had a charmed life. He might have got hit. Anyway, about a half hour after, they shelled the house where we had passed through and it was a heap of bricks by the time they finished. I learnt after we got out and was relieved there was about 100 Jerries down in the cellars, all took prisoners. We had left them for the moppers up.

Just after that incident a Sergeant and fifty men came and reported to me with rations, boxes of ammo, sandbags, picks, shovels, barbed wire and a rum issue, for when things were quiet. The Sergeant said to me. I am to deliver these supplies to you and return back to my Company. My Officer's orders. I told him to forget that and take orders from me. I want you here so split up your men along the line and tell them to dig in as fast as they can. His answer was to the alternative, saying he would get into trouble through not carrying out his orders. I explained my position, loss of men, not enough to beat off a counter attack. That's why I ordered him to stay, no Officers, and that I was in charge of this lot and warned him that if he refused I would report him and that would be as good as deserting the front line.

I called one of my Sergeants to witness what orders I gave him – wasting my time, Yes or No. He saw the right side of it and they got stuck in with the rest, but I was expecting a counter attack at any time. Had plenty of lookouts and plenty of wire going up in front of the trench. They were digging nice soft ground and was well down to four feet and connecting up with one another. Plenty of earth on parapet, filled sandbags and the men were getting real cover made all for their own good. I crossed the brook about six times to see how No. 5 Platoon was getting on. Sgt. Jimmy Lewis, the ex-CID man at Eastville Police Station, he was OK, nothing to report, just a patrol had to be driven off with Lewis gun fire. I jumped the stream to keep my feet and legs dry. My runner waded across.

There was a little cottage at the back of their trench and Jerry was putting a salvo of shell there now and again. There was a trench all ready there for them. Just had to make a few alterations and we're out in front. I was just returning from a visit there, got to the stream, threw my rifle over and prepared to jump and half way through that jump over came

The grave of Lt Noel Armitage one of the officers killed during the capture of 'Gloucester Farm' on 25th/26th April 1918. Although from the Scottish Horse Regiment, he was drafted to 'Bristol's Own' to fill gaps in Officer Ranks. *(Author's own collection)*

a salvo of shells and I landed in the middle of the stream. I was soaked up to the waist, lost my tin hat but my rifle and ammo was dry. I got back to my usual place about half way so that I could be found if wanted – a converted deep shell hole – nice and dry.

Took my equipment off, great coat, all my clothes, puttees, socks, boots. Told my runner to scrounge around for a steel helmet. Cut the bottom of two sandbags, put my legs into them, then put my trousers on again. Wrapped a couple around my waist and I was soon back in fighting trim again with another tin hat. I often wondered if anyone else had

```
37821 C./S./M.G. PINE, 12th Bn.
Glouc. R. (Bristol).
   During most of the period he
has been acting as C./S./M. and
he has throughout shown the
highest example of keeness and
devotion to duty at all times.
His courage under fire has been
a very fine example to the men.
On two occasions, when all the
officers of his company had
become casualties, he has taken
command and led his company in
the attack, afterwards successfully
consolidating the position won,
the success of his company being
largely due to his ability and
pluck.
```

George's DCM citation as reported in the *London Gazette*. **The other occasion referred to in the citation is believed to be the capture of Le Cornet Perdu on 28th/29th June 1918.**

done that in the front line. I read in the *Sunday People* if you have an amusing incident that happened in the front line let us know in so many words and win £10. I was tempted; I had a few in my time. But I never bothered.

No one came to see how we were getting on. Took it for granted that everything was OK with the messages I sent back. The men had done well to consolidate against the threat of counter attack and it was drummed into them as midnight approached. All slit trenches were connected up with a traverse now and again, and everyone had plenty of cover – it was a moonlit night and we got the warning. Enemy movements in no-man's land. I put a Verey light up, Jerry was a good way away. So I waited for a time just to make them think they were not spotted and I passed a message for left and right of me – prepare for rapid fire on the word. So they were keyed up and ready. Then I shouted Rapid Fire. The surprise attack of the Germans was certainly a surprise for them for they never expected so much resistance and hearing our heavy rifle fire those at the back areas got through for field gun support and they never got so near as our barbed wire. They were well and truly beaten off, and at daylight, it became quiet and calm, I ran up and down the line on the top congratulating the men. 'Well done!' I shouted and we held on for a few days before being relieved. The morning of the last

day at stand to, the Captain and Sergeant Major put in an appearance.

Not a word of praise but finding fault. The men themselves were shocked and what they said about them… proper army talk. My popularity with those men was unbounding and all the NCOs were going to write out a recommendation for my good leadership, but I told them that would get nowhere. For those had to be sent in by an Officer and that was sent in by Captain Chapman whose company I joined later, and I was also promoted by him in the front line to Company Sergeant Major (CSM) with pay. That was another great honour for me. Down came the three stripes and up went the Crown, Warrant Officer, Second Class.

May 1918
We were relieved and went way back for a long rest in a village where the civvies were and also the Portuguese soldiers. There was trouble with them and our Tommies when the estaminets cafes were open, so we had to put out pickets of a dozen men (Police) to keep order.

28/29th June 1918
I remember once we went into action to drive Jerry back over a river and blow up a bridge. Waiting for zero hour he pasted us with tear gas shells. So that was a good send off when it came. Stick to me Sergeant Pine, my Officer said. We had a runner with us, hadn't got very far when the runner caught a packet. I bent down and turned him over – he was deathly white. I said to the Officer, "I am afraid he is finished." Though his eyes were closed, he said "No. I am not." It made us smile. We left him for the stretcher bearers and carried on for our men were advancing very rapid. Got to our objective, officers and men detailed to destroy the bridge, did their job and we established a front line about 100 yards

The grave of Lt Reginald Guise. *(Author's own collection)*

from the river, in full view of the enemy the other side. I went forward with the Officer, Capt. Guise – very good man he was – to have a look around at the other side of the river. Quite visible, we were, hugging the ground, side by side. Saw a road opposite us and in it was a small gun – a Pom-Pom. They must have spotted us and fired it. My Officer caught the full blast right in his face. He must have been killed instantly.

I laid there for a bit, shouted out to the men to concentrate fire on the road. That drove them away from the gun. I moved a little, turned my Officer over and the sight I saw, although nearly 50 years has passed, it still makes me shudder, and my thoughts

were, what a narrow one for your humble. Right from the start of us going abroad I always had that in my mind, if your name and number was on a shot or shell, you had it. But at times it was a miracle that anyone survived, the amount of iron that was flung at us. The least I want to write about this First World War the better pleased I am, for I never spoke about it much in after years.

We had a good rest and we were getting ready to hit back at Jerry on a large scale. I was back with my Company. I had acted CSM for all four Companies in the Battalion. Now I was CSM rank confirmed of my own Company.

August to September 1918

Now, this preparation for the big push of ours. We had everything – guns, tanks, ammunition, planes and men, and our position was on the way to Cambrai. Our troops had reached that far when we used tanks first – that was 1916. Then they went miles, the tanks were a surprise for the Germans. Then our big brass hats made a big mistake for they moved too fast for supplies to keep up with them. Ran out of petrol, ammo, food and water, and the Germans made a quick counter attack and our troops were back to where they started from. That was a few years before. But once we got Jerry on the move about August 1918, we had learnt a lesson.

We were hitting the Germans hard and they were packing up in hundreds and we were moving forward every day over the ground we had lost a few years back. This time, as the troops moved forward so everything behind moved with it, and there was plenty of supplies, air and artillery support, and Jerry was moving back fast and we kept it that way until we reached Welsh Ridge – Cambrai was a mile off.

My Company Officer was Captain Roberts – not built for a soldier, but nevertheless knew the way to treat his men. We had reached our objective for

The push towards Cambrai in September 1918.
(Author's own collection)

we wanted and ordered the men out and make their own way back with the information, each man in case anyone got bowled off. I was the last to leave, and it was getting daylight.

I had not got far when I copped it – back of the head. That put me out, for a time I could remember sinking into oblivion. How long I was like that I don't know but when I came around I at once realised where I was and that I was badly wounded in my head and I must try to get as far away from the German trench because I never wanted to be taken a prisoner. I got out my field dressings and began to bandage up my head. Had just finished it when a Jerry had me through the right shoulder, so that finished it.

I managed to crawl to a deep shell hole and slid down it and was again out to the world. I had been in the shell hole for one whole day. Troops had advanced again that night, with little opposition and it was thanks to the message my men took back. This was told to me by the Lance Corporal I met at the Investiture at College Green after the war. I told him what happened to me. He said that they advanced the next night and must have gone over the ground where I was in the shell hole.

The first thing I thought of was home, the next my surroundings. Which way have I got to go? It was dark and I never realised there was something wrong with my eyes. I was searching the sky for the North Star to be on my right going back but it was no use, my eyes were not strong enough. Then I remembered our new eighteen pounder field guns that were pounding away at Jerry all the time. They had a familiar crack when firing and I thought, if I walked in the direction of those gun flashes, I should be going in the right direction.

So that's what I did and it was a nightmare. Good job it was dark. I started off, falling down, getting tangled in barbed wire, and finally slid into a deep

that day and I, full of energy the way we had advanced without many casualties, volunteered to go forward to find out how far Jerry had gone back, which is the usual procedure when you take ground from the enemy. The Captain agreed and away we went. It was dark early morning and I knew I had the North Star on my left. We had not got far when we ran into a mob of Jerrys, about three hundred, no arms, marching towards our lines to give themselves up. What a defeated lot. I shouted: "Anyone speak English?" out stepped a 6th officer. "We wish to surrender." I told him to carry straight on with them, after taking his word that all had laid down their arms and bombs, then forward we went as it would be soon getting daylight. Me, a Lance Corporal, four men, plenty of Mills bombs and spread out for 20 yards in speaking distance. Our guns were pasting the Jerry back areas. Finally we reached the Jerry trenches. I was the first in, passed the word back to throw a bomb down any dugout we passed, but it was not long before we had bombs hurled at us. So, I had got the information trench. I wasn't there long when someone came along. "Who are you," I said, with as commanding a voice as possible. The answer: "A runner on an important message." My thoughts: English, thank God for that. He certainly guided me in the right direction. The runner told me to follow the trench he had come up and it would lead me to a First Aid post in a sunken road. I found it all right and collapsed. The next thing I found I was in a field ambulance going back out of the front line to a First Aid dressing station a few miles back and got myself put tidy and labelled for a hospital train journey to the Australian General Hospital in Rouen.

The operation to take the bullet out my shoulder was done in France. My steel helmet saved me from a more serious head wound. Bad enough as it was. Four days there and then to Blighty across the Channel to UK – swathed in bandages around the old napper and shoulder, loaded on to the Hospital Train.

I had been through this lot in July 1916. So, when the RAMC Orderly came to attend to me, I asked him where the train was going. His answer: "Bristol", my remark: "Oh, my God." Then quiet. The orderly said "What's up chum?" I said: "My home town." Our train eventually arrived at Temple Meads station and it was getting dusk.

We were on the platform on stretchers for a time, and then loaded up in ambulance transport. My thoughts: I could not see out the window, as my sight was very poor. I did get a glimpse of some tall trees as we were pulling in to some place.

It was a hospital and it was Saturday night. So near and not so far. My wounds were re-dressed, washed and put comfortable for the night after the Doctor had been around, and I had a fairly good night's sleep. Sunday morning came – nurses fussing around and breakfast. I could spot the Tommies walking about the ward so I beckoned to one. He came over to my bed. I asked him for the name of

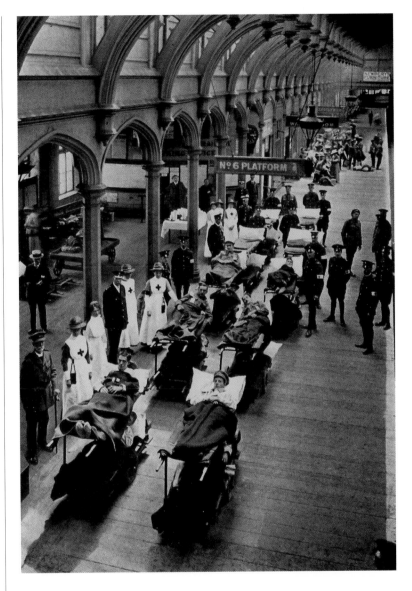

Wounded troops arriving at Temple Meads station, Bristol. This is how George arrived back in Bristol. *('Bristol in the Great War' 1920)*

this hospital. His reply: "Beaufort War Hospital, Stapleton", which is now called Glenside. I told him my home was only a mile away, could he take a message to my wife to let her know where I was.

I explained to him that I could not see very well. So I told him what to put on the note, name, address and the direction to take to Eastville, Greenbank Hotel, prominent place well known, Pine, name

Shortly after arriving at Temple Meads, George was transported to the Beaufort War Hospital. Newly arrived patients are shown here being tended to by RAMC staff. The walking wounded are also looking on. *(Author's own collection)*

popular. He had to walk all the way – Sunday, no trams, war on. But he found it. Knocked at the door. They had already received a telegram from the War Office – seriously wounded. The wife answered it; saw a Tommy in hospital blues. He noticed her go white. He said, "All right, Mother. You Mrs Pine? Here's a message from him. He is at Beaufort Hospital, arrived last night." My father lived around the corner. The wife thanked the Tommy. He would not take anything and was gone. Up she tore to Dad, told him the good news. He said, "Get yourself ready. Away we will go, out to Beaufort."

The wife had her Sunday joint in the oven. Ration for two. Her mother had gone up to her relations at St George to tell them about me. They were not very long getting out to the hospital and at first the gatekeeper would not let them in. Explained to him that I had been brought there the previous night; how the wounded Tommy had brought the news, and that I was in Ward 5, no visiting card. But my father asked him to ring through to the ward and they were allowed in after a bit of red tape at the gate. What a greeting I got what little they could see of me.

Time for them to go and when she finally got home, her first words were: "Oh, my Sunday joint!" – burnt to a cinder in the coal-fire oven.

The wife was out to the hospital every day after that. She had a white visitor's card. A coincidence occurred on the Saturday I arrived at Beaufort. The wife and my eldest half-sister, Mable, was out on Stapleton Road with young George in the pram and a big convoy of ambulances were going by in the direction of Stapleton. Mable said to the baby: "Wave to your Daddy, Georgie." "Oh, don't say that, Mable," was the reply from the baby's mother, but she might have been right, and it was often spoke of after.

We had a lot of Yankee soldiers wounded there. They were some cases. The Sister told the wife she was only to come on visiting days and took her white card away. Up spoke a Yankee Sergeant: "Devil shoot me, she will come as often as she likes, and you won't stop her."

Unfortunately, they had an epidemic of a germ called Spanish Flu. People were going down with it – whole families, and no one would venture to look after them for fear of catching the germ. There was a Remount depot for horses at Shirehampton and we had a lot come in from there, in Isolation Wards they were dying off, and I noticed after the war there was a few buried at Greenbank Cemetery.

I was beginning to get stronger and was allowed out of bed. It was a nice big ward but the side wards in the corridors were padded as it was really termed the Asylum. We used to watch the poor men that were a bit queer out in the grounds working sweeping up leaves from the tall trees. A Yankee Tommy changed a big basket they were putting the leaves in for one that had no bottom, and they couldn't make out why the leaves were still there when they lifted the basket, but an attendant came along and discovered their trouble and the Yanks had a telling off, I was glad to say.

George (middle row, seated far left) with fellow patients and nurses at the Beaufort War Hospital in around November 1918. *(Robin Pine)*

Well, I was at the hospital when the Armistice was signed, 11-11-1918, two days after my 27th birthday. All the family were down with Spanish Flu, too ill to come out to see me. I was told though the wife was so ill she was always coming down Channon's Hill, Fishponds and paying me an imaginary visit to the hospital. It was the weak state she was in. Anyway, as soon as she recovered she was out there visiting day or not. I used to walk through a wide corridor to some steps leading to the glass doors to the grounds. But the Sister warned me – no further Mr Pine, promise you won't go down those steps, or I shall have to keep you in the ward – on account of giddiness and the severe pain I suffered in my head, and my loss of sight.

The doctor sent me to the BRI to see the eye specialist. That was when I found out that the nerve chords running from the back of my head were damaged – destroyed. So I just had to watch my step, look down and where I was going and nothing to fall over or knock against, but I have overcome that now, but still knocks myself about. Relaxes too much and too careless when moving around. Had a good Christmas at the hospital, 1918 and they let me out for a day on New Year's Day. A taxi to the wife's relations and there was plenty of frivolity, being the festive season. It was too much for me. I was glad to get back to the hospital again – a sigh of relief.

Author's Notes

Italy and the Western Front again – January to March 1918

'Bristol's Own' spent the first quarter of 1918 in Italy. The contrast between mud-caked Flanders and the relative calm and beauty of Italian hills and mountains could not have been more marked. 'Bristol's Own' relieved Italian troops in the Piave area. On the night of relief, and long after 'Bristol's Own' had taken up their new positions, the Italians remained in place and asked when the British relief was coming. They were startled when told that it had already arrived – around 100 'Bristol's Own' troops took over positions previously held by 500 Italians.

Unfortunately for George, he was sick with 'trench fever' for most of the period and was unable to share some of the experiences of his comrades.

Trenches on the Italian Front in early 1918. *(Bristol and the Great War' 1920)*

The Italian language posed a problem or two. What did prove useful was the knowledge that the adding of 'io' to some English or French words might achieve the desired effect. Whilst on the way to reconnoitre the mountains near Asiago a group of 'Bristol's Own' paid a visit to a small restaurant. Keen on some cheese to accompany their meal, 'cheeseio' brought a blank expression from their host – 'fromagio' met with more success!

Up against 'Bristol's Own' were Austro-Hungarian troops who were regarded as an 'inferior crowd and slip-shod' soldiers. Some of the night raids carried out by 'Bristol's Own' across the Rivers Brenta and Piave would not have been carried out if well-trained German troops had been opposite them. With little action and very few casualties, 'Bristol's Own' had a relatively relaxed and enjoyable time in Italy.

April to June 1918

With much regret, on 1st April 1918, 'Bristol's Own' started their exodus from the apparent calm of Italy for the torments of France. Leaving Vicenza Station on 2nd April, the Battalion arrived back in France on 6th April. Its original objective was the occupation of a section of the line south of Arras. However, after marching 18km in the direction of the town, orders suddenly changed. The Battalion had to retrace its steps and on 11th April, took a train north to Thiennes. Destined for Nieppe Forest, its task was to help stem the last major German offensive of the war – known as the Battle of the Lys.

On 9th April 1918, following a two-day artillery bombardment, 50,000 German troops completely overran around 20,000 Portuguese soldiers who were holding the line along the Lys Valley. The town of Merville was captured and the Germans now had their eyes on the strategic railway junction at Hazebrouck. The Allies were forced to retreat over five miles and there was an urgent need for reinforcements to help plug the gap in the defences.

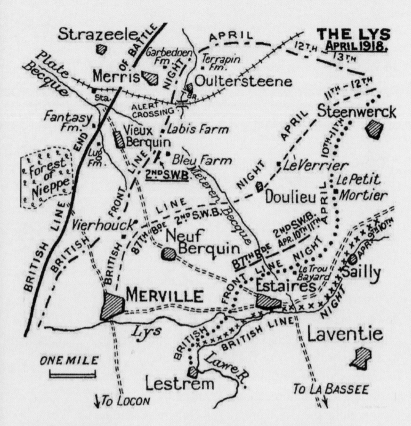

Map showing the retreat of Fred Pine's Battalion between the 9th to 13th April 1918. From studying the Battalion's War Diary and other accounts, it appears that Fred fell somewhere between Le Petit Mortier and Le Verrier on 11th April 1918. He has no known grave. *(The History of the South Wales Borderers 1914–1918)*

On their march to Nieppe Forest, George and the rest of 'Bristol's Own' encountered hundreds of refugees who had been driven from Merville and neighbouring villages. The elderly and footsore youngsters had left their homes in a rush, had nowhere to go and could carry few belongings with them. 'Bristol's Own' arrived in the Forest on 12th April 1918. The previous day and only a few miles away, George's brother Fred Pine and 350 of his fellow 2nd South Wales Borderers were killed whilst helping to stop the German advance.

George never knew where his brother fell or how close he was to the exact spot.

With the help of crack troops from the Guards Brigade, the German advance was halted around 500 yards in front of Nieppe Forest. However, this was not before B Company of 'Bristol's Own' had suffered whilst rushing across flat open countryside to reinforce the line – 12 were killed and 56 were wounded by machine gun fire in the action on 13th April 1918. There then followed a series of exchanges as the new front line continued to be fiercely contested. On 25th/26th April 1918, with the aim of straightening the line, capturing a series of German outposts and taking out a troublesome sniping position, George took part in the capture of the hamlet of Le Vert Bois and a series of farms – one of which was nicknamed 'Gloucester Farm'. In his memoirs, George describes his part in the attack in some detail.

From the War Diary account, it appears that George was in the 'Right' attacking party of A Company that comprised No. 2 Platoon under Lt N Armitage and No. 3 Platoon under 2/Lt E G Wills. During the raid, Lt Armitage was killed and 2/Lt Wills was wounded. Several times during the attack, when these Officers became casualties, George took control and helped consolidate the newly won ground. A further 21 'Bristol's Own' troops were killed and 30 were wounded during the attack. On the German side, dozens were killed, 39 were captured and three machine guns were also taken.

The attack was a success and General Hacking sent a Telegram the following day congratulating the 12th Battalion on achieving the objectives. The Telegram mentioned Capt Chapman's part in the raid and it was Capt Chapman who later put George's name forward for the award of the Distinguished Conduct Medal – notification of which was published formally in the *London Gazette* on 3rd September 1919.

During the assault, an old lady was found in 'Gloucester Farm'. She had lived in the house, which was practically in No Man's Land, throughout the previous two weeks of fighting. She was carried away safely in a wheelbarrow. The 'old lady' is believed to have been Madame Wambergue. With her husband Jules, the couple had lived on the farm with their 14 children throughout the War – only leaving when it was destroyed

The page from George's Pay Book showing Lt R E Guises's signature, authorising a 20-franc wage payment on 26th June 1918. *(Ken Pine)*

were apparently sent to 'In Flanders Fields Museum' in Ypres with a note saying that they came from La Ferme du Vert Bois – otherwise known as 'Gloucester Farm'.

At the end of April 1918, 'Bristol's Own' was relieved for some well deserved time out of the line and for most of May 1918 the Battalion was held in reserve.

In early June 1918, CSM James Lewis – the former CID man from Eastville Police Station who George recognised when he joined 'Bristol's Own' and who George mentioned in the attack of 25th/26th April, was killed by a trench mortar. CSM Lewis was also awarded the DCM for his part in the capture of 'Gloucester Farm' on 25th/26th April 1918.

On the morning of 28th June 1918, the Battalion took part in a two-brigade attack on the German front line and penetrated to a depth of over 2,000 yards, capturing the village of Le Cornet Perdu and blowing up several bridges across the River Plate Becque. The following day, the Battalion spent time improving its position and communications. Whilst crawling with George along the riverbank, Lt R E Guise was shot in the face and killed. George turned his Officer over and the horror of the image stayed with George for the rest of his life. Lt Guise was also decorated for his part in the capture of Gloucester Farm on 25th/26th April – receiving the Military Cross. Three days before he was killed, Lt Guise wrote his name in George's Pay Book – authorising a 20-franc wage payment. Reginald Guise's family had been connected with the Gloucestershire Regiment for generations – Lt Col John Guise being 2nd in Command of the South Gloucestershire Militia when it was raised in 1768. Members of the Guise family had held Commissions in the Regiment from then on and almost without break right up to the First World War.

July and August 1918

Most of July was spent in reserve in the Nieppe Forest area and there were relatively few casualties during the month. Between 19th and 22nd July 1918, whilst the

during the fierce fighting of April 1918. The only part of the farm to survive was the 'germoire de pomme de terre' – the potato store where British Soldiers used to sleep.

By 1921, the farm had been rebuilt on exactly the same spot and the Wambergue family returned and continued to farm the land. In 2003, Hubert Wambergue – one of the 14 children – was still living alone in the farmhouse. He recalled that whilst cultivating his land one day, he found two boots – one belonging to a British Soldier and the other to a German Soldier. The boots

George would have been among this group of 'Bristol's Own' as it advanced in artillery formation alongside the road towards Achiet-le-Petit on 21st August 1918.
(Soldiers of Gloucestershire Museum)

Battalion was in training, its deficiencies in personnel and command structure were made up and George was promoted to Acting Company Sergeant Major for A Company on 22nd July 1918.

The early days of August 1918 were characterised in the War Diary as… 'Usual trench warfare. Enemy fairly quiet and nothing of importance to report. Usual shelling of our back areas every evening'. However, between 7th and the 14th August 1918 the Battalion went into training at Orchard Camp, near Racquinghem and the 'usual' nature of trench warfare was about to change. During this period, the Battalion concentrated its training on 'Open Warfare Attacks' – a feature of the following six weeks as 'Bristol's Own' prepared to take part in its final great battle.

The Battle of the Ancre, stretching from the Somme to Arras opened on 21st August 1918 in thick misty weather. Unlike previous engagements, there was no preliminary bombardment. Instead, the infantry was supposed to advance under a creeping barrage, supported by Tanks. However, dense fog considerably hampered the effectiveness of artillery support and the use of Tanks and 'Bristol's Own' went forward with only Lewis guns providing cover. Closing in on the rising

ground around Achiet le Petit, 'Bristol's Own' came under heavy machine gun fire and had to dig in to take cover. Here they stayed until darkness when they met up with units of the East Surreys who had followed a wandering Tank into the village. During the course of the day, 'Bristol's Own' had suffered just over 100 casualties.

Heavy fighting continued on the following morning when German forces counter-attacked. Although initially successful in regaining some lost ground, the attacking party was out-flanked and cut-off. It suffered heavy casualties and two platoons of George's A Company managed to capture around 180 Germans and five machine guns. In the same action, the 1st Devons also captured around 200 prisoners.

On 23rd August 1918, 'Bristol's Own' was again sent into the attack. With heavy losses, it managed to eventually cross the Arras-Albert railway line with its steep embankments. D Company suffered badly during this attack and the German machine guns were only put out of action when they were outflanked. The village of Irles was the next objective. It was strongly held and took six hours to capture – eventually falling at around 7.30pm. 'Bristol's Own' was then relieved having suffered another 200 casualties on the 23rd August alone.

Over the three days of fierce fighting, the Battalion lost more than 300 men and of the 20 officers who had gone into the line on the 21st August, only three remained.

George's promotion to Company Sergeant Major was confirmed when he was made a Warrant Officer, Class II from 24th August 1918.

For much of the rest of the month, the Battalion was held in reserve and rested and re-organised as much as possible. It also undertook 'battlefield salvaging and clearance' duties. During this process, one howitzer, two field guns and 40 German machine guns were recovered.

The final entry in George's Pay Book – it would be more than four months before George would be re-united with the 40 francs. *(Ken Pine)*

The end of 'Bristol's Own' and almost the end of George

During the first two weeks of September 1918 'Bristol's Own' was held in reserve and the opportunity was taken to continue with its reorganisation and to undertake specialist training. Although the Battalion was depleted by over 300 Officers and men, it was being made ready for what would be its final act of the war – an assault on the heavily fortified Hindenburg Line. The last entry in

George's Pay Book was on 26th September 1918 when he was paid 40 French francs. It would be over four months before he would see the two 20-franc notes again. Following a rapid advance towards the Hindenburg Line near Neuville the previous week, the 26th September was a quiet day that saw the Battalion cleaning up, paying its troops and generally reorganising itself.

Battalion Headquarters was established in Neuville, and on the morning of 27th September 1918, the Battalion left its reserve positions and went into the trenches again. The 5th Division's orders were to capture 'Beaucamp Ridge' and 'Highland Ridge' and if the advance of troops to the west of Marcoing was successful, then to advance to 'Welsh Ridge', that overlooked Cambrai.

'Bristol's Own' stayed in the trenches throughout 27th and 28th September and started to move into position from 11pm on the 28th. The three attacking companies – A (George's company) B and D were ordered to capture a length of the Front Line incorporating a sunken road – after which, the advance was to be continued by another Brigade. However, the orders were subsequently altered but not adequately relayed to the troops.

The Battalion War Diary continues the account… "At zero hour – 3.30am (on 29th September 1918) – a creeping barrage came down 300 yards in front of our line and remained there three minutes, then moving on at rate of 100 yards per three minutes. Owing to the late hour at which orders were received and distance Battalion had to march, the companies only arrived in the assembly position as barrage commenced and the Sections and communications could not be properly organised in the darkness. This and the fact that the men had no respite whatsoever made it difficult to obtain complete control. Attack commenced but owing to facts already stated and the darkness, direction was extremely difficult to maintain. Progress was good and casualties small. At 4.30am a report was received that objective had been gained and it was not for some hours that this information was found to be incorrect – sunken road having apparently been taken for the real objective. The Battalion came under very intense MG fire frontally and from both flanks, especially from Gonnelieu on the right. At first, touch could not be obtained with units on flanks but eventually, 1st Devon and Cornwall Light Infantry (1/DCLI) came up on left but all reports agreed that no one came up on right, thus leaving this flank entirely exposed. Casualties – two Officers wounded, 12 Ordinary Ranks killed, 28 wounded – this number in view of the heavy machine gun fire encountered, must be considered very small. Enemy shelling very slight. About 120 prisoners captured. Owing to incomplete mopping up by Division on our left, isolated enemy machine gun posts existed which caused us considerable trouble. Men could be seen handling these guns although it was known that Division on left had gone forward. These posts had to be disposed of by means of Rifle Grenades. Field Guns firing from top of Ridge in front of us were silenced by our counter-batteries."

From George's recollections and the War Diary account, George would have been shot twice at around daybreak on 29th September 1918. Semi-conscious, he remained out of sight in the relative safety of a shell-hole for the rest of the day. His 'Bristol's Own' colleagues carried out patrols during the day but didn't come across him. In the evening, patrols from the 1/DCLI entered La Vacquerie and found the enemy in the SE corner only. It was quite possibly a messenger from the 1/DCLI who helped to guide George back to the safety of the Sunken Road First Aid Post during the night.

Almost certainly presumed dead or missing after not returning to his Battalion for around 18 hours, George has the distinction of being one of the last, if not the last casualty of 'Bristol's Own' to emerge alive from the First World War battlefield. The Battalion's contribution in helping to break through the Hindenburg Line on 29th September 1918 – just six weeks before the War

ended – was to be its final offensive act. By the following morning, German forces had retreated from the whole of the immediate front and during the day 'Bristol's Own' was relieved and withdrew to the Metz area.

On 1st October 1918, whilst George was on his way to the Australian Military Hospital in Rouen, the Battalion marched to hutments in Velu Wood where it stayed until it was disbanded. Reviewed by Major General Ponsonby on 4th October, orders to disband were received the following day. A ceremonial church parade was held on 6th October, after which the surviving 792 soldiers of 'Bristol's Own' were transferred to seven other units within the 5th Division.

Beaufort War Hospital

On 4th February 1915 the War Office contacted the Committee of Visitors to Bristol Asylum and asked for its help in providing more beds for sick and wounded soldiers in the Bristol area. It was suggested that patients at Bristol Asylum, Fishponds, (later known as Glenside Hospital) should be sent to other asylums in the West - thus freeing the building for use as a military hospital. The request was immediately accepted and the building was converted to its new use. Two operating theatres were constructed and with 24 wards and some beds

A stamp used on correspondence from the Beaufort War Hospital.
(Roger Angerson Collection)

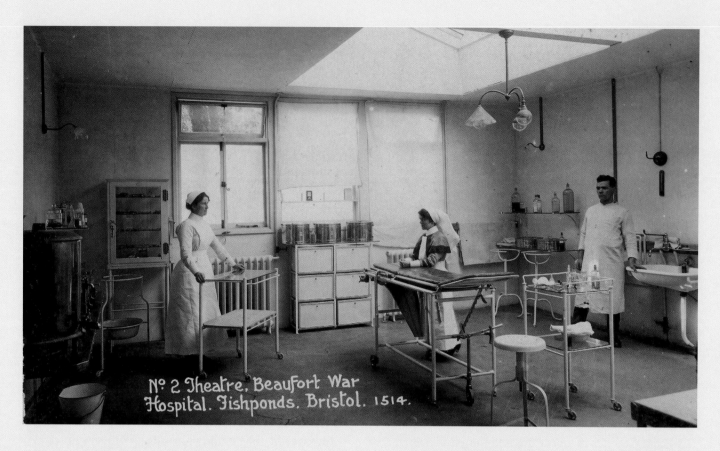

No 2 Theatre. Beaufort War Hospital. Fishponds. Bristol. 1514.

George had another operation on his shoulder performed in one of these theatres. (Roger Angerson Collection)

placed in corridors and day rooms, the Hospital was able to accommodate 1,045 patients.

The Duke of Beaufort agreed to his name being given to the Hospital and Dr. J. V. Blatchford, Medical Superintendent of the Asylum, was appointed to command the Beaufort War Hospital, with the rank of Lt. Colonel. The War Office appointed Miss A. C. Gibson as Matron and supplied sisters and nurses from the Queen Alexandra's Imperial Military Nursing Staff Reserve. The first convoy of wounded soldiers arrived on 24th May 1915.

By the autumn of 1915, with casualties continuing to increase, a further 200 beds were provided by converting the Female Infirmary block at the workhouse into a home for the sisters and nurses. In addition, 180 emergency beds were provided, and this brought the number of beds available to 1,640. In the summer of

1916, an Orthopaedic Centre for the area was established at the hospital with 500 beds allotted for orthopaedic cases. The existence of workshops and other buildings which could easily be adapted was a key factor in the selection of the Beaufort as the first Orthopaedic Hospital in Bristol. Another 30 beds were reserved for mental cases among local troops and in 1917 a ward of ten beds was established for cases of sickness among German prisoners of war who were detained in the labour camps around Bristol.

To help keep the soldiers spirits up, those who could travel were treated to outings to events across the City and performances were also staged at the hospital too.

As the number of soldiers needing treatment continued to grow, the authorities tried to send men

"Won't you shake hands.?" NO!

Not until. Your hands are Clean!

AMERICAN RED CROSS.

BEAUFORT WAR HOSPITAL,

FISHPONDS, BRISTOL

Some of the c1,600 patients in the grounds of the hospital. The Chapel – now home to the excellent Glenside Hospital Museum – can be seen top left. *(Glenside Hospital Museum)*

Wounded soldiers preparing to leave the Hospital on an outing. *(Glenside Hospital Museum)*

needing treatment as near to their own homes as possible. It was this change in approach that allowed George to be sent to a hospital so close to his home in early October 1918. This must have been a great comfort to George and his family during a very difficult time.

The work of the Beaufort War Hospital came to an end on 28th February 1919 – just over five weeks after George had been discharged. The number of patients treated

during the War was 29,434 and total deaths numbered 164. Of these, 30 were locally admitted cases suffering from influenza and pneumonia during the Spanish Flu epidemic of the autumn and winter of 1918-19.

The British and American Red Cross Societies supplied address postcards for soldiers to write messages to family, friends and loved ones. Some wounded patients used the cards to convey other feelings. *(Roger Angerson Collection)*

34831 Coy. Sgt. Major George William Pine D.C.M

Gloucestershire Regiment

Served with honour and was disabled in the Great War.

Honourably discharged on 14th January 1919.

George R.I.

Chapter 9
Adjusting to Civvy Street – Another Battle
1919–1920

I was getting stronger as the days went along and it was getting on time for me to get my discharge from hospital. One thing about it, the war had finished, and the men were having their Demob papers. So, out of four brothers there were only two of us left. Harry and myself. Fred was killed in France, wife and child he never saw for she was born whilst he was on active service. Tom was killed in Gallipoli (single). My name was put forward for a Medical Board, Ministry of Pensions, and it was not very long before my career in the Army finished, and I got my final discharge, unfit for further services in the armed forces, and was honourably discharged, January 1919.

I was fitted with a Civvy suit, coat, waistcoat, trousers, indigo blue serge, overcoat, Civvy boots. Also a suit of khaki. I had my photo took before I discarded it and was home, 89 Bellevue Road, to share it with the wife, her mother and baby George. After being parted for three years of hardship and worry, and suffering for us all, and now I was wondering how I should get on in Civvy life – to fight this battle of handicap of being more or less a physical and mental wreck.

What I had been through destroyed the sense of logic, leaving suspicion and dread of those around me, those who cared for me. I realised I had to snap out of it if I was going to get back to normal life and health, a feeling I had never experienced before. The reaction had set in but I was determined not to let it beat me. The battle was on to take interest in life and those around me. My war wounds made me dull and retarded, especially in dull heavy weather, and those around me wondered what was the matter with me. So it was a case of get to it George.

But it was a struggle that I had a hard job to hide, by the sudden reaction to pain. I had a good doctor, Dr. Mora, and he was very concerned about me and

The certificate George received that confirmed his 'Honourable Discharge' and that he was disabled in the Great War. (*Robin Pine*)

37831 C.S.M. Pine Geo. Willm 12th Glosters

To be attached to Page 2 of A.F. B. 179A. A.F. B. 179P. (Additional).

The answer to this question 16 should be copied from A.F. B. 179A and signed by the Officer in Medical charge of the case and the Officer in charge of Hospital before the papers are despatched from the Hospital.

16. Was an operation performed? Yes.

If so, what? F. B. removed from rt. Shoulder

W.A.Smith.

Officer in Medical charge of case.

Date 8. 1. 19

To be detached and handed to the man on his discharge from the Hospital.

Lt. B......... Lt Col...... A.M.C.

Officer in charge of Central Hospital.

(2569) Wt W4953/PP1312 500m 9/18 J.F.W. E3744

A note signed by Lt Col Blatchford at Beaufort War Hospital confirming that George received an operation whilst a patient. The note was attached to his discharge papers on 14th January 1919. *(Ken Pine)*

very careful of the medicine or tablets he gave me. Ministry of Pensions (MOP) assessed my disability at 50 per cent. So that was a good start off and my rank made it more. Warrant Officer, Class II. So much for the child, so much for the wife, added on. I had plenty of notices from the MOP saying that if I went back to work it would not make any difference to my Pension.

I was getting letters, long envelopes from the Regimental Pay and Records Office; they were very acceptable for there was money orders in them to be cashed at the Post Office. Quite good sums, and amounts higher for longer service and rank. Then I had £20 from the Chelsea Pensions Hospital for the DCM award. I also received a parcel at my home, labelled 'OHMS wounded soldiers kit'. It was kit that

I had in my haversack and the pockets of my tunic – knife, fork, spoon, lather brush, shaving soap, three German hollow-ground razors and one army issue. These German razors wanted some beating. I sold them to the Civvy barber for a good profit as my nerves were too bad to trust myself with a razor – too shaky. Also there was a bigger surprise, two army pay books. One filled out and the other part full. In the back were two 20 franc notes which I was not long turning them into English money at the Foreign Exchange Offices in town. I have still got the pay books and the label, in my possession now, and part of a hard-tack biscuit from our rations. Like

The only surviving souvenir from George's First World War collection. Being a bugler, George would have been interested in the German variety, so he removed this badge from a Prussian Bugle. *(Ken Pine)*

a dog biscuit – oblong shape, size about three inches by two inches with a hole in. I threaded wool through the holes and I kept it for a long time. I brought home many souvenirs from France and they dwindled away as the boys grew up. One was a German saw bayonet. I brought that home and gave it to my boss at the shoe factory. When I went back to the factory I saw it hung up in his office. The wife kept all my letters I sent her during 1914-18, one big drawer full of field cards, which were the quick ones. Write address on one side and cross out what never applied on the other side, such as, I am well, I am not well, I have got or received your letter, vice versa and so on. Ordinary letters, these were censored. Green envelopes these were not censored, only once in a while, always put a nice big letter in them and plenty love in them. We used to get one once a fortnight. Many a green envelope was exchanged for a fag. When the Smokers' Ration was short then I sent a lot of French silk cards home of different designs, chiefly cap badges. The wife thought the world of them, but they all disappeared from the drawer they were kept in. The young-un had been on the scrounge.

Of course, when I got home like every returned soldier, we celebrated but I found it was too much for me, night after night a couple of hours in the pub. I had to suffer for it the next day. So I cut that lot out or it would have cut me out. I should have found myself in the asylum. It was doing me a lot of harm. I wanted to go back to hospital again so those that read this could guess how I felt, but the wife wasn't

having any, saying I had been away long enough - no more. But I had to go into hospital in later years. MOP sent me to different hospitals for nervous breakdowns, and the National Health people sent me to Barrow Gurney (Dundry Villa) for five months.

Now back to my pension. Times were very hard and the cash never went very far and, of course, there was the rationing. Ration books for everything. Plenty of Black Market and the wife politely told me she was afraid I should have to go back to work.

George and Violet pictured on George's discharge from the Army. George with his new suit of 'khaki' and Violet proudly wearing George's Imperial Service Badge. *(Robin Pine)*

Two silk postcards of the type George would have sent home to Violet but which were all 'scrounged' by his children – none survived. *(Soldiers of Gloucestershire Museum. Tom Wiltshire Collection)*

Well, I took it in good part. Made up my mind to go up and see my old boss at the shoe factory as he promised me my job would be kept open for me. But I knew I could not stick it. But I was not going to be a fibber. I had an interview with the boss and he told me he never had a light job he could offer me, but he was willing to let me have a go on my own machines I used to work on, which needed a lot of judgement. My eyes were the main handicap and my right arm was weakened – the vibration of the machine shook my whole body. The noise was awful and being shut up in the factory. I just had to give it my best. I was disheartened. One night after I finished at 5.30pm I got home 8.30pm. On my way I had to go through St George's Park. I collapsed, exhausted on a seat for a couple of hours and finally got home.

I went to my Doctor the next day and he told me an open air job would be the best for my handicaps. The Labour Exchange was in being then, ours was in Neasely Road by the Rovers Ground. There was a special place for the disabled men. Sign on every morning and unemployment pay every Friday, so that helped a bit. One job I was offered was a night watchman on road repair jobs, sat by the coke bay and seeing to the lamp. But when I applied for it

the Corporation had already filled the vacancy. So I had my card stamped and took it back to the Labour Exchange for them to check.

During the meantime things began to hot up at the MOP Medical Board and what a do. As I was not working I could not put in a claim for travelling expenses as it was in Park Street. Different men to see for different wounds. My biggest problem was eyesight – much had been destroyed. The specialist I saw was Mr Eyles and he gave me a good examination. Reassessment of my Pension came by post in a few weeks. No change, so that was that. Still 100 per cent pension and a date for the next Medical Board – they were determined not to let me rest.

There was formed an Old Comrades Association. We had meetings every morning and the main topic was getting jobs for the ex-servicemen and we sent a deputation to the Council. One thing allowed were the barrow boys on certain pitches and it was run by the Club, at a reduced price they were both sides of the road. Bacon, meat, vegetables, but the men were getting restless out of work, and the next target were getting the girls off the back of the trams and replacing them with the ex-servicemen. The Tramways Company held fast, so the men started the rough stuff, marched to Redcliffe Street and as the trams came in, pulled the trolley off the wire then

St George's Park, where George collapsed exhausted one evening on his way home from trying out his old job at J H Woodington, Boot Manufacturer. *(Vaughan Collection at Bristol Record Office)*

smashed the windows. I said to myself, no place for you George – home out of it. But in time men were getting their jobs back and replacing the girls.

So I made up my mind to go down the Tramways Office and get a conductor's job when I found there was nothing else doing as they were taking on the ex-servicemen. That was in April 1920. The man I had to see was, to my surprise, the ex-RSM, 12th Gloucesters, Mr. A Bailey. He said, "Well, never thought of seeing you again, Micky", that was my nickname in the Mess. "Why haven't you been before now?" I told him (my last resource) – but I kept my handicaps and war wounds to myself and I camouflaged them as well as I could, even to my own people. A picture of health, a smile on my face, a natural one.

I often wondered if this was the right thing, now I am gone past 80. My worry was the Medical Examination and reading the card. I got through that OK. Had they tested my vision I should have failed for that's where the trouble was, a blank, but they never did. I passed, got my uniform next day and went to the School of Instruction to learn the road and was put on the route I asked for – Eastville, Old Market, and Durdham Downs. A conductor who was with the company pre-1914 lived a few doors from us and he came in a few nights to help me along. I got through my exam OK, and was posted to Eastville Depot.

Author's Notes

Some recognition

On 19th February 1919 – just a month after being discharged from Beaufort War Hospital and the Army – George and his brother Harry attended a Reception and Investiture at the Colston Hall that was organised at the request of Lord Mayor Twiggs on behalf of the Citizens of Bristol. The event honoured Bristol Officers, NCOs and all other men who had received military decorations during the First World War. The souvenir booklet produced for the occasion included the names of George, Harry and Fred Pine. Along with George's award, Harry received the French Croix de Guerre and Fred the Military Medal.

The Colston Hall was decorated with the flags of the allies and the event got under way with the singing of the National Anthem followed by a musical programme with songs sung by Miss Gertrude Winchester. For the occasion, Fred Weatherly re-wrote verse three and the final chorus of 'Bravo Bristol'. The new words summed up the feelings at the time…

> *"And now the seas are free again, and the bloody fields are won*
> *We tell our children's children what Bristol men have done*
> *And their deeds shall ring forever down Avon to the sea*
> *And the sound of the march of the Bristol men the song of their sons shall be…*
> *Twas a rough, long road to travel, twas a tough, long job to do*
> *But, please God, they meant to do it, And by God they've done it too*
> *The cost? – who stopped to count it? They knew and played the game*
> *They fought for the Empire's Honour and the glory of Bristol's name!"*

The certificate that Lord Mayor Twiggs presented to George on 19th February 1919. *(Bristol Record Office)*

Picking up the mood, on the same day, the Lord Mayor received a letter from King George V who offered his own congratulations… "I desire to congratulate all those whom you are honouring today on their magnificent achievements, and at the same time I wish to associate myself with the feelings of pride aroused in the hearts of your fellow citizens at the splendid record of Bristol's gallant sons, who have added fresh lustre to your city's great traditions"

The Lord Mayor presented George with a certificate to mark the occasion.

George was rightly very proud of his wartime achievements and the five medals he received. As well as 'Pip', 'Squeak' and 'Wilfred' – the nicknames given to the 1914-15 Star, the British War Medal, and the British Victory Medal, George was awarded the Distinguished Conduct Medal and the Territorial Force Efficiency Medal. In addition, George also received the Silver

Lord Mayor Twiggs. *('Bristol and the Great War', 1920)*

George's Medals. From left to right – DCM, 1914-15 Star, British War Medal, British Victory Medal, Territorial Force Efficiency Medal. *(M Shed)*

War Badge that was issued to servicemen who were discharged from the military as a result of sickness or injury caused by the war.

The struggle to make ends meet

George and his family were not alone in trying to cope with the tribulations of post-war life in Bristol. The situation was pretty desperate throughout 1919. The winter of 1918-19 was dominated by the Spanish Flu epidemic that killed thousands across the City. Thankfully, none of George's family died but for many Bristol families this was yet another tragedy following so soon after the First World War.

Food was in short supply, not only from rationing but from natural famines. The potato crop for example was the worst since 1876 and retailers across Bristol were struggling. The retail cost of certain essential food items such as potatoes was fixed at a particular level, whereas the wholesale cost was not. Many retailers ignored the regulations and charged what they considered the market

rate. Some were caught by Inspectors from the Bristol Food Committee and were prosecuted for charging customers higher than the prescribed prices. Despite several prosecutions, the President of the Bristol Retail Fruiterers' Association said in court that the Association had instructed members to defy the law… "We are entitled to a living as well as the scavenger and the food inspector".

Protests by retailers highlighted the growing sense of desperation that was felt across the City. Not all businesses were re-employing returning serviceman and jobs were hard to find. The City Council was keen that its large spending departments could absorb as much labour as possible and it established a Special Committee on Unemployment. The Committee made recommendations for job creation schemes in an effort to ease the burden for some of the 8,000 unemployed

The crowded Peace Day Celebration on the City Centre in Bristol on 19th July 1919 that gave the Old Comrades an opportunity to protest at the lack of jobs for ex-servicemen. *(Vaughan Collection at Bristol Record Office)*

men in Bristol. Schemes suggested included the employment of 20 men for five weeks to fill in the trenches on Brandon Hill that were made during the training of Bristol troops before and during the war; roadway work at Portishead that would occupy 40 men for two months; housing schemes at Fishponds, Shirehampton and Knowle that would employ around 150 men; and the construction of cart roads and railway sidings at Avonmouth Docks.

Some councillors were disappointed at the impact these proposals would have on reducing unemployment and suggested that if something more material was not done, then there would be trouble. One councillor went a little further. Criticising some 'unpatriotic' Bristol businesses for not re-employing returning servicemen, Mr Senington said that if something was not done voluntarily, then something would have to be done by force – and with 8,000 unemployed men in the City, there would be tumult. Not everybody on the Council shared Mr Senington's views but it reflected the tension of the time.

The Peace Day Celebrations in Bristol on 19th July 1919 also gave Bristol's Ex-Servicemen an opportunity to parade around the City and to make their feelings known about the plight of their members.

Against this background, the Bristol Tramways & Carriage Company was under increasing pressure to dismiss its female conductresses and to re-employ men who had returned from war service and to find jobs for other unemployed men. About a quarter (2,280) of its male employees had fought in the war and 132 were killed. By the middle of 1919, the company had re-employed around 650 of its ex-servicemen. However, progress in re-employing more men at the expense of female conductresses was not as rapid as some had hoped and this caused much unrest – leading to the type of tumult predicted by Mr Senington.

On Monday 26th April 1920, Edward Harwood, Thomas Paicy and James Bush were arrested for disorderly conduct in Nelson Street and Colston Avenue after protesting vigorously against the refusal of some Bristol companies to relieve female workers of their jobs in favour of unemployed ex-servicemen. The three men were due to appear in the Magistrates Court at 11am the following day, but by 10am on 27th April a crowd of several thousand protesters had gathered outside Bridewell Police Station where the men were being held. The crowd was made up of ex-soldiers and other sympathisers, including women and young people of both sexes. The crowd decided to send a deputation to the Magistrates' Court, demanding that the three men be released immediately. The request was refused and the men were remanded in custody for a week.

The crowd turned angry and stormed off. In Lower Maudlin Street, a tram on its way to The Centre was stopped by the demonstrators. The passengers, the driver and the female conductress were taken off the Tram and the crowd hurled stones, smashing all of the tram's windows. The crowd then gathered in The Horsefair to plan its next move. A spokesman suggested they should protest at an Insurance Company where an ex-serviceman had been offered a wage of only £50 a year. The crowd set off for Corn Street and a deputation confronted the management of the insurance company.

This was a peaceful protest and after the meeting the leader of the demonstration addressed the crowd and said that they had given the management eight days to discharge all female employees and to engage disabled ex-servicemen at a minimum of £3 per week.

During lunchtime, groups of girls and women employed at factories and works along the tram routes gathered in crowds. The conductress of each tram as it passed was the object of loud and prolonged outbursts of hooting – punctuated by remarks of 'an uncomplimentary character'. In the afternoon, many of the men who had demonstrated in the morning attended the funeral of an ex-soldier who had died at Stapleton Workhouse – allegedly of starvation.

Throughout the day, reports came in of several more trams being attacked. Trams in Eastville and St George were particularly affected and considerable damage was also done to a shelter belonging to the BT&CC at Eastville. George witnessed some of these events but didn't want any part of it.

Speaking to the press, The Hon Secretary of the International Union of Ex-servicemen issued an ultimatum to the BT&CC: "All female labour must be replaced by ex-servicemen within a week."

How the Western Daily Press reported the troubles on 27th April 1920. *(Bristol Reference Library)*

MORE BRISTOL TRAMS ATTACKED

Exciting Scenes at Several Centres.

Ultimatum as to Women Labour.

ARISING OUT OF THE DEMAND OF THE EX-SERVICE MEN IN BRISTOL WHO ARE OUT OF EMPLOY, THAT GIRLS SHOULD BE NO LONGER ENGAGED AS CONDUCTORS ON THE BRISTOL TRAM SYSTEM, THERE WERE FURTHER DISORDERLY SCENES YESTERDAY, AND SEVERAL CARS WERE ATTACKED AND THE WINDOWS BROKEN. SOME OF THE CONDUCTORS WERE HUSTLED AND JEERED AT, BUT NOT STRUCK.

Some of Bristol's 'Clippies' who lost their jobs to make way for returning and disabled soldiers. *(Peter Davey Collection)*

On 28th April 1920 things got worse when an angry crowd of around 2,000 gathered in the City Centre to watch a deputation of ex-servicemen who were in 'desperate straits' being received by officials of the BT&CC. Public sympathy was with the men and 30 trams were damaged during some ugly scenes. This direct action and the threat of further reprisals accelerated the dismissal of the remaining conductresses and the company paid them £5 each to go away quietly – some thanks for helping to keep Bristol on the move during the war. Although partial emancipation had arrived in the form of the vote in 1918 for women who were aged over 30, it would be generations before there would be anything resembling parity in the workplace.

The abrupt and somewhat brutal dismissal of the 'Clippies' helped George secure his job with the company. In response to an advert he applied for a job as a tram conductor and was interviewed by someone he knew quite well – ex-RSM Arthur Bailey, of 'Bristol's Own' who had the distinction of being crowned the best individual rifle shot within the 'New Army' during the war. George joined the Bristol Tramways and Carriage Company as a tram conductor around 20th May 1920.

Chapter 10
Tram Conducting
1920s–1930s

started off with another conductor for a week, showing me the ins and outs and how to do this and that. I got on fairly well. But when I got home, my poor old napper. I was going round and around though I was sat down in the arm chair. Up early the next day. Posh up over night, polish satchel, punch strap, buttons, double breasted, book of rules laid down by the Tramway Company for we were public servants and had to serve them to the best of our ability.

I had to announce the tram stops when we were approaching them. That I did in the old Sergeant Major style. Very often I had a remark said – you would make a good Sergeant Major – if you only knew my thoughts. When the crowds were about, pass right inside, sit close together, full up inside, top deck only, and it was only three lots of tickets, 1d, 2d,

One month into his job, George pictured with driver 'Smash' Sheppard on Tram 31 on Upper Belgrave Road, Durdham Downs. George kept a copy of this photo on him throughout his working life. (*Author's own collection*)

3d. Carry them between the fingers of your left hand and get out what ticket you want with your right hand, put it in the slot and press down to punch a hole in it – bell would ring, and it would register.

As time went on I got more used to it. What I had to look out for was the people inside with their legs stretched out, or over I would go. And another thing, the conductor had to give the bell, signalling the driver to go with the left hand, our backs facing the way the tram was going. That was a big handicap to me because my right side vision was the worst, but I did make sure and look down at the steps before I gave the signal. It made me slow and that never worried me, though you would get a rap from the driver if you were not quick on the bell. They had a schedule to keep and wanted to keep to it.

Discipline was very strict in those days. You were down on the mat for the least thing – reported by passengers, inspectors, failing to pick up used tickets by the end of journeys and leaving people. You were

Service No. 3 collecting passengers from outside the Empire Theatre in the 1920s. *(Peter Davey Collection)*

The Campbells steamer Westward Ho! about to take passengers from the trams waiting near the Clifton Rocks Railway in Hotwells. *(Peter Davey Collection)*

expected to shout to intended passengers "Ride Sir?" or "Ride Lady?"

Holiday times we were very busy taking people to Durdham Downs, the nearest point on the tram for the Bristol Zoological Gardens. We used to get the excursion trains up from South Wales and they alighted at Stapleton Road for the No. 3 service to take them to the Zoo or the Pantomime when it was on. There was several attractions that pulled in the crowds where our service passed – Kings Cinema, Empire Theatre, Odeon, Skating Rink, Art Gallery, Dance Hall, and The Glen. Our early turns were six journeys and late duties were seven straight duties.

Then there were split duties, so many hours morning and so many evenings, when the workpeople were about, called 'Spread over Duty', start 6am till 9.30am then 3pm till 6pm, extra cash for those duties. They were called Rush Cars, and there was six of them. After the work people were cleared away the Station Inspector would have you for a special run to the City or Rovers Ground with a crowd, or over to the Speedway at Knowle, or down to Hotwells to meet the Campbells Steamer, and pick up the people. We used to take the QEH boys over to Westbury for their Recreation Ground at Eastfield

Road. The Tramways had their ground in the next field. Jimmy Hyman was our groundsman – he was an old Rovers Centre forward.

I took part in some of the sport that was going and I was Secretary of the Eastville Depot Sports Club. All the Depots had them, inter-Depot football, cricket, bowls, skittles, cribbage, whist, and a rifle club. Just after we started back after the war we had a company Sports Day at Eastfield Road – all kinds of events.

One event I was keen on was the Tug of War. It was advertised around all the Depots, the different events, and entry had to be sent in by a certain date. I got together about eight men and trained them for the Tug of War. Got the use of a rope and the Engineer at Eastville Depot fixed up a tripod with weights for the men to practice on. But I got in touch with the Bristol Police who were champions of all England at that time. Their practice ground was at Brookes Dye Works. We went over there a few times to train with them and picked up a few useful hints in the art of Tug of War. I asked the Sergeant Police Trainer Coach what he thought of the men I had. He said, you got a good side; they got the style OK, lays their eight on the rope, digs in together and pulls together, and watches your signals, no shouting "heave", that gives the opposition a clue.

I was the coach and I had quite a lot of experience in the Army sports, so I had a busy time until the day of the Tramway Sports on Saturday afternoon. I had a lot of running about to do with regards the men on late duties changing their duties for an early turn. All that week it was a proper headache. I managed to get my Tug of War team all together in Old Market Street and caught a special tram going over to Westbury. I had high hopes of pulling this lot off with the training the men had and the interest they took in it.

But my hopes of success was dashed. When we got off the tram at Westbury and walked to Eastfield Road Sports Ground we had to pass a pub, some of the team went in to have a drink and that was their team's downfall. We got to the ground – the other events had started, and the loudspeaker was shouting for the Tug of War teams to get ready. "First to pull, Eastville Depot versus Staple Hill Depot. Teams not on time will be disqualified". So my men went in to change into shorts and jerseys. The Staple Hill coach told me that they had a scratch team, just managed to make the weight, just their tunic and collars off.

The pitch was on a bit of a slope. Best of three pulls. So all eyes on me and I stood where every man could see me. I lost the toss of ends and they decided to pull us down hill. They pulled us over after a long hang on. One up to Staple Hill and two to go. I knew we were beat – that beer in the pub did it. We just managed to pull them over the second pull after a see-saw long pull, first them then us. I could see our fellows were finished when the third pull started. It was not very long before Staple Hill had us over and that was the finish to Eastville Depot Tug of War team. My hopes of a winning team were finished, and I was a very disappointed man. It was not good enough. The time I had put in to get them fit and

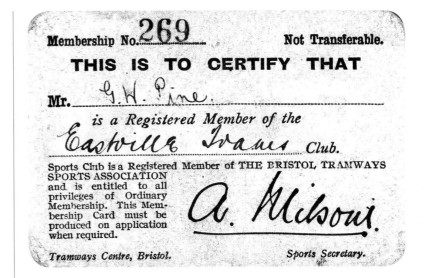

George's membership card for the Sports Association. *(Edith's Trunk)*

trained up to perfection the week previous. I just packed up and went from Eastfield Road to Eastville. Proper fed right up.

Good job it was Sunday the next day and I never had to get up early. But we very often had a leg pull from the Staple Hill and Fishponds men when we passed them on the road, for we got beat by more or less a scratch team of men, picked at random. The Permanent Way Men (Navvies) that kept the tram lines in repair won it that year.

I thought never again, but I had another disappointment. I was Captain of the Inter-Depot Skittles Team and we were running for league champions. There was only a couple of points difference at the top and only a couple of games to finish the season. The day and night on which we had a football and skittle match some of the best skittlers were playing football and promised to get down to the club in time. The last pair to go on at skittles were playing Fishponds Trams and their position in the League – bottom – so we had nothing to fear. My motto as captain was, two good men on first against theirs to get a lead, and then put them on according to how the game's going. Two good reliable men last to pull back if down by a few pins. So I had my reserves in case the footballers could not make it in time. Well, they never made it, the reserves had to play, and I am sorry to say it lost us the match by one pin, and the Championship at the end of the season. That was the other disappointment for me as the captain of the skittles team, but I have got two runners-up medals for skittles.

We had a good football team and Eastville did well at cricket as well. Several of our players were very often picked to represent the Bristol Trams against other town's tramways at both games. I gave up the Secretary job to someone else, it was too much for me and the men wanted a lot of nursing, but I still went on playing skittles for the Depot.

I was getting a bit of trouble with my eyes and my Doctor advised me to have an eye test. So I went to the optician, had a pair for all times, and a pair for reading, which meant I had to keep changing them when filling in the numbers at every fare stage and journey's end. So I got a pair of bi-focals; two in one and they wanted some getting used to.

Then I had to go for another MOP Medical Board. I was at work, so I was expecting a drop in pension. First the Eye Specialist, he scrapped my glasses, what I was wearing, and I had another pair for all times distant from the Ministry of Pensions, and my pension was finally fixed at 50 per cent for life, with no further reduction, unless I was sent to prison. So, I drew my pension Wednesdays and my working wages Fridays – enough coming in to live comfortable.

The men that were engaged as conductors the same time as me were putting in for tram driving, and passing. I knew it was no good for me to put in for it, for when the test came for my sight I should fail, and it might mean losing my job. Lucky I had a good record, no serious accidents. But I wanted to get on but this put a stop to improving my position. We had two power stations, one at the Counterslip, St Phillips,

and one at the St George Depot. One station had a serious breakdown and they had to take so many trams off each service. That meant those that were took on last were made redundant. I was put on night work at Eastville Depot, washing single deck buses. Malmesbury, Tetbury, Clevedon, Weston. Hard work, a lot of bending down. Clogs, oilskin, overalls, bucket, hand brush, hose pipe and mucky weather, it was terrible. And when the roads were tarred it was a job to get it off the wheels – tar with chippings.

Then I was transferred to North Road, Cheltenham Road Arches Taxi-cab Depot. Start over Westbury Bus Depot only two buses there, one Gloucester, two Thornbury. Clean them, start 8pm, three of us, finish at 11.30pm, catch the last tram from Westbury running into Horfield Depot. Then down Zetland Road, jump off at North Road and clock on there, have dinner, then start on the taxis. All night until 6.30am. There was in use at that Depot the Taxi-cab that Tapler, the murderer, took with a bullet hole in it.

I was back at Eastville Depot again on the wash, and we had another flu epidemic and a lot of the uniform staff were down ill. So I went to the office to get my conductor's job back again, and was successful, and was the means of getting all the others back in uniform that had been made redundant through the power breakdown. So, I was back on the No. 3 service again, and I learnt after I should never have been transferred owing to an error at Records Office, for there were men my junior it never affected.

I was glad to get off the wash job and the trouble was I could not sleep during that summer, we had a heat wave. There was a water shortage in the Depot. They had a water trough in the shed along the tram lines. There were four sets of lines, six on each line, ready for use when we started, for it was turned off at 6pm everywhere. No hose pipes, they were forbidden. It made it harder for us. I used to go to bed after I had my breakfast and stay there until a

couple of hours to return to work again. Bedroom windows open wide, perhaps young George would be playing out the back garden with the boy next door. A blow and a bellow and bedlam with the two mothers for a few minutes, then someone doing repairs, banging in nails. So you see why I was glad to get back on the road. But I was dreading one thing that those at the Centre Record Office would notice that I had not put in for tram driving. It happened.

I was warned by the Depot Foreman that I had to report to the staff manager on the Monday morning. This was Saturday. He could not tell me what it was about, so I was wondering what I had done, for we were reported for the least thing by the public, and down on the mat in front of the bosses, and they would give a day's notice of dismissal. Monday came, and down I went. A clerk saw me, took me in a room, took my weight, then my height, then I guessed what it was about – tram driving – but I said nothing to him. I thought, let him carry on. What I got to say I will to the Staff Manager.

At last I was ushered into his private office. So he started off: "Well, Pine, you have got a very good record for the past four years, you are on the short side rather, but I think I can manage to recommend you for tram driving. Why haven't you put in for it?" So I told him, my eyesight and weak right arm caused through war wounds. I told him my front view was all right but field of vision was a blank. He said: "I am sorry Pine; I knew you were badly wounded in the war, but not to that extent". Now it was my turn to say something. He knew my Army record, so I just told him that I wanted to get as high as possible with

The Tramway Generating Station at Counterslip, St Phillips seen here just after it was built in 1901. *(Bristol Record Office)*

Two BT&CC employees cleaning a single-deck bus in around 1925 – just about the same time as George was doing exactly the same when temporarily laid off from his tram conducting duties. *(Bristol Record Office)*

Clara Winterson (George's mother-in-law) holding baby Joan – George and Violet's second child born on 4th February 1922. George and Violet also had another daughter who was born on 24th April 1929. Unfortunately, she died a day later. *(Robin Pine)*

George, in his Tram Conductor's uniform, poses for the camera in the late 1920s. *(Robin Pine)*

the firm, but with regards the uniform staff, this was out of the question, could not do driving, therefore I could not put in for promotion to Inspector. Was there any other job I could be put to such as clerk in the Depot, and learn the office work? He replied: "Pine, I will make a note of this for further reference. You are quite happy for the time being." If you never did anything wrong, and never had to go down on the mat, they forgot you were working for them and time went on.

Years passed by, good days, bad days, had a few accidents, people jumping off and on the wrong way – before the tram stopped. Had to take particulars, and get witnesses, that were important for it was amazing how the people would put in for a claim.

Have a collision with a lorry and it would scratch the sides of the tram. Had to be reported. We had safety fenders, both ends of the tram and the driver could touch a handle, and down it would go perhaps to catch a dog or cat that ran in front of the tram. I remember an accident that happened at Upper Maudlin Street. It was winter, light covering of snow on the road and ice, the tram lines wet. We were travelling down hill towards the Bristol Royal Infirmary, there was a man riding a bicycle, carrier on the front. He overtook a horse and cart going steady on account of the bad state of the road. As soon as his front wheel touched the tram line, off he came a yard in front of my driver. Down went the fender, driver applied the wheel brake, track brake, and sand but she was skidding, and we took him about fifty yards before the tram stopped, almost at the bend by the Infirmary.

It was my job to get him out and to my amazement he could stand up and talk and just shook up. I knew the man for he delivered our Sunday papers and was very deaf, and speech was affected. Also he would not go to the Infirmary to have a check up, and I had to make a report and the driver, it shook him up and we lost a lot of time. Anyway, the man was at our door with our papers the following Sunday, full of praise for the driver. I told him to go and see him, as he only lived a few streets away.

But the worse one was a young fellow about 16 years old. We were drifting down towards the Arches at Stapleton Road. I believe there was a football match at Eastville and the down track did come in close to the pavement. We were moving slowly, this lad passed me on his bike, must have fell off, and his leg went between the nearside front and back wheels, and the back wheel went over his foot. My driver knew nothing about it because all this happened behind him. Not until I gave him the five bells. That was another big hold up. The lad belonged to the Hoopers, big sweet shop in Robertson Road. The lad had to have a false foot. The father put in for damages. Neglect on the driver's part.

The next serious one was a little youngster about three years old out for a ride with her Granfer. This happened at Stapleton Road Station. After we left the stop at Warwick Road (Hodders) I checked how many people we had, there was a few inside, and when I went on top only the gent and little girl. There was an intersection – so that if the tram was coming

up you had to wait until it crossed to the double track, then we could move away. The gent asked me to stop at the Station Railway Inn. So I gave the driver the bell to stop, which he did, and waited for them to come down. I was stood under the stairs looking up towards Warwick Road, when suddenly the youngster flopped face down flat on the platform. A man on the pavement jumped on the tram and picked her up. How it happened I don't know. The tram was stationary for a few minutes and they were sat on the first seat on the left at the top of the stairs. Whether the old man had her in his arms and let her go or she was trying to come down by herself.

Anyway, I saw the youngster was being attended to and then was busy getting witnesses to prove we were stationary, and I managed to get those inside to state that the tram was stationary when the accident happened. The youngster was in a very bad state and it was very serious. Our reports had to go in. Police went to my driver's house and to me. The old man said and swore the tram moved when he was coming down, it went on for a long time. The people put in a claim but it was not proven. My next serious accident was when we changed to buses so that will come later on.

I was a keen gardener. Started off with all sorts of vegetables, spuds, cabbage, peas, beans, broccoli. But the wife never wanted them, too many cats around. So I concentrated on flowers. I had a lovely show of flowers and my specials were Chrysanths. About July I had blooms as big as a saucer, incurve and

The Notice that appeared on duty cards, advising drivers and conductors what to do in the event of an accident. *(Dean Marks Collection)*

NOTICE

Drivers and Conductors are reminded that it is in their interests that all requests from any person whatsoever for a <u>detailed Statement</u> of any accident in which the Company may be concerned, should be referred to the Company's Head Office. Such requests will be dealt with from that Office immediately.

The potential for accidents is clear from this late 1920s photograph of Tram 27 on George's route in Broadmead. *(Peter Davey Collection)*

outcurve, and they were bronze. I bought from the nurseries at Hanham. They wanted a lot of looking after, not to let grow wild, not too many side shoots, and about four buds on a plant. I had smaller ones that bloomed November – lates – and stood the winter very well, so that I was picking them for the table or sideboard for five months, then cut them down to an inch above the roots, cover them with fine ashes that had been out ready for a month. This helped to keep the frost away from the roots. Sticks around them to keep the cat off.

By the following March, time for transplanting. About half a dozen new shoots on each root and this went on year after year until the garden was spoilt through having to have an Anderson Shelter put in. I will tell you more about that later on. That was my hobby. I kept fowls for a time, reared them, never short of a meal. I used to kill them myself – learnt the art off my father, and to bleed them properly.

I became a victim of arthritis in my right knee and he got very weak. I had to go to the doctor about it several times. He gave out as I was coming down the stairs of the tram and it put the wind up me. I had visions of being flung out in the road. The doctor asked me if I played football. I said before the 1914 war. He said I had misplaced cartilage and would have to get them seen to. I asked for a note to go to the BRI. He put me on the Club and I saw Mr Priddy, the specialist. Massive big fellow – about 6ft 4in, played rugger for Bristol, and he played rugger with me. "Get down there my man"– caught hold of my right leg and put it out straight. Bang with the palm of his mauler, one side of my foot then the other side, then twisted it: "Does it hurt?" ("No sir", meekly). Then the final act, he still had hold of my foot, a sudden jerk, doubled my leg up in underneath. I let out a Sergeant Major shout and nearly put him on his back, as big as he was. Then I had to step up and down on a chair. I could do it with the left leg but not the right. He termed it osteoarthritis, had to go to the BRI for electric treatment twice a week. Massage with Iodex black ointment. Diet and medicated iodine on sugar. Start off 1 drop, increase daily. By the time I finished I was counting up to 60 drops on a spoonful of sugar, but it did it good and I was soon back to work again, about three months. There was no National Health in those days. I was in a couple of Sick Clubs. The Bristol City and the Order of the Druids. That made up my loss of wages. I had quite a good run then of fairly good health.

We had an addition to the family, Joan, and then Ronald followed after. More mouths to feed and our family grew to five – four boys, one girl. There was always plenty of overtime such as working a rest day. If we worked Sundays we had a rest day in the week. Time and a half if we worked it. A single conductor always used to be after me when I had a week of earlies with a rest day Sundays to change over with him for the week. Both of us had to see the foreman on duty mid-week before to ask for the change over duty. If OK, five bob for your humble and it suited him, he was courting and the cash came in handy in those days.

We used to have a new uniform every summer and put it on Whit Sunday, in addition white hat covers. I well remember one Whit Sunday (June) and a boiling hot day. I was working that day. Had first tram out from the Depot 1.30pm. That was the time of starting, no morning trams, Sundays. Weekdays 5.30am. All poshed up in my new clothes, nice polished bag and punch strap, white top

George looking very dapper in his suit and proudly wearing the lapel badge of the DCM League that was formed in the early 1930s. The League was established to help find work for DCM holders who were seeking such help. It's likely that George was suited-and-booted in preparation for his attendance at the First Annual Dinner of the Bristol Branch of the DCM League on 23rd May 1936. *(Ken Pine)*

cover on my hat and away I went. I always got to the Depot about a half hour before clocking in time so as to get my ticket box full of tickets, way bills, total sheet, way bill rack. Check the ticket numbers on the total sheet to see if they were correct. They were done up in bundles of 100, two 10s, nailed at the bottom to keep them together, and any default it was marked up to the conductor. Tidy up the box – have the ticket numbers following so as to dap your hand on the following bundle of 50. It was best to do this as you never had time to do it when you were out on the road. You had a Duty Card for the week with time of reporting, times of each half journey, Eastville, Durdham Downs. Vice versa return. That

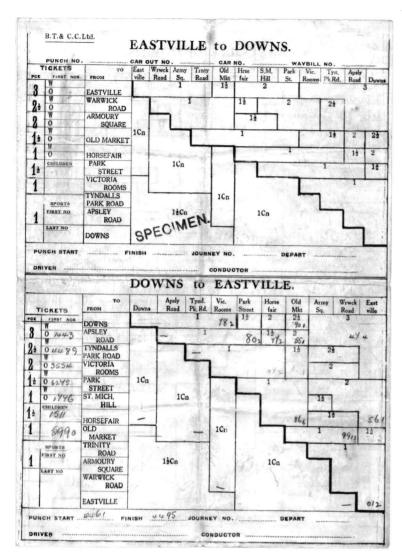

Believed to be a Specimen
Waybill for the Eastville
– Downs route. George
would have used a similar
document every day. The
Waybill recorded details
of each journey including
passenger numbers, the
number and value of tickets
sold. The Waybill was
supposed to be completed
at every Fare Stage and at
the end of the shift. The
Waybill and the cash would
be handed in at the depot.
(Dr Michael Walker)

was one journey, Waybill One, date,
tram out, tram number, journey number,
driver's name, conductor's name. If this
was not entered and an Inspector got on
to check, name in his book. So, you see,
there was plenty of preparation, apart
from taking fares.

Now I will tell you about this Whit
Sunday. It was the June week that Lord
Derby's horse won the Derby. As I said
previous, boiling hot day, and all the

women were out in their flimsy dresses. We left the
Depot, took a number of people up to the Downs OK.
Dark clouds were appearing after we left Old Market.
We had a cloud burst; the rain came down in torrents.
Driver had his mac and sou'wester and the roads
were surfaced with wood blocks the size of ordinary
builders bricks. Water got under them and they
swelled up like a small hill along Stapleton, especially
by the entrance to the Rovers Ground. There was a
marker there showing previous flooding.

When we arrived near our journey's end a
manhole cover shot up in the air just in front of the
driver, right in the tram track. My driver opened the
doors his end, told me to get the trolley rope down
as we had to change over to another wire. I said:
"You got oilskins, I got nothing." He went up and got
him down for me, but I had to stay on the platform,
trolley rope in my hand and watch the trolley when
he sent the tram back on the main road prior to
going up to Eastville Depot. Outside there was a
cross-over line for us to get on the right track to start
our second journey.

Rain still ticking down but not quite so hard.
The work house, long wall of about a hundred yards
was like a huge waterfall and when we got down
by the gates up went another manhole cover and
a spout of water – what a life. We got down as far
as Eastville Police Station and in the dip right to the
Rovers Ground entrance, Black Swan was nearly
three foot of floods. My driver would not chance it
so stopped there. A Greyhound single deck bus came
from Fishponds Causeway and he stopped alongside
us. They had just started in Bristol – opposition to the
tramways. Along came an Inspector, got on the tram.
"What are you stopped here for driver?" he said.
When he saw the flood, oh Blimey, my driver was
afraid of it getting in the generator.

The Greyhound bus was moving off, his journey
was Old Market via Robertson Road, first turning left.

I said to the Inspector Johnnie Buck: "The opposition is taking the Mickey out of us." So he said: "Driver, take her through steady". All the people were in shop doorways in their flimsy Sunday summer best and away we went, and the waves were created like the steamers going along on the river in the shop doorways, splashing. Up went the wearing apparel of the women. Screams galore. Wood blocks floating about, and we pulled out of it just the other side of the Rovers Ground on our way to the Downs. The rain had gone off and we heard that they had it very bad at Zetland Road. So the tram service was put out of schedule there also. This affected Horfield's service, Durdham Downs service via Zetland Road, Staple Hill at Eastville and Zetland Road, Fishponds to Centre. What a shambles the road was in – mud and wood blocks and what a Whit Sunday. Our poor uniform got covered in trolley juice, dabs of oil off the trolley wheel. My hat cover was black and blue – I was glad to finish.

The Second World War was creeping up on us and the children growing up. The wife had to go in hospital for blood poisoning. With the children I had a job to get in to see her. I could only see her at night and her mother did most of the visiting with her sisters. She was very ill but thank God she got over it OK. There was an Inspector's wife in the next bed to her and she and her husband were very kind to the wife. She was in there about a month and soon recovered.

The children were going to school, Greenbank, and with their health, generally, we were lucky. Joan had a couple of spells in the BRI, and Ron once. His was Rheumatic Fever that affected his heart but thank goodness, he grew out of it in later years. I remember they sent our Bill up the corner shop to get some cheese for supper and the shop was supposed to be closed, 6pm. But the shopkeeper did pull down his blind, have a little light burning and keep the door

Flooding outside the Black Swan was a regular occurrence, and happened again in exactly the way George described on Thursday 15th July 1937. *(Bristol Record Office Film Archive)*

Flooding was a constant menace to the Tramways system at Cheltenham Road throughout the 1920s and 1930s. *(Bristol Record Office)*

shut. But the Police had been watching the shop for a long time. This particular night a Sergeant and a new copper was about and he wanted to get the copper a court case, so they saw Bill go in the shop, waited for him to come out and nabbed him. "What have you got in your hand son?" Bill started to cry – blurted out "Cheese" and bolted down home, but Ron came in first. "Coppers got our Bill," and collapsed in an armchair. Then Bill followed and put the cheese on the table and doubled out to the WC and locked himself in. I happened to be home. Their mother was seeing to Ron when a knock came at the door. I answered it – Sergeant and the copper was there. "You are the tenant of this house? That your son just ran in?" "Yes." "He made a purchase at the corner shop (cheese) when he was asked what he had." I said "You are wrong; the constable mistook what the lad said 'change' not 'cheese', so he never made a purchase."

The Sergeant turned to the copper "Did you see the cheese in the boy's possession?"

"No, Sergeant."

"Where's the lad?"

"In the toilet."

"How long will he be?"

"God knows, you have frightened the life out of him."

So I heard the Sergeant say to the copper "You have made a mess of it, forget it mister."

Ron recovered from his fright but his mother was worried about him for a long time after. They had their school sports at Gordon Road

George and Violet with family friend Edna and George Jnr in his 6th Gloucesters uniform pictured in around 1937.
(Ken Pine)

Playing Fields and Ron had entered in several races. I happened to have an afternoon off so I went up to watch it and to see what sort of show Ron would put up. When it was over he had collected four certificates. He gave them to me. I went on home, left him with the boys. When I got in the kitchen, his mother was there, I threw the certificates on the table "Now, Mother, will this stop you from worrying about Ron's heart?" She had a good cry, mother-like. The youngest of the lot, young Ken, he met it when he went with the people on the Downs. Playing cricket, the ball struck him on the nose. Had a nose bleed, went to bed at night and it must have burst out again during the night. He was covered in blood. More panic from mother – fetch the doctor – he came. He said Ken wouldn't die from a nosebleed, he will be all right.

Another time he was stood by the front door and the same people had come back from a coach outing. Stopped the other side of the road. The old lady called him over, showed him a stick of rock, got knocked down by a motor car. BRI. Had a nasty lacerated ankle. That was journeys up and down to the BRI, but take it on the whole we were very fortunate with regards their health. They all did fairly well at school. Bill was of an inferior type when playing with other boys. Ron would have no messing and if he saw other boys taking the Mickey out of Bill he got stuck into them. Several mothers came to the door and said your Ron has beaten my boy up. He was not a bully, but he had guts. The bigger the better. They always had a good inside lining, good food and plenty of it. I always said there can be nothing wrong with them if they got a good appetite. George Jnr left school, had a few jobs and then followed his father's footsteps and got a job with the Tramways Company at Lawrence Hill Depot in 1936-37. He also joined the Territorial Force, 6th Gloucesters as a Bugler.

There was talk of finishing with the trams and

Tram 31 on Blackboy Hill. Photographed on 6th April 1938 – just a month before Tram Service No. 3 was replaced by buses. *(Author's own collection)*

going over to double-deck buses. Tram drivers were given the privilege to go over Lawrence Hill Depot to learn bus driving in their own time so as to be ready when the great changeover came.

We had quite a few tram bus drivers and tram conductor drivers; so that when a bus driver went on loan to Lawrence Hill his place was taken by a tram conductor driver. In time everyone had to go down to see the Staff Manager, whether they wanted driving or not. So, down I had to go again. As I said before they forgot you are working for them unless you do something wrong. Says the boss: "Well, Pine, we are having you all here regardless of whether you want bus driving or not."

I mentioned my previous visit and the promise of a good few years back. His reply: "Pine, we have drivers bordering on the edge of retirement we have to find jobs for when the changeover comes." That was 1938-39.

Our route was one of the first to change, Eastville – Durdham Downs. Oh, what a change. Talk about sea legs and being thrown about. Bus went faster, in and out, might have a driver that had just passed his test; get threw all over the show. Gear clanging and braking. Pulling up – had a job to keep our balance. Had to dig them in well, a driver might not get along very well, lose time, along come the next bus, overtake and pick up the passengers. You could not do that on the old tram, so they had their advantages. It got better when the new drivers mastered the gears and clutch, a lot faster; more people riding. Fares went up, no priced tickets and longer racks.

Author's Notes

George's Route and Tramway Outings

Tram Service No.3 – Eastville and Durdham Downs – took passengers along Stapleton Road, Trinity Road, West Street, Old Market, Lower Castle Street, Broadweir, Merchant Street, Broadmead, Horsefair, Maudlin Street, Perry Road, Park Row, Queen's Road, Whiteladies Road, Blackboy Hill and finally onto Durdham Downs. The wage for a tram conductor in June 1920 was 65 shillings per week.

As well as transporting passengers along this route to attractions and places of work, George also helped to collect visitors who were on special excursion trips to the City. In its annual booklet that showed its services and a map of Bristol, the BT&CC highlighted the various attractions available to visitors and provided advertising space for local businesses.

A ticket from Tram Service No. 3. *(Peter Davey Collection)*

An advert placed by Bristol Zoo in the BT&CC annual booklet. *(Author's own collection)*

The early 1920s was a particularly popular period for excursions. Motor transport and the travel opportunities it provided was in its infancy and the BT&CC capitalised on new ways of attracting passengers and business. As well as operating over 200 trams in Bristol alone, by 1922, the company had a fleet of 177 motorbuses and 56 charabancs.

During the summer months daily charabanc tours were run to places such as Bournemouth, Sidmouth, Ascot Races, the Severn and Wye Valleys and closer to Bristol, to Wells, Glastonbury, Cheddar Gorge and Burrington Combe. A substantial private-party business for Charabanc tours developed for church groups, sports clubs and work group outings.

Trams to Buses

The writing was on the wall for Bristol's Trams long before a German bomb intervened and brought about the slightly premature end to the service. By 1932, tram services in many towns across the country were being replaced by more flexible and quieter bus or trolleybus services. The first totally enclosed double-deck buses started to appear on Bristol's streets between 1932 and 1934. Although the number of buses continued to increase, by the mid 1930s Bristol's tram fleet of 232 vehicles was regarded as the world's largest.

However, in 1936 when plans for the major re-development of the Tramways Centre came before the City Corporation, decisions about the future of the tram service took a new turn. The Corporation began to consider whether it should exercise its option to buy the tram and bus services from the BT&CC. In anticipation of this move, on 10th May 1937, the BT&CC signed an agreement with the Transport and General Workers Union (TGWU) that guaranteed the future security of tram employees should the service be abandoned. Any employee under the age of 50 that was found unsuitable for bus handling would be offered training as

A convoy of 15 Charabancs and eight motorbuses in Burrington Combe, Somerset with dozens of day-trippers on the hillside. *(Bristol Record Office)*

Around 15 Trams waiting to be scrapped at Kingswood Depot. The upper decks have been stripped of their seats. This batch of trams was broken up between 17th July and 19th September 1939. *(Author's own collection)*

a conductor or for any other duty as may be available – nearly 1,000 men came within the ambit of the agreement. Just two weeks later, on 24th May 1937, Bristol ratepayers had an opportunity to express their views on the intended purchase by the Corporation at a special meeting at the Colston Hall. Over 400 people attended and voted in favour of giving the Corporation the authority to promote a Tramway Bill in Parliament to allow the acquisition of the tramway undertaking for £1,125,000, plus £235,600 towards replacement bus services. Aged 45 at the time and probably fearful for his job and prospects owing to his war injuries, George quickly joined the TGWU the day after the vote at the Colston Hall.

The Bristol Transport Act received Royal Assent on 30th July 1937 when the Corporation became joint operator. The Act provided for a Joint Committee of three Corporation and three Company representatives. The Company was to own the trams as agents for the Corporation until the service was abandoned. The Act also stated that the replacement of all trams by buses should be completed in two to three years.

George was right to fear the worst, because his route (Eastville and Durdham Downs) was one of the first to succumb to buses. The other routes replaced by buses at the end of the day on Saturday 7th May 1938 were the Tramway Centre and Westbury and the Hotwells to Centre section of the Brislington service. Tram Service No. 3 that George worked on changed to Bus Service

BRISTOL TRAMWAYS REPLACEMENT SCHEME

Third Stage—Commencing 16th July, 1939

The following Tram Routes will be replaced by Buses :

CENTRE—FILTON	CENTRE—OLD MARKET
CENTRE—DURDHAM DOWN	ZETLAND ROAD—OLD MARKET

FREE LEAFLET GIVING DETAILS OF THE NEW BUS SERVICES AND ALTERATIONS TO EXISTING BUS SERVICES OBTAINABLE FROM CONDUCTORS OR FROM THE COMPANY'S OFFICES

THE BRISTOL TRAMWAYS & CARRIAGE CO., LTD.

One of the posters that was attached to a Tram window to inform passengers about the impending replacement of the service. *(Peter Davey Collection)*

The first bus Ttcket issued on the Centre to Westbury route following the retirement of the Tram Service. *(Bristol Record Office)*

No. 2 – Eastville, Old Market, Durdham Downs – and it followed a very similar route. On Sunday 8th May 1938, the first of the 271 buses to replace the trams were seen on Bristol's streets.

The 34 Trams that retired from service that Saturday night were driven straight to scrap sidings laid specially at the rear of Kingswood Depot. By 24th June 1938, all 34 trams had been broken up. Apart from a few trams destroyed by enemy action during the Second World War, it was at Kingswood Depot that Bristol's Trams met their maker – all were destroyed and not one remained intact. As the Tram Replacement Scheme progressed, members of the travelling public were kept informed of developments through leaflets, posters and notices in the local newspapers. The windows of the trams that were due to be replaced also carried posters advising passengers of the replacement timetable.

Tram No. 31 on its last day of service. The children are Peter Davey and his sister Melody. The Driver is Walter Bishop, and the name of the conductor is unknown. *(Peter Davey Collection)*

The tram on which George started his career 19 years earlier, is pictured above on 15th July 1939 on the last day of the Filton, Downs and Centre to Old Market section of the Kingswood route. It was in a batch of 50 trams broken up between 17th July and 19th September 1939. The outbreak of the Second World War reprieved the remaining trams that were due to be replaced in October 1939. The scrappage scheme had reduced the fleet of trams to 64, and these continued to work the surviving routes to Bedminster, Ashton, Kingswood and Hanham. By the same time, the new double-deck bus fleet had grown by around 300 vehicles.

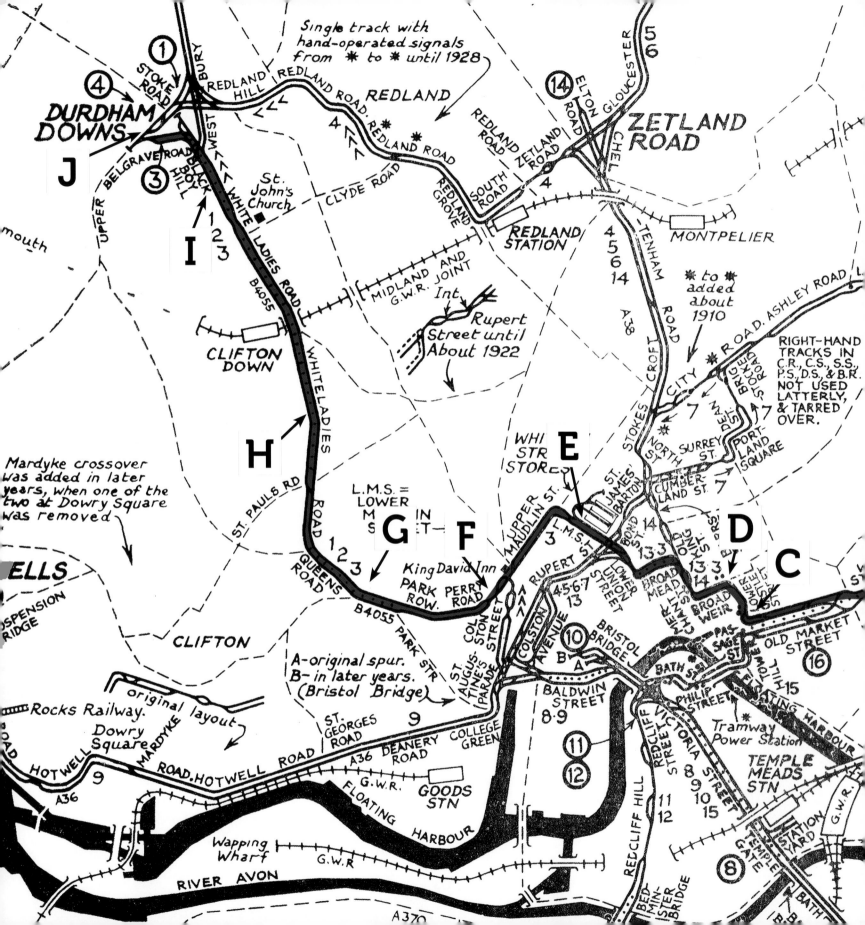

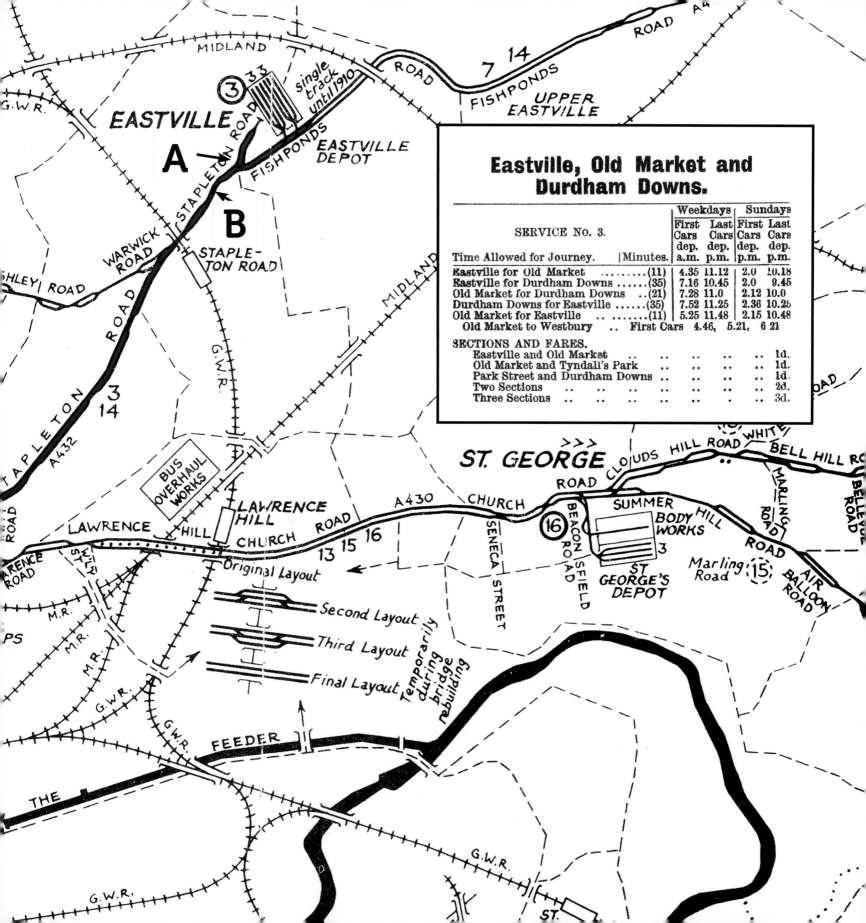

MIDLAND ROAD

ROAD A4

7 14

FISHPONDS

UPPER EASTVILLE

single track until 1910

③ 33

EASTVILLE

A

B

EASTVILLE DEPOT

FISHPONDS

STAPLETON ROAD

G.W.R.

WARWICK ROAD

ASHLEY ROAD

STAPLETON ROAD A432

3 14

STAPLE-TON ROAD

G.W.R.

MIDLAND

BUS OVERHAUL WORKS

LAWRENCE HILL

LAWRENCE HILL

CHURCH ROAD

A430

CHURCH ROAD

13 15 16

ST. GEORGE >>>

CLOUDS HILL ROAD WHITE

BELL HILL RO

BEACONSFIELD ROAD

SUMMER

BODY WORKS

ST GEORGE'S DEPOT

3

MARLING ROAD

ROAD

Marling Road

⑮

AIR BALLOON ROAD

BELLE

ROAD

16

SENECA STREET

LAWRENCE ROAD

M.R.

M.R.

M.R.

G.W.R.

PS

Original Layout

Second Layout

Third Layout

Final Layout

Temporarily during bridge rebuilding

FEEDER

G.W.R.

G.W.R.

THE

G.W.R.

ST.

Eastville, Old Market and Durdham Downs.

SERVICE No. 3.		Weekdays		Sundays	
		First Cars dep. a.m.	Last Cars dep. p.m.	First Cars dep. p.m.	Last Cars dep. p.m.
Time Allowed for Journey.	Minutes.				
Eastville for Old Market	(11)	4.35	11.12	2.0	10.18
Eastville for Durdham Downs	(35)	7.16	10.45	2.0	9.45
Old Market for Durdham Downs	(21)	7.28	11.0	2.12	10.0
Durdham Downs for Eastville	(35)	7.52	11.25	2.36	10.25
Old Market for Eastville	(11)	5.25	11.48	2.15	10.48
Old Market to Westbury	First Cars 4.46, 5.21, 6 21				

SECTIONS AND FARES.

Eastville and Old Market	..	..	..	..	..	1d.
Old Market and Tyndall's Park	..	..	..	..	..	1d.
Park Street and Durdham Downs	..	..	..	..	..	1d.
Two Sections	..	..	..	..	..	2d.
Three Sections	..	..	..	..	..	3d.

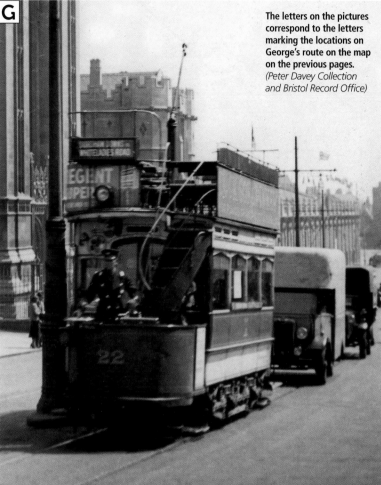

The letters on the pictures correspond to the letters marking the locations on George's route on the map on the previous pages.
(Peter Davey Collection and Bristol Record Office)

Chapter 11
Tramway and Family Life in World War Two
1939–1945

Well, the 1939 War came and that made a big difference to the staff of the Bristol Tramways & Carriage Company. Away they had to go and it made the firm short of men – not enough to man the buses. George Jnr had to go too. He joined the 44th Royal Tank Corps, and was trained first as a messenger on a motor bike. Powerful thing – he came home on it a few times. He went over to the east coast, East Grinstead, I believe.

Ron was at the Cathedral Garage – he was in a reserved occupation – Joan was at a firm in Newfoundland Road. Bill and Ken were the only ones at school and the war put them back quite a lot, for they spent a lot of time down in the shelters. Their mother had a full-time job looking after their Gran, as

she was getting on in years and was an invalid. I could see that it was going to be a difficult job for she was up and down all the time. We fixed up a bed-sitting room for her in the parlour.

I had to go for a tribunal to get exempt from ARP work owing to my handicaps through War wounds 1914-18. So, when not at work I was a Fire Watcher for our District – ours was number 395.

The most awkward part of it for us civilians were the air raid warnings. Daytime was the worst for the women and children. But at night when they were sounded, most of the men-folk were at home, if not on night work. Everybody had to have an air raid shelter, so I put in for one, consisting of about 10 pieces of steel sheets of corrugated steel and angle irons. They were brought to the door, dumped out the back yard and we had to get on with it and fix it up ourselves. Being an old campaigner of the 1914-18 war I knew how to get stuck into the job. The hardest job was digging the hole for it had to go down to

One of the new double-decked buses on George's route on the corner of Whiteladies Road and Burlington Road following an air raid on 2nd December 1940. Fortunately nobody was injured because the bus was empty at the time. *(Jim Facey Collection at Bristol Record Office)*

A Fire Watcher at Ashton during the Blitz. (Jim Facey Collection Bristol Record Office)

a depth of four foot. That took a time. But, anyway we made a good show of the shelter and I added a little more on to it to make it bigger and easier to go in and out of it. When it was finished we christened it 'The Pine's Retreat' and downed a couple of pints of wallop from the Greenbank Hotel. The Landlord was George Jenkins, the then City football manager.

At night the alarm went, out everyone would go to the shelter, and take army blankets, cushions and eatables. We always had this ready and we all had our allotted thing to take. We could hear the tunes being played at Filton Aeroplane Works. It was 'Marching Through Georgia' for the Alarm and 'Colonel Bogey' for the All Clear. There was plenty of room for us down the shelter. Gran, mother, Joan, Bill, Ken – we were supplied with beds, two each side, a small one across the bottom of the shelter for the youngest. I fixed up a door and a blanket inside to stop the candle light showing out – strict blackout.

The family next door refused to have a shelter – they always went across to a friend's opposite for

they had cellars to go down. God help them if they had a direct hit. The houses were nearly 100 years old. Even the anti-aircraft gun firing would make them shake. We had a gate made out in the garden so that they could pass in and out, and one night we had it so bad it was not safe for them to go down the cellar across the road, so they flocked down ours – 12 all told. Then they decided to have one of their own.

One thing that hurt me was that it spoiled my flower garden, finished. We had plenty of earth on top of the shelter, so I put a few flower seeds in there, including a marrow seed. I was a proper Green Fingers. He came up, flowered, then the marrow formed. When he was a couple of inches long I scratched Bill's name on it with a pin. As the marrow grew so Bill's name grew with it and he was a tidy size. But when the sirens went we had a house of panic for very often the anti-aircraft gun would open up straight away before they could get out. There were mobile guns along the main road outside, then there was an anti-aircraft unit at Purdown nicknamed Purdown Percy. Up the top of our garden was the garden of the first house in the side turning. The man there was an ex-artillery man from the 1914-18 War. He used to shout out to the flack or shell bursts when they had the Jerry in the searchlights. "Up a bit. 15 degrees lift" and vice versa, it was amusing.

One of the worst jobs I had on the double-deck buses was when we stopped at Stapleton Road Station just as a load of Tommies came down the incline, all the way from the Dunkirk evacuation. What a shambles, plastered in mud. I almost thought I was one of them. We were right for them as we were going to Stapleton and there was a camp for them in Eastville Park. No Inspector about so I crammed them on and just stood back and away we went. Dropped them at the park gates and, of course, the Fishponds and Staple Hill bus took them to the top gates. I never bothered about fares, I just took it as matter of fact

Government will pay, jotted near enough the number I carried down on my Waybill and that cleared me. They were all cleared away by the time we got back to the station. They were at the park quite a time; Jerry dropped a few bombs out in the Park.

We were in a spot of bother when the sirens sounded. We had to stop and order the passengers to go into a shelter then restart when the all clear came. We had some narrow squeaks at times.

4TH JULY 1940

We had a close shave at Stapleton, Merchant's Arms, about mid-day. We were waiting to start our journey, sat on the wall surrounding the pub when I heard a plane. I shouted: "Bob, it's a Jerry!" I knew by the sound of his engine and no warning, a bomb dropped the other side of the pub and he passed right over us – I could see the pilot as plain as day. It crossed over Farmer Owen's House straight on the way to the gun sight at Purdown. Whether that was his mission to destroy that or not, but the guns never opened fire all the time the raid was on. A hit and run job but a proper mystery about the anti-aircraft guns at Purdown. It was the talk for some time after. Me and Bob Horne, the driver, went around the back of the pub, done a bit of damage there, but the building stopped the blast from us.

25TH AND 27TH SEPTEMBER 1940

Another of the double-deck thrills was when Jerry came over in mass formation with bombers and fighters, to bomb Filton and Patchway. Daylight raids on a Wednesday and Friday, approx. 11am. I was on early turn. Our duty was six journeys Eastville – Durdham Downs, and the last journey, return to Old Market Street and then go to Patchway to pick up the workers who finished at 2pm and bring them back to Old Market. But on the Wednesday we got to hear of the raid, and got out to Filton Church. There we could

look across to Patchway – it was all in flames and what was left of the workers had gone home. We just picked up a few that were doing shift work. Jerry had an easy job that day, no opposition at all. We never had the planes to put up against them.

They tried the same again on the Friday, but they never got off so light that time – our play of wait for it came off. We were on our way to Old Market from

George pictured during the Second World War in his conductor's uniform.
(Ken Pine)

Eastville to Durdham Downs. Our stop was outside the Engineers' Union Offices. Sirens had sounded and the people had gone to the shelter. Over came the Jerry bombers, with fighter escort. They certainly ruled it at the time, right overhead, bombers going straight in the direction of Patchway. Fighters going backward and forward on the lookout for our planes but nothing happened, not even a bomb dropped over the city. I have never seen so many planes collectively in the sky before, not until later on in the War. I said to my driver "Going to stop here?" He said "Why not". He was one of the new Tram Bus Drivers. So I said – from one who knows –"Let's get as far away from the centre of town as possible" for

the near ones may drop their visiting cards (bombs) and they were still coming over from the direction of Temple Meads.

We got up as far as Perry Road and the ARP Warden stopped us. So we had to walk down Stoney Hill by the Savages Club and could look over a good part of Bristol in the direction Jerry had come. We had not been there long before we heard machine gun fire. I said to my driver it had started. What happened was, our planes waited until they had got clear of the city, then got stuck into them, fighters first, then bombers. It was a proper shambles. Bombs were dropped anywhere so as to get clear of our fighters and the ack-ack. What we saw of the routed Jerry planes going back and the dog fights were worth seeing for we must have had the famous Battle of Britain pilots waiting for them and what they thought was another easy piece of cake was a proper rout for the Luftwaffe. Jerry's wings were well and truly clipped that Friday. We finished about a couple of hours late.

24TH NOVEMBER 1940

One Sunday, a friend of Ken's was killed when a bomb hit the swimming baths in Eastville Park. The marks can be seen now, though the baths has been closed for years. In that raid they also dropped one in Daisy Road by Joan's house. It was quite early and a daylight alarm went. We were sat at the tea table. Up I jumps. Bill was at the kitchen door and he was past me, steel helmet on and out. But Jerry was on top of us and was dropping his stuff. What made things worse was that our house was in line with Stapleton Road Station and the gas meters, three of them, a proper target at the gas works. I often marvelled at the pluck that Joan showed during the raids – in that big house all by herself at night for her husband, Ron, was on night work. Her mother pleaded with her to come down home. But she stuck it out. Made herself a shelter under the stairs, I believe.

George Jnr's Regiment were ordered overseas, Middle East, and when home on leave he got married – a quiet wedding at St George's Church. They were just a few days together, him and Eileen, his wife, and then away. So that was another worry for his mother, Gran and Eileen. She had changed her job as a servant and got on the telephone exchange as a telephone operator and did well. Got rooms at Cooperage Road and started to build a home straight away. Ron and Joan at work, Bill and Ken at school. We were getting no peace with the German raids, rarely we had a

The dawn scene on 25th November 1940 at the bottom of Union Street, with Broadmead ablaze. *(Jim Facey Collection at Bristol Record Office)*

peaceful night. I remember they went to shelter one winter's night and never left it until near day break the next morning. That killed mother Pine's nerve and she spent more time with me and Bill on top and her mother used to shout out in the shelter in the lane "Violet, is it safe to go along and get a pint of bitter along Greenbank?" It got so much of a custom that if quiet, no sirens or alarm, mother went along the road. Bill had an old steel helmet of mine he did wear and if the sirens went, Bill dashed along the road, opened the door, shout come on Ma, sirens gone. Old George Jenkins used to cuss him blind for it did empty the pub and that's how it went on.

3RD AND 4TH JANUARY 1941

Sirens went one night when we were on the Downs waiting to start our return journey back to Old Market Street, where we were to have our tea break. We got relieved; I paid in my cash and went down the stairs to the basement we used for our meals for some time before the war – next door to the Olympia Picture House in Careys Lane. We had just ordered our tea and sat down to eat our bread and jam when an Inspector came down: "Everybody out of the building and get as far away as you can from the centre of town. They are dropping incendiary bombs." I had just got up to the top of the stairs when a shower came down. One pitched on the pavement right by the entrance. The wall of the Picture House jutted out about a yard and a couple of our dustbins were stood there waiting to be taken down by the yardman. A fellow in front of me in seconds had a cover off a bin and down on the bomb – it was proper quick action and presence of mind. It put paid to that bomb.

My driver, Alf Bishop, caught hold of my hand; come on George, along Redcross Street to the stone shelters at the Ropewalk Park. The excitement brought on the pain in my chest. I had no tablets to put under my tongue then. The fire bombs were still dropping. Buildings were on fire all around us. The factories at the back of the shelter – one big blaze. My driver said: "Out of this, George. He will be over with his bombs. Let's make our way for Eastville Depot." So he caught hold my hand and we ran along to Lawfords Gate to Stapleton Road and got in the shelter at Armoury Square. Jerry had started to drop his bombs. One was quite near, a great big one, and it made the shelter shake. We learnt after that it dropped down on John Street and had flattened a big area around where the Easton Road coal pit used to be. Anyway, when it was getting quiet but the All Clear had not gone, we made our way to Eastville Depot to report our whereabouts, as orders now were drivers were to use their own discretion whether to stop or carry on and give the passengers a warning that if they carry on it was at their own risk, but advised to take shelter.

28TH AUGUST 1942

On one early turn our bus had left Old Market Street and the alarm had sounded. We were stopped at

Ref. 2/41.

THE BRISTOL TRAMWAYS AND CARRIAGE COMPANY, LIMITED.

NOTICE TO BUS DRIVERS.

Partially filled sand bags are being provided on each Omnibus. These are only for use to deal with INCENDIARY BOMBS.

The sand bags may be given to any constable, fireman, A.R.P worker or recognized fire fighter for use on a bomb.

If an Incendiary Bomb is seen on or near the road:-

(1)   DRAW VEHICLE TO SIDE OF ROAD, WELL CLEAR OF BOMB.

(2)   TAKE SAND BAG FROM BUS AND CARRY IT TO BOMB, HOLDING THE BAG IN FRONT TO PROTECT YOUR HEAD AND FACE.

(3)   DROP SANDBAG ON BOMB AND MAKE SURE THAT BOMB IS WELL COVERED AND LEAVE. IF MORE THAN ONE BOMB, DEAL FIRST WITH THE ONE IN THE MOST DANGEROUS POSITION.

(4)   REPORT POSITION OF BOMB TO ANY WARDEN OR FIRE WATCHER PRESENT AND LEAVE THEM TO CLEAR WHEN BURNT OUT.

(5)   SEE THAT NEW SANDBAGS ARE REPLACED ON VEHICLE AS SOON AS POSSIBLE SO THAT YOU MAY BE READY FOR FURTHER BOMBS IF ENCOUNTERED. (SUPPLIES WILL BE KEPT AT ALL DEPOTS FOR THIS PURPOSE.

5th February, 1941.

BT&CC Notice to Bus Drivers advising them what to do if they came across an incendiary bomb. (Bristol Record Office)

Cotham Playing Fields, Kellaway Avenue, by the wardens. Plenty of ack-ack going. We learnt when we got down to Old Market that Jerry had hit two double-deck buses in Broad Weir. One of them was an Eastville – Durdham Downs bus and both driver, Reg Broadribb and conductor Bert Tanner, were killed.

Things were not going well in East Africa and Eileen had a notice from the War Office saying that George had been taken a prisoner by the Italians. After a rather long period this was confirmed by the Vatican so that was a bit of a relief to Eileen and us at home.

The last thrill on the double-decker was caused by the weather on our way to Durdham Downs. It had started to snow and by the time we had got to the bottom of Blackboy Hill there was a good covering of snow. There was a compulsory stop at St John's Church. Driver changed down to first gear and kept

The terrible scene at Broad Weir on 28th August 1942 around an hour after the bomb destroyed buses and lives. *(Bristol Record Office)*

going but on the brow of the hill the bus stopped, brakes on and started to skid backwards. Luck was with us as the near side was clear of stationary cars. After going back for a while the driver put over to the left lock and I thought we were right for the shop plate glass window but the kerb stopped us. A good job I had a driver that knew the job.

The double-decker was getting a bit too much for me. My legs would not stick it. I heard they would not give you a changeover to single decks unless you had something wrong with your legs. This is where my osteoarthritis knee came in – no trouble to get a certificate and I was transferred to the 83 Service (single deck – no stairs to climb) running from Old Market to the top of Gloucester Road and then to Durdham Downs and the Suspension Bridge. We had a proper job on them. As petrol was wanted for the services, we ran on gas for a while – the gas gadget at the rear made from a form of charcoal. But it had no pulling power and we had to give up gas.

In about 1944 the Yanks were over here in force. Their wagons, monster great big things they were, with headlights like those on a lighthouse and they used them too at night, whether Jerry was about or not. We were going down towards Ashley Down Station Arch off Muller Road when a convoy of them passed us and turned left into a big field which was used as a sports ground, so we had to stop until they

Cartoon from 'Omnibus', the BT&CC's Staff Magazine. George welcomed the move to a single-deck bus. *(Bristol Record Office)*

Drawn by H. DANCEY (M/M)

" Say! How about a swop, chum?"

finished going around the field to their allotted place – lights full on, whereas ours was dimmed to the size of a half crown. They were a proper danger on the road. I had an early turn, finished 1am. Going from Old Market to the Downs; Muller Road, cross over Gloucester Road to the Wellington Hotel; Kellaway Avenue, and just past Cotham Playing Fields, when we met it with one of them. He had just come out of a side turning, ignored the halt sign to cross over the main road that we were using – bang! – I wondered what hit us. Took us right into the side turning. I was stood by the door and got flung down the steps but managed to get a grip on the hand rail or I should have been flat out on my face in the road. I wrenched myself very bad, but I wanted to get around to the driver, for they hit him right in the driver's cabin door.

The Yanks stopped about three lengths away. Sergeant came along, "Can't stop long buddy." I said: "Hold it, you are stopping here until the Police and Tramway Officials come along."

A crowd had collected and the ambulance was

phoned for. My driver was right out and we were afraid to move him until they came. I had taken particulars off the Yanks. Got witnesses, saw the driver off to the BRI then a gent called me in his house, as I wanted to ring up the Chief Inspector. He said you can use my phone, but have a drink first and rest yourself before phoning. I got through to the Chief, told him what had happened, where we were, number of our bus, all about the driver, only five passengers on the bus, and no complaints from them. Put them on the next bus following.

They were no time coming on the scene – Traffic Manager, Chief Inspector, half dozen Inspectors. I just sat on the wall of a garden and let them carry on with the Yanks. Got out a fag and had a smoke to calm my nerves for I could not stop myself from shaking. I really ought to have gone to the hospital for a check up, but what rattled me was, the maintenance gang brought another bus along, for ours was a write off, and wanted me to carry on with an Inspector driving down to Old Market to pick up passengers on the way down. I refused and told them straight I was not fit to do it so they gave way and we went back to Old Market Street (Light) which meant no passengers.

When we arrived the Inspector asked me what I was going to do as I had an hour and a half to spare, so I told him I would go and have a cup of tea in the canteen, then get the sheets ready for the other relief conductor, make out the accident report and hand it into the Station Inspector at Old Market. By the time I had got this done my relief had arrived, so home I went. I had to tell the story to Mother, as she could see there was something wrong with me. I turned up next morning for first bus out and, of course, had a fresh driver. But going through Kellaway Avenue and Coldharbour Road, we watched the side turnings for the mad Yanks. On the following Sunday night about 7.30pm (dark) we were sat at the table. Ken, Bill, their Mother and me. A knock at the door – I answered it.

There was a massive big Yankee Officer there – over the other side of the road was his Jeep. He told me his business so I called him in. He was the Attorney General for the US Army for our district and he came in for a statement from me, which he took down in shorthand, then typed out on a small typewriter. He read it through then got me to sign it after asking if it was correct. After that we had a chat. He was from Texas, owned a big ranch there. This thrilled the boys.

I asked him how the driver would get on. Looked as if he will get the rope for he is on a charge or will be for murder if our driver dies from injuries received from the crash. He was in hospital for three months, but his driving was finished when he was fit to return to work. The Union fought his case against the US Army and he received £750 compensation and the company gave him a light job – bill sticking on bus windows. I had to go in hospital a couple of months after for a hernia operation – BRI, Dr Tasker – and I thought that wrench I had at the accident may have caused it.

Time went on and when I was on late turn and passing our house I used to give a whistle if the alarm was on, knowing they were out the back yard shelter. I went in for a radio set and got one on the weekly. Of course the programmes were limited, mostly all records. Tune in to Luxembourg – get a good programme. Then there was Tommy Handley with Jack Train in Colonel Chinstrap, a proper mimic. Much Binding In The Marsh, Richard Murdoch, Sam Costa, Robert Horne. They helped to blow away the blues. Then their Gran Winterson passed away, so that the home was beginning to look empty. Their mother broke down in the January as her mother died in the December. We turned the front room into a living room and the back room for us two and Bill and Ken upstairs. That helped her a bit when she was able to move around.

Night times were passed away by playing cards

The inside of a POW hut at Stalag 11B *(George Morley)*

and Eileen, George Jnr's wife, used to come down from Cooperage Road, St George and I learnt them how to play cribbage – one of my favourite card games, that and solo whist. When it was time for her to go Bill or Ken went part way with her. The War was coming to a close. We did always stop playing cards just before 9pm to listen to the news. Our troops were advancing, driving Jerry back and the end of the war was in sight.

Every time they were announcing the Prisoner of War Camps that had been relieved the suspense must have been great for Eileen. George Jnr's was Stalag 11B. He had been a prisoner for three years and his wife had built up a lovely home for them both. Well it came at last. 9pm approaching, cards finished, wireless switched on, and the announcer started: "This is the BBC 9 O'clock News. Stalag 11B has been relieved."

What uproar for ten minutes, 52 playing cards went up in the air. Eileen was putting her clothes on, won't stop for a cup of coffee. I must go up and tell Gran, she was stopping with Eileen at the time. Two days later Eileen had a telegram from George Jnr to say he would be home on leave in a couple of days.

The liberation of Stalag 11B on 14th April 1945. George Jnr had already escaped. *(George Morley)*

It appeared that he and a mate had made their escape a fortnight before the camp was relieved. They were getting close, heavy guns were being fired and the lads plotted their escape one night, for their job was digging up mangel-wurzels in a big field and at the time their guards were old sweats from the 1914 War, Anglo Saxons – easy going. Their plan was, whilst working in the field, to ask the guard to excuse them time to go to the toilet, which was a quarter of a mile away in the direction from which our troops were advancing.

When they got there, in the shack, they started to knock out the back wood planks and the noise they made was drowned by our guns firing. They kept under cover of the building and the Jerry only spotted them when they were a good distance away, fired a few rounds of rifle fire at them first to make a show, to cover themselves. Never ran so fast in his life.

George Jnr had a job to convince the Yanks they were British Tommies but after a while they were hustled down to the back areas and handed over to British troops. They gave the Yanks the position of Stalag 11B so as to avoid shelling and it was captured a fortnight after. So that's how and why George Jnr got home a fortnight before. He got home about two days after getting the news he was coming. So I had to work fast to organise a welcome home for him.

People next door started a collection. I trimmed up the front window with 'Welcome Home George from Stalag 11B'. Flags flying from every house either side the road, and bunting across the road, high enough for the double-deck buses going to the BAC to pass under. We let him have a couple of days at his home then the day at 89 Bellevue Road. Had the press photographer and what a crowd. I had the day off and put my medals up and the photos were very good. The little boy next door (Terry McCoy) handed over a cheque for £20, collected from around the district, to George Jnr. At the time he was suffering with a poisoned thumb and had it in a sling. Had a few weeks' sick leave and then reported back again until the finish and to get demobilised, and went back to his old job conducting at Lawrence Hill.

All happenings were beginning to play up with my nerves and reaction from the First World War, and the end was not far off.

Now the Armistice. When that was signed and the 1939-45 War was over we had celebrations by Firewatch District. We had concerts out in the street – music, dancing, all kinds of music. I organised a march around the houses. I got the boys that had bugles and side drums and formed a band. I was the Drum Major with a new mop for a Mace. All the children from around and about formed up and away we marched, a nice little crowd of 100 children, your humble swinging the mace – up in the air he did go, and up would go a shout. This would last from 6.30pm to 7.30pm, go somewhere different every night for a week, and then our concert would carry on after. The children they were down after tea: "So, Mr Pine, taking us for a march tonight?" I enjoyed it and the children, and the same thing happened when the Japanese War finished.

The scene outside 89 Bellevue Road on 5th May 1945 as George Jnr is welcomed home by family, friends and neighbours. George is proudly wearing his BT&CC uniform and his WW1 medals. *(Edith's Trunk)*

Author's Notes

Scares during the Blitz

JULY 4TH 1940

The pilot George saw on July 4th was Lt Hans-Heinrich Delfs. The Heinkel He 111 plane he was flying was on a lone mission to bomb the Bristol Aeroplane Company (BAC) at Filton. During the raid, as well as dropping two bombs on an ash tip near Eastville Park (the incident George witnessed), a bomb was dropped on Gloucester Road. Two bombs also fell in the vicinity of the BAC Rodney Works – injuring eight people in the factory and three RAF operators at the nearby barrage balloon site.

The Heinkel attempted to make its escape but it had already been tracked. Three Spitfires on daytime deployment at Filton had been scrambled and were in pursuit. Two of the Spitfires, flown by Pilot Officer H.D. Edwards and Sergeant R.H. Fokes caught up with the Heinkel and eventually shot it down. It crashed into trees on Longmoor Farm near Gillingham in Dorset. The pilot, seen so clearly by George a little earlier, was the only member of the crew to survive. Although injured, he was arrested by Pilot Officer Edwards who had landed his Spitfire in an adjacent field.

SEPTEMBER 25TH & 27TH 1940

The daylight raid on the BAC site on 25th September 1940 was huge. From German bases in France, 68 Heinkel He 111 bombers took part in the attack. They were accompanied by 52 Messerschmitt Bf 110 fighter planes who escorted the bombers to and from their target. The attack on the BAC site started at 11.45am and although 41 Spitfires and Hurricanes were scrambled to engage the enemy, it wasn't until the raiders were on their way back to their bases that British fighters had some success. However, only eight of the 110 attacking planes failed to make their way back across the English Channel and one RAF pilot was lost during the exchanges. According to the claims of the returning German pilots, 81.7 tonnes of high explosives had been dropped on the factory and the Luftwaffe's own magazine, *Der Adler*, soon after proudly proclaimed "this factory will not produce many more aircraft".

However, this was not the case. Although five assembly shops had been destroyed and a further eight damaged, of the 50 or so completed aircraft in various parts of the factory at the time, only eight were completely destroyed. A further 24 aircraft received minor damage that was soon repaired. The greatest impact was on personnel, with 91 BAC workers being killed. In addition, 13 soldiers from the 4th Battalion, Royal Berkshire Regiment were killed whilst on a route march along Gloucester Road between Patchway and Filton; a searchlight operator was killed at the 'Dazzle Defence' site battery in Filton and an RAF operator died at the Barrage Balloon site in Filton. A further 16 civilians died in nearby areas and over 300 people were injured.

The 'Flap' room, 504 Squadron, Filton September 1940. Pictured from left to right are Pilot Officer Hunt, Pilot Officer Trevor Parsons, Squadron Leader Johnny Sample (CO), Flight Lieutenant Tony Rook (OC 'A' Flt), Flying Officer Michael 'Scruffy' Royce and Sgt 'Wag' Haw. *(Mac Hawkins Collection)*

Pilots of 504 Squadron examine the MG17 machine guns from the Bf110 shot down over Fishponds on 27th September 1940. Pictured from left to right are Flying Officer Trevor Parsons, Flying Officer Michael Royce, Sgt 'Wag' Haw and Sgt B.M. Bush. Royce, Haw and Bush took part in the dogfight over Bristol on 27th September 1940. *(Mac Hawkins Collection)*

The damage and loss of life inflicted at Filton on Wednesday 25th September 1940 prompted RAF Fighter Command to act quickly to shore up the defences around the BAC factory. The following day, 504 Squadron – equipped with 17 Hurricane Fighters and 12 pilots – was transferred from Hendon to Filton and the heavy anti-aircraft gun ring around the BAC plant was supplemented by the addition of eight semi-mobile guns from elsewhere across the city.

As George had rightly surmised, 504 Squadron arrived in Bristol, fresh from taking part in the Battle of Britain. On 15th September 1940, it was credited with destroying five enemy aircraft and damaging six others over South East England. The Squadron arrived in Bristol at 3pm on 26th September 1940 and before they landed, most of the craters on the landing area caused by the previous day's bombing had been filled in. Ground and support personnel with equipment and spares arrived from Hendon in the early hours of 27th September.

At 11.23am on the morning of Friday 27th September, sirens were heard again across Bristol and almost immediately, 12 of the Hurricanes of 504 Squadron were scrambled. The first six planes were airborne by 11.25am followed closely by the second group. A total of 52 German aircraft appeared again in daylight over Bristol. This time, their target was not the BAC site as initially thought, but Parnall's Aircraft Factory at Yate. The arrival of the Hurricanes was timely as, in relatively good weather, George and thousands of people across Bristol witnessed a classic dog-fight over the city. The newly arrived Hurricanes completely routed the raiders – forcing them to jettison their bombs and run for home. The hurriedly released bombs fell mainly in open countryside around North Bristol and in the Filton area, although four people were killed. Four other

RAF Squadrons – two Spitfire and two Hurricane – also took part in the defence of Bristol and continued to attack the raiders as they fled south across the Somerset and Dorset skies.

By the end of the action, 10 of the German planes had been brought down – one in Fishponds in Bristol, one near Radstock, six in Dorset and two in the English Channel. Of the German Airmen who took part in the raid, 14 were killed and 6 were captured – five of whom were wounded. The only British Airman to perish was Pilot Officer Miller whose Spitfire collided with a Luftwaffe plane over the skies of Dorset.

By around mid-day on 27th September 1940, 10 of the Hurricanes from 504 Squadron had returned to Filton. One plane had force landed at Axminster and another had landed at Weston Airport short of fuel. The BAC workers were full of admiration for the pilots of 504 Squadron and organised a collection to buy beer and cigarettes as a token of their appreciation for their magnificent work. The gifts were handed to the pilots on 28th September and the next day, the Lord Mayor of Bristol paid a visit to Filton to personally thank the Squadron's pilots for their gallant efforts above the skies of Bristol.

Sadly, but perhaps not surprisingly, five of the 12 pilots who had bravely defended Bristol on 27th September 1940 were killed in action or on active service before the end of the war.

NOVEMBER 24TH 1940

With the aim of eliminating Bristol as an importing port for supplying much of the Midlands and the South of England, the 24th November 1940 saw the first major bombing raid on the city. With 135 bombers dropping a claimed 156 tonnes of high explosives, nearly five tonnes of oil bombs and 12,500 incendiary bombs between 6.30pm and 11pm, the impact on Bristol was devastating – both in loss of life and architectural gems like St. Peters' Hospital and the Old Dutch House. Some

200 people were killed and 890 were injured during the onslaught which saw the loss of much of Castle Street, Wine Street and High Street. Serious damage was also caused in Knowle, Temple, Barton Hill and Eastville.

One of the first high explosive bombs fell near the Corporation Baths at Eastville Park. It was this bomb that killed Ken Pine's friend Herbert Bennett (17), and three of the friends he was playing with – Alice Leonard (17), Doreen Vickery (14) and Joyce Trotman (13).

JANUARY 3RD & 4TH 1941

The raid George referred to was the single biggest attack on Bristol during the Second World War. More than 200 German planes took part and bombs fell across the city in two waves from 6.35pm on 3rd January until 5.51am the following morning. The attack was aimed at completing the destruction of harbour installations, large mills, warehouses and cold stores, and to paralyse Bristol as a trading centre supplying Southern England. In total, the German bombers dropped 152 tonnes of high explosives, two tonnes of oil bombs and 53,568 incendiary bombs during the longest raid of the war so far. Bedminster,

The devastation at John Street. *('The Bombing of Bristol' 1943)*

St Philips, Hotwells and Cotham were particularly badly affected and 149 people were killed and 315 injured.

George was fortunate to make his way back to Eastville Depot unscathed given the scale of the attack. It was a good job that George was in the shelter at Armoury Square. The bomb that dropped on nearby John Street destroyed 10 houses and killed 24 people, including entire families like the Dytes and the Palmers with six and five family members killed respectively. Fire Watcher, Sid Watkins of Chaplin Road, Easton was also killed in the blast.

AUGUST 28ᵀᴴ 1942

Had George been on a different shift, he might well have been killed in the inferno that accompanied the bomb blast in Broad Weir at 9.21am on 28th August 1942. Two of his colleagues on the Eastville – Durdham Downs route perished, three other BT&CC employees were killed and two others were injured. Two buses were completely engulfed in flames and another one was badly damaged. Many passengers were burnt alive and in total 45 lives were lost, 25 people were seriously wounded

The terrible scene at Broad Weir around an hour after the bomb destroyed buses and lives. *(Bristol Record Office Film Archive)*

and a further 30 received minor injuries. The daylight raid and the dropping of a single 250 kilogramme bomb came without warning. Believed to be an experimental raid targeting Bristol Docks, the effect was devastating. In terms of loss of life, it was the single most serious incident to occur in the City during the World War Two.

Escape from Stalag 11b

Like his father before him, George Pine Jnr joined the 6th Battalion Gloucestershire Regiment at St Michael's Hill, Bristol as a bugler in the Territorials. This was in April 1935. Also like his father, George Jnr joined the Bristol Tramways and Carriage Company and worked as a Bus Conductor until the start of the Second World War.

When war broke out, George Jnr had already transferred to the Royal Tank Regiment as a reservist and was at camp in 1939 when war was declared. He was sent to Brighton for training for much of 1940 and married Eileen on 12th December 1940. A few weeks later on 1st January 1941 George Jnr and the rest of the Royal Tank Regiment left the country on the SS Sobeski – a Polish troopship – and eventually landed in Egypt in March 1941. It would be four and a half years before George Jnr could return home and the following paragraphs briefly describe his war experience.

Under the overall command of General Wavell, a 40,000 strong force of British, Australian and New Zealand soldiers made their way across the desert to places like Sidi Barrani and Fort Maddalena – utilising captured Italian lorries and stores as their own equipment had difficulty in keeping up with the pace of their advance.

They moved to Benghazi, Derna and Tobruk on the way to Tripoli and captured thousands of Italian troops who had given up after relatively short exchanges. Life got tougher when the German Afrika Korps under General Rommel arrived and George Jnr and the rest of the Allied Forces had to retreat to Tobruk. Surrounded by German forces the siege was eventually lifted in

December 1941 after considerable fighting around Sidi Omar and Sidi Rezegh where a massive tank battle took place. George Jnr's regiment suffered many casualties in tanks and crews, but the German Forces retreated back to El Agheila.

Following a brief rest, George Jnr celebrated Christmas 1941 in Benghazi.

On 27th May 1942, the German Army launched a massive offensive along the Gazala Line, forcing the Allies to retreat towards Tobruk, Knightsbridge and Gazala. In the battle for Knightsbridge, George Jnr's battalion was particularly badly hit, being left with only one fit troop of tanks including his own. Told to deny the Germans the only piece of coast road, George Jnr's Squadron Leader was badly wounded shortly after taking up the defensive position. George Jnr managed to get him to the nearest Regimental Aid Post before returning to defend the road.

Shortly after, George Jnr's tank came under attack and although he and his crew managed to get out, the Gunner and Wireless Operator were wounded. The tank was completely destroyed. The crew got into a drainage ditch and hoped to hide there until dark. However, travelling up the ditch was a strong contingent of German forces and the crew had little choice but to surrender. The Germans were very good to the wounded crew and George Jnr and the rest of those able to walk were passed down to the rear of the fighting to mainly Italian soldiers who "were braver soldiers when you were prisoners than they were in battle."

George Jnr was taken to Derna Airfield from where he and a large contingent of British and Australian prisoners were flown to Tripoli, and then by boat to Italy and an Italian Prisoner of War Camp. In 1943, George Jnr was transferred to Stalag 11b near Fallingbostel in Germany, where he spent the next two years. On one night, his name was read out during a broadcast by the infamous Nazi propaganda announcer Lord Haw-Haw, during the *Germany Calling* radio programme.

On 7th April 1945, with Allied Forces closing in on the POW camp, George Jnr escaped. He and a few others asked the Captain who was watching them if they could go to the toilet. They went in through the front of the toilet block and broke their way out through the back. This was nine days before the camp was liberated by British Troops. They ran off and eventually met up with the American 5th Army at Hildesheim Aerodrome, some 50 miles away. George Jnr was flown back to High Wycombe on 27th April 1945.

George Jnr arrived in Bristol on 2nd May 1945 and following a few quiet days at home with his wife Eileen, the scene was set for a major family celebration. The event was captured by a press photographer and next door neighbour – a young Terry McCoy – presented George Jnr with £20 collected from friends and neighbours from Bellevue Road and surrounding streets. After he was 'de-mobbed', George Jnr went back to work with the BT&CC – initially as a bus conductor, then as a bus driver.

Bristol Tramways and Carriage Company During World War Two

As well as picking up thousands of Dunkirk survivors from Stapleton and Temple Meads stations in early June 1940 and taking the soldiers to barracks and a temporary camp at Eastville Park, the company also transported 21,500 women and children who had been evacuated from London.

Although the introduction of fuel rationing in September 1939 caused the reduction and cessation of some services, the company maintained its 'rush hour' timetable throughout the war and helped to keep the citizens of Bristol on the move ensuring Bristol's businesses could continue to function. In 1939, the company transported 138 million passengers across the City – 32 million on trams and 106 million on buses. The Blitz years, a curfew on operating times and the cessation of Sunday morning services took their toll on

One of the Bristol Conductresses going about her business on a Bristol Bus in 1942. *(Bristol Record Office Film Archive)*

passenger numbers. They saw a steady decline, reaching their lowest point in 1941 when 123 million passengers were carried. By 1944, passenger numbers had risen again to a massive 153 million – around four times the number currently carried on Bristol's buses.

The Company lost relatively few bus drivers to the Armed Services as bus driving was a reserved occupation. Most of the shortage in male drivers was filled by the engagement of around 400 men who had little say in the matter as they were under the direction of the Ministry of Labour. Most of these men were heavy goods drivers and according to the company did not want to be bus drivers. They were regarded as unwilling workers with an apparent detrimental effect on service operation.

A large number of women were also trained as bus drivers, although only 20 were eventually selected. The company's war history almost grudgingly accepts that some of these women were actually good drivers… "These women did some very good work, and despite the difficult nature of the routes on which they were operating were remarkably accident free."

However, the Company lose a significant number of male conductors to the Services – 1,244 in total. Bearing in mind his age (48 at the time) and his First World War injuries, there was no question of George being called up, so he remained a bus conductor for the duration of the war. Overall, 1,953 employees were required to serve in the War and of these, 53 were killed on active service.

To cope with the exodus of male conductors, female employees were recruited to take their place. However, in the company's war history, it was less than complimentary about the impact of the female influx… "Whilst a small proportion of female conductors have done very excellent work it must be said that this type of labour has been generally unsatisfactory and wastage has been heavy." Of the 4,055 female conductors recruited, 2,604 left the company's employment before the war had ended. To help take some of the strain off female conductors, particularly during busy periods when fare collection was reportedly not carried out properly, the company recruited 1,200 male auxiliary conductors. These were volunteers

The damage outside Lawrence Hill Depot caused on 16th/17th March 1941. *(Jim Facey Collection at Bristol Record Office)*

155

Bedminster Tram Dept looking pristine on 29th July 1901.
(Bristol Record Office)

who helped when riding to and from their normal place of work during peak periods. Duties included bell signalling and the safe loading and offloading of passengers – leaving the regular conductor to concentrate on fare collection. Although at first their help was resented by the female conducting staff, their assistance and presence was eventually accepted.

As George mentioned, owing to petrol rationing, the company experimented with the use of producer gas as a fuel to power some of the buses. Some 29 single-deck buses and one double-deck bus were converted and each vehicle had a trailer attached to it. The drivers were not enthusiastic about the performance and operation of the converted buses and the experiment was eventually

dropped. The impact of the war on the company's fleet, its buildings and its people was huge. As well as losing vehicles and buildings to Luftwaffe bombing, 28 of the company's single-deck vehicles and two of its garages were requisitioned for the war effort. During the air raids, 456 company vehicles were damaged including 14 destroyed, 26 seriously damaged, 14 requiring major repairs and 402 receiving minor damage.

The Tram Depot in Bedminster was destroyed by a bomb at around 6am on 4th January 1941, killing tram driver Albert Humpry who was about to start his day's work. The bomb also severed tram tracks in the

Bedminster Tram Dept after it was destroyed on 4th January 1941. *(Bristol Record Office)*

The last major raid on Bristol finally put an end to the City's tram services. *(Jim Facey Collection at Bristol Record Office)*

vicinity and most of the rolling stock was damaged including four trams that were completely wrecked. These were broken up where they stood and the rest were towed to Kingswood Depot for the breakers to complete the scrappage. Trams never left Bedminster Depot again. Two days later, the bus service took over.

The company's main depot at Lawrence Hill was also severely damaged on 16th and17th March 1941. Although there were no company casualties, the Training School was completely destroyed.

The last heavy raid on Bristol on 11th April 1941 destroyed St Phillips Bridge, which was adjacent to the Tramway Power Station. This finally brought an end to Bristol's Trams. Given a stay of execution owing to the outbreak of the war, it is ironic that it was the war that finally killed off the tram service. The power cables for the then last remaining section of the tramways operating between Old Market Street, Kingswood and Hanham were destroyed and the Bristol tram services were replaced the following morning by bus services.

Then, without warning, on 28th August 1942 a lone German bomber dropped a single bomb over the City.

It fell in Broad Weir, near Old Market, which was the terminal point for a number of company bus services. There were five double-deck buses in the vicinity at the time and three were destroyed. The bomb killed three bus drivers, and one male and one female conductor. A bus driver and female conductor were seriously injured.

Overall, 20 company employees, including seven who were on duty, were killed during the air raids on Bristol. The company was rightly proud of the fact that apart from two days when Bedminster Tram Depot was destroyed and the roads in the immediate area were impassable, all services were maintained by the company throughout the war. The operation of services, particularly for workers at Munitions and Aircraft Factories and at the Docks was the prime concern. Except when they were in immediate danger, company employees worked through air raid warnings. Even during the heaviest of bombing raids, they were determined to keep services running.

George played his part in helping to keep Bristol on the move during the Second World War.

Chapter 12
Winding Down to Retirement
1945–1956

My sister, Edie, was living quite comfortable in her flat, retired from service, and she used to get letters from my brother, Harry, in Australia. He got mixed up in the war against the Japs, for they had their eyes on Australia.

I had a letter from him later on and in it a rather tall order. He had joined an Old Comrades Association and he wanted his birth certificate and war medals. I was looking after his medals. But his certificate was a problem, for the Registry Office had been bombed at St Peters. There was a temporary one in the old Weights and Measures Office, Merchant Street. They gave me the address of Somerset House, London, and they sent me a big one, with the family history on it. Whilst I was waiting for that I got his medals fixed up at the House of Lewis, Military Tailors, and

they looked posh, ready to pin on his coat – Croix de Guerre, 1914, Bronze Star and three others. He wanted them for Anzac Day, the big day for the Aussie ex-soldiers, or servicemen, so I had to work fast. Packed them both up, medals, certificate, a nice long letter from the home front, took it along to the Post Office, had it registered and air mailed. I had a letter from him later to say he had received them OK in time for the big parade.

I was delighted to get that letter. I took it down to my sister as she only lived ten minutes away. She thought the world of it and wanted to pay the expenses, but my sister was one of the cheerful givers and she never let us brothers go without during the First World War years.

Bill had finished school, and got a job at Patchway Aerodrome, but it was too much for him, but he wanted to try it. Then he had a few more jobs and landed at Robinsons Wax Factory. When Bill reached 18 years old he did two years with the Royal Pioneer

George and his half-sister Dora visiting him at Headington Hospital in the early 1950s. *(Ken Pine)*

Ron Pine (left), Bill Pine (centre) and Ken Pine. All of George's sons wore the King's uniform. *(Author's own collection, Eileen Pine, Ken Pine)*

He stuck it fairly well and could have made a good soldier but the Army never really appealed to him. There was a proper bully of a Drill Sergeant for the new recruits on parade. The story goes, Ken was on parade one day, did something wrong. "Pine!" bawled the Sergeant "Come out here!" Gave Ken a good rollicking, on the point of bursting a blood vessel, noses touching, then he stepped back and said: "Pine, you're a clot. What are you?" Ken in a smart answer "A clot sir", not a bit disturbed at the way the Drill Sergeant carried on, it never affected him at the least. So the Drill Sergeant said "Why, Pine?" Ken's reply was "My father was Company Sergeant Major, DCM in the 1914 War. I have been used to being shouted at all my life Sir." About turn, double back to the ranks. He was happy go lucky, the same as in his civvy job. He had one stripe but never kept it. It never appealed to him to be apart from his pals.

When he finished his two years in the Army which also made a man of him, he went back to his old firm. They took him back OK but Ken could see that there was no chance of improving himself there. Smartened himself up and went down to the Redcliff Street offices, got an interview and, within a week, was at work with the big firm, and is still there now. So, Bill and Ken at Robinsons – one wax and the other cardboard factories at Fishponds.

Ron went to East Africa doing his two years National Service with the Royal Electrical and Mechanical Engineers (REME). So we had four sons that wore the then King's Uniform. George Jnr was back to work, also Ron. Joan was working at Packers Chocolate Factory, on advice from her doctor.

I had a spell in the Infirmary for a hernia operation and that finished me on the buses. They only had one light job opened for me and that was at the Club. When I went down for an interview the Chief Steward told me, "George, this is not an invalid's job – if you can stick it, so well and good". He

Corps up in Nottingham. So he got to learn all about Maid Marion and the Sherwood Foresters.

His Regiment gained honours fighting the floods at Gainsborough. I believe it was the River Trent burst its banks and caused serious flooding in the city. Bill went in for promotion and he rose to the rank of Sergeant. I told him I would give him 10/- for every stripe – he got 30/- out of me – a lot of money in those days. Their chief job was vehicle recovery. They wanted him to soldier on but Bill had enough.

When Ken left school he went into the shoe trade to learn 'clicking' but he was clicking with the girls at the factory too much. The Welfare Man there used to call in to see me or his mother to tell us that Ken was not getting on very well and would not take his job serious enough. At the age of 18 it came to Ken's turn to go away with the Gloucesters.

A City Centre bus queue on a wet Saturday afternoon on 15th December 1945. This would have been a familiar site to George when he worked on Service No. 2. Note the uniformed servicemen standing in the queue. *(Bristol Record Office)*

was an ex-coach driver that had to give up through poor eyesight. He was a proper driver at getting the place clean. There were three of us men and we had allotted floors to clean. Mornings I was down in the basement, two skittle alleys to bees wax and polish, and the bar, as we were licensed for all kinds of drinks and cigarettes. That was the hardest of the lot – collect all the empty bottles in the cases and carry them upstairs, clean and polish the glasses. Sweep out, but use the brush so as not to create dust and make more work.

The bar used to open at 12.30pm, the same as the pubs outside. I finished at 1pm, back at 6pm until 10pm, like a spread over duty – Monday to Saturday, Sunday off. Another man was cleaning the entrance hall and the cloak rooms. Then on the same floor one

long dance hall stage that was also used for whist drives, concerts, shows and meetings – 60 tables, four chairs to each, so you can guess what we had to shift after it had been used. Of course he had a system of working that would make it easier, all four of us were in action them winter nights, and I found out to my sorrow the Chief Steward was right, it was a hard job. For I was a conscientious worker and made that bar look nice and clean, and night times, wear a coach driver's summer dust coat.

I was nervous at the start, behind the bar, serving up the pints, but soon shook it off. I was and still is TT and now and again it would be: "Have one yourself!"

George worked on this single-deck bus from Service No. 83 pictured here in Haberfield Street, Bristol on Monday 25th March 1946, shortly before George finished working as a bus conductor. *(Bristol Record Office)*

George in the garden of 89 Bellevue Road in around 1946 with his neighbour's Anderson shelter in the background. *(Andy Pine)*

I did say I would later, but take 6d and put them on one side. When enough, packet of fags. There was always a certain amount of fumes coming from the beer barrels. We did draw straight from the wood.

Five 28 gallons of liquor on a long hose, three tapped, two spare – Georges Bitter, Pale Ale, Whitbread's PA, Draught Bass, Stout in Bottles, and all

the other brands. All this was for tramway men only. Pay two pence at the entrance hall to admit a friend, a pass for that evening. The Steward there also had to look after four full-sized billiard and snooker tables and a small room for table tennis. A rather large committee room for meetings. All had to be kept spotless, so it was no pushover, but it got me down in the finish.

I had a breakdown and the Ministry of Pensions sent me over to Oxford – a place a mile outside the city, Headington. It was a big mansion on top of a hill in immense grounds – one of the early Victorian estates with big carriage roads, all private. There was a bridge going over the main Headington Road leading from there to London. The Tramway buses used to pass there via Oxford. The Yanks had commandeered it whilst the 1939-45 War was on. Trust them.

Then the Red Cross took it over as a rehabilitation centre for disabled ex-servicemen. They were mostly men that wore callipers on the leg. So I was back in hospital blues again. I had about five months there and we all had our allotted jobs to do. I chose gardening to be outside. They grew everything, vegetables, all kinds, and my job was to look after a large straw bed. That was better than being in the workshops, mat making or carpentry. One day out in the grounds I had a black out and down I went. The Matron happened to be looking out her window and saw what happened, so that they soon had me indoors about a day in bed and I was on my feet again. It went in the report book as I was complaining about pains in my head, and giddiness.

They sent me four miles away to Wheatley Military Hospital. Not to my liking, hospital for head injuries. Now I was there and could not go to sleep. Orderly came around, male nurse: "Can't sleep, Dad?" I said: "No, but I can hear babies crying". He said: "You are right, they are in the next ward" – serving soldier's children with meningitis of the brain. He said: "I tell you another thing, an old soldier, 84 years old, has been operated on for a tumour on the brain."

They gave me a lumber punch and took so much fluid away, a certain place in the spine, a very careful job, a big needle, on my side, knees up touching my chin, no movement, all over, then relax, and that relieved the pressure on the head. Anyway, I was at the military hospital for head injuries for two weeks (long enough for me). Too much khaki about – Military Nurses and RAMC orderlies. I was glad to get back to Headington.

We used to get paid 6d a day for working, and the well-to-do people used to send to the home for men to come to their places to do fruit picking. Our Red Cross was well patronised by the students at the college and I went to Radcliffe Hospital several times. The famous doctors in England were there.

Went on a trip to Churchill's House at Blenheim Palace, Woodstock. They were holding a fete in the grounds 2/6 entrance fee, side shows, and the big attraction was a lady diving into a tank of flames from a great height. Then the people gathered around the front entrance to the mansion as the son was in residence there. He was sorry that the people could not look over it because the military were still occupying three parts of it. They could not call their home their own.

I used to get a haircut and a shave in a barber's shop and like all barbers he was very talkative. Sport was the topic, and he was telling me about the good football team Headington had. He was one of the big men on the management. Quite early on he told me they were starting a team again. That was stopped during the War and on the Friday that I left Headington Hospital I read a notice from the football club inviting us to a football match, free, and whilst at home I followed their progress. Did very well and now they are in the Second Division English League

– now named Oxford United. I had a few visitors whilst I was there, though far away from Bristol. Mother came once with little grandson, John and his mother Audrey. We were watching television, it had just started then, and those in a certain radius could get it. All of a sudden young John went missing. He was out on the veranda playing in amongst the Tommies stripped to the waist, laid down sunning themselves, quite enjoying himself. And as I am writing this memoire for him he has just passed his 24th birthday, June 25th. How times fly. I have got a few snaps of The Hall in my album. A lovely place and well planned out. Lovely landscaped gardens reaching quite a long way down with a lodge at the bottom, used by the gardener, and a gate. There was a big gate at the top on the Headington Road. At approx

George at Headington Hospital in the early 1950s. *(Ken Pine)*

George and Violet with their children and grandchildren photographed on 25th March 1950 on the occasion of Bill and Kath's wedding. George's children standing are, from left to right – George Jnr, Ken, Joan Pymm, Bill, Ron. The two grandchildren are Roger Pine, with Violet and John Pine, sat on George's lap. *(Ken Pine)*

6pm I did go across the road and wait for the bus to Bristol, and if the driver knew me he would stop and have a chat.

It was getting on time for me to have my discharge and I had to go and see the Medical Orderly for examination and investigation. When I told him what I was doing at the Club, he suggested writing to the firm and that is how I got my job in the School of Instruction for Drivers and Conductors, as an Office Clerk. It was just up my alley, marvel, and I was there for seven years.

This was just right for me, for I soon learnt the ropes of the office work and my job at first was cleaning the office. It looked more like a junk stores than an office, the stuff they had in there. This was at Lawrence Hill Depot and there was paint shops, carpenter shop, electric shop, all for bus repairs. Through the Chief Instructor, G A Downes, I could get anything done. Cleared all the rubbish out and had a store room made outside. Had the rotten coconut mat out, an immense big thing, replaced by thick lino that they did use for the bus floors, and painted inside and

out, all done by the Central Repairs at the Berkeley Street end of the big yard. Our office was in a corner of the coach shed where they used to bed down for the night and get cleaned. I made that office look like a palace after a time, and then I started on the outside of the office. A certain amount of space was allotted to us and was marked off by a four-inch white line on the surrounds. I got to work on them and cleaned off all the grease with petrol. Over to the paint shop with a chit signed by the boss. Gallon of white paint and a three inch brush. When the boss came in off one of his examining jobs, he saw it. "Well done, George".

When I was working outside I had to keep my mind on the phone ringing, because there was calls from the branches – Swindon, Cheltenham, Stroud, Gloucester, Bath, Weston, Highbridge. They used to have a boy there before me, and those young lads were not trustworthy, and were often away from the office when the phone went. Our switchboard was at the Berkeley Street entrance. I got the hang of the phone OK. Pencil and paper always ready and pick the phone up left hand, pencil with the right to put down messages.

Time of starting was 8.30pm and often I was home by 4pm. Inspector would say, I am not going out no more, so you can shove off home. The easiest job I had on the Tramways Company, and as the years went on I was never idle. We had a Remington typewriter, when they were out. I self taught and mastered him, not very swift, but I improved. Mondays were the day for that, when the new arrivals came in. Drivers and conductors, the names of these were submitted by Head Office on the Saturday previous. That was what we always waited for, a bit close at times, for we closed down 12.30pm Saturdays.

Charley was full of praise for me and if he heard one of the instructors trying to take the Mickey out of me, he was down on them and he could let it go. The

Trainee female drivers with Chief Instructor G A Downes (far right) and Assistant Instructor. *(Bristol Record Office)*

School staff was one Chief Instructor, one Assistant Chief Instructor, one Inspector, five Instructors, five double-deck learner buses, and one single-deck bus used for men conductors learning to drive. This they did do in their own time. That was one of my jobs to keep a record of them and an Instructor for the preliminary drivers. Two hours a day suitable for their ordinary duty at their respective Depot. A conductor had to put in 30 hours – that would take him about six weeks. Then he would be recommended by his Instructor for full time training on the double-deck buses that usually took two weeks. Of course it is all different now, new gadgets for training.

When new men make application for driving or conducting they have to fill in a Public Service Vehicle form and there are some very tricky questions. They were given to them at Head Office on the Saturday and handed to us at the School, Monday. Drivers' ordinary licence, no more than three endorsements, and they won't employ a man that had been to prison. I looked through a form one day and found one man had done four years for manslaughter. I explained the rule to him, he told me it was not his fault, but I had

A single-deck Learner Bus outside the Bush Warehouse in Prince Street in the 1950s. *(Peter Davey Collection)*

How 'Omnibus' the BT&CC's staff magazine characterised the relationship between Instructors and learner bus drivers. *(Bristol Record Office)*

to refer him back to Administration. Send him down at once. So he was taken down to the Head Office and was not engaged. I felt sorry for him.

Then the conductors that had been turned down by the Chief Examiner after doing 30 hours preliminary training, then two weeks full time training. Failed. Send back to their Depot to carry on

conducting. Perhaps have another go later on. Start all over again.

Conductors, well there was hardly any failures. They had a week's training. Mon, Tues school, Wed out on the road with another conductor at the Depot they were going, Thurs some country service, Friday School, Saturday town, passed out, then on their own. Of course, with the machines now it is a lot easier. When I left the company there were only six roller ticket machines in operation and they used them on the queues going home from work during the rush hours. Well, I had got on fairly well at the office. Chief Instructor G A Downes was promoted to Chief Inspector at the Centre Office. Assistant Instructor Watts was promoted in his place, so that made one less at the school. More work for me but I was fairly well established in to the office work. Any queries on the phone, make a note, tell them Mr Watts would give them a ring.

As I was still on Lawrence Hill Traffic books and they wanted me over there so that the school office did all for a shilling a week rise. Mark you, I enjoyed it, and it was coming on time for me to finish.

In April 1954 I had a spell in Southmead Hospital. I was in there a month. In the same ward was Tony Cook the Bristol City goalkeeper in the bed opposite me. He was in for an operation for appendix. Mine was a major operation – water trouble. The City footballers used to come in to see him and on his locker was a big fancy basket with a tall handle with the red and white colours of the Bristol City Football Club. He knew me right from the time he was a schoolboy for he lived down one of the side turnings at Durdham Downs. I used to pull his leg about the City and the Rovers, and it was at the time that Geoff Bradford was about to make his comeback.

He was a very popular player with the Rovers; local product and an international. He was seriously injured in a game against Plymouth, the full back deliberately fouled him and it was so bad that it was said his footballing days were over for he was in hospital for a long time. This comeback day in April was against Stoke and I am not certain but it was timed for an evening game, and we all had our headphones on, listen to the game on the special wire for the hospital relayed from the Rovers ground, it was very exciting for the Rovers ran out winners, 3 goals to 2 and Geoff Bradford scored all three. What a comeback! He played some good games for the Rovers after, though still good, was never the same.

I saw him a few times but both his legs were always supported with knee pads or caps. I used to go over with the boys until the excitement got too much for me and I had to cry off. Joan used to forfeit her stand pass and I went with Ron, her husband, but as soon as the game finished and I started to come home the pain started in my chest. I had no white tablets to put under my tongue in those days.

Now back to the Hospital. Tony Cook was discharged before me and eventually I got mine, and there was nothing military about it, thank God – for I wanted to forget all about that.

Mr Watts was very glad to see me back at the office and I soon got used to the old routine. They had an Inspector in whilst I was away and in 1956, two years later, I retired from the Bristol Tramways and Carriage Company.

Went down the Records Office, told them, they said I could leave the day I was 65, on a Wednesday. They never wanted me to leave. I was told I could stay on as long as I liked at the Instruction School. But I had quite a long chat with mother and asked her if she could manage to live on Retirement and Army Pension. She left it to me and I finished. To be my own boss, at home doing the chores, getting housemaid's knees, and mother was able to relax her crippled legs.

Well they gave me a good send off from the school. Chief, two Inspectors, six Instructors, glasses,

George and John Pine in the back garden of 89 Bellevue Road in around 1954. *(Eileen Pine)*

bottles of champagne. Drank my health. Chief made a little speech. I responded, a bit emotional. Handed me a packet, £5, and one sent up from the Centre Office. This was after the dinner hour. Staff went back to their jobs and one single-deck bus was waiting to take me home to 89 Bellevue Road. So that was that.

Now to start a life of retirement...

Author's Notes

Ministry of Pensions

Throughout his life, George was never afraid to do battle with officialdom. He was fiercely determined to do the best he possibly could for himself and his family and the Civil Servants from the Ministry of Pensions (MOP) were used to receiving regular letters from him. He was keen to ensure the maintenance of the allowances he received for his bravery award and for his First World War injuries that left him permanently disabled.

With occasional breakdowns that required spells at places like Barrow Gurney near Bristol and Headington near Oxford, George continued to suffer psychologically as well as physically from his part in the First World War.

No wonder then that George was a regular client of the MOP.

One of the many letters George received from the MOP between 1948 and 1952. *(Edith's Trunk)*

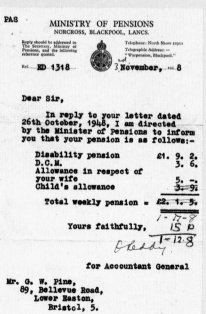

Banter on the Buses

Omnibus, the monthly staff magazine of the Bristol Tramways & Carriage Company started in the mid 1940s. It contained the typical mix of serious and humorous articles and included sports and social news from the various company depots. There appeared to be a tremendous amount of camaraderie and friendly banter among the employees who, judging by the quality of sketches submitted by employees from the various depots, were quite adept at recounting every day scenes and experiences.

Although George's retirement after 36 years of service didn't apparently warrant a mention in either the November or December 1956 editions of *Omnibus*, he would have been amused at the regular contributions portraying the life of a BT&CC Conductor. His close colleagues however, were extremely appreciative of the work he did for the company and they conveyed their feelings in messages on his retirement.

"HURRY ALONG TH — ER — AHEM! TAKE YOUR TIME MISS"

The Bristol Tramways & Carriage Co., Ltd.

DEPARTMENTAL CORRESPONDENCE.

From

The Motor Instruction School.

To

Mr. G.W. PINE

Ref................

Ref................

Date........8th November, 1956.

TO OUR FRIEND GEORGE.

WE, YOUR COLLEAGUES OF THE BRISTOL TRAMWAYS SCHOOL
WISH TO TELL YOU, ON PARTING, HOW MUCH WE HAVE APPRECIATED
YOUR ALWAYS READY HELP AND NEVER-FAILING CHEERFULNESS.
WE ARE VERY SORRY YOU ARE OLD ENOUGH TO LEAVE US.
AND WE SHALL MISS YOU VERY MUCH.
A SMALL PRESENT IS ENCLOSED AND WE WISH YOU, OLD
FRIEND, AND YOUR WIFE, A LONG AND HAPPY RETIREMENT.

A. Bevan
W. J. Ball.
E. Rennolds
W. Tovey
A.W. Watts
R. Yates Parne
N. Weeks
W. F. Watts.

Messages from friends and colleagues in the Motor Instruction School and the Records Department when George retired on 8th November 1956. They clearly thought a lot of him

To: George PINE on his retirement.

A very small but nevertheless greatly sincere token
of thanks for the unfailing courtesy, efficiency,
effort and good humour always extended to us in the
course of our long liaison with him at the School.

Good Health and all happiness.

From: His Friends in the Records Department.

Messrs: Braund, Drew, Emery,
Hyde, Jordan, Mills,
Steeds and Stoneman.

8th November 1956.

Chapter 13
The Last Word
1956–1972

Now to start a life of retirement… George started writing his life story when he was 80 and, sadly, just a few words after reaching this point he died suddenly and left his recollections incomplete. He had finished writing about his working life and when he died, it was as though he was taking a momentary pause before writing about more relaxing times.

After the struggle he had endured throughout his life George was entitled to some rest and relaxation. However, being an old soldier from the First World War he was not about to sit idly by. 'Mother', with her leg problems, was becoming less mobile and required regular visits to Frenchay Hospital. George re-arranged the house to make the accommodation more manageable – moving the bedroom downstairs so everything Violet needed was on the ground floor.

George having a dance with the Warden at Greystoke Elderly Persons' Home.
(Andy Pine)

George soon got into the swing of domestic life and was always first up in the morning. Kettle on and a brew, with cups of tea and a few biscuits. Then he got stuck into the chores. Even though they were not used, he cleaned the upstairs bedrooms once a week and he had a system of working – living room, long passage, back kitchen, and back yard with plenty of disinfectant. Next chore was breakfast and once that had been cleared away, he made sure Violet was comfortable and ready to receive her regular visitors – and couldn't they natter!

After lunch had been prepared and cleared away it was time for George to have a well deserved cat nap. He'd then posh himself up, have a light tea, read the paper and put Violet's favourites on the radio – Tommy Handley, The Archers and Much Binding In The Marsh. If she was able, Violet went along to the local to chat with her regulars and have a drink.

George could always find something to do, and he spent a lot of time in the garden getting it

George and Violet in their back garden, shortly after he retired from the BT&CC. *(Ken Pine)*

Bellevue Road in the 1960s showing the type of house George and Violet lived in. Their house was opposite this rank of houses. *(Veronica Smith)*

shipshape again. He got the landlord to make a few improvements to the house by putting in a water tap for the back garden that was separate from the neighbour's and by enlarging the back kitchen to include a proper sink.

He got stuck into the washing on Wednesdays and hung it out and hoped for the best, for a quick dry. Friday was ironing day but he couldn't get on with that very well. Violet used to do it sometimes, if she felt well enough, but had to do it sat down. A neighbour used to come in to give Violet a hand to mangle and hang out the washing, and it was a breather for George as he was also doing the other errands and preparing the meals.

Away from domestic chores, George and Violet used to stay at Bill and Kath's house in Frenchay for a week towards the end of the year. George wasn't keen on attending Old Comrade Association functions – they weren't for him – but he attended any relevant ceremony where he could pay his respects to his fallen colleagues. On 29th March 1958, he was proud to wear his War medals at a ceremony to mark the granting of the Freedom of the City and County of Bristol to the Gloucestershire Regiment.

Back in Easton, 89 Bellevue Road was not in the best of condition and the roof was barely rainproof. George was sure that one day, when the double decker buses passed the house at 5.30 in the morning on their way to Patchway and Filton, he would find the bed sliding out of the window. He often said that the old house was only held together by a mystery.

John Pine had very fond memories of his Gran and Grampher's house and the welcome that awaited family and friends…

"I remember the front door was always open to the street both metaphorically and literally so that anyone could walk in at any time of the day. I never remember the front door closed, although I am sure it must have been sometimes (perhaps even locked at

Ian St. John and Roger Hunt start to celebrate Hills' own goal in the last first team match that George watched. *(Mike Jay Collection)*

night). There was always a cheery welcome from Gran and Grampher. Gran would, more often than not, be sitting in her comfy chair in the small front room, legs heavily bandaged and Grampher waiting on her every need.

Looking back now I am sure that they were not very well off, but everyone was always welcome and well fed. Gran and Grampher Pine's house was where I first tasted bread and lard, and bread and margarine with sugar, which, as a child, I loved. I was always fascinated by the garden with the outside loo, in which Grampher grew chrysanthemums. He was very proud of his ability to produce such large blooms from his small garden.

I recall Christmas Eve with all of the extended family at Bellevue Road. This was the start of our Christmas. At first there would be the excited conversations and then Grampher Pine would be playing his accordion. Who would have guessed that he was still suffering from injuries inflicted so many years before and still had shrapnel inside him.

Away from the house, I remember going to the Bristol Rovers Ground, Eastville with Grampher and his five children and their other halves to watch Geoff Bradford, Vic Lamden, Bill Roost, Harry Bamford and co. I remember the smell of the gas from the gas works and the thrill of being lifted over the turnstiles. We always stood in the enclosure and Grampher

would make sure that I was passed down to the front so that I could see my hero Peter Hooper and cheer on Bristol Rovers."

The last first-team game that George saw was the home match against Liverpool on 19th August 1961. Rovers lost 2-0 and Liverpool included Ian St John and Ron Yeats who were making their debuts in the game. Liverpool went on to win the Second Division title that season and Rovers were relegated.

George saw a few reserve games afterwards – these were a lot quieter for him – but he eventually had to give it up through poor health. When the first team was playing at home, all the family called in. Cup of tea and biscuits and they told George all about the match and it was quite a crowd for an hour or so.

On 10th June 1966, George and Violet moved from 89 Bellevue Road – their home for 50 years – to a Prefab at 68 Nuthatch Drive, Frenchay. As well as the house being on its last legs and due for demolition as part of the redevelopment of Easton, George and Violet needed more suitable accommodation.

Early in 1967, George arranged the use of a Home Help for the first time as he and Violet

George and Violet's 50th Wedding Anniversary was reported in the Bristol Evening Post on 10th June 1966. *(Ken Pine)*

Mr. and Mrs. G. Pine

GOLDEN DAY FOR EX-C.S.M.

The only survivor of the four Pine brothers who went to war in 1914 celebrates his golden wedding today.

He is 74-year-old Mr. George Pine, of 68, Nuthatch Drive, Frenchay.

Two of the brothers were killed.

Mr. Pine's elder brother, Harry, won the French Croix de Guerre, and George won the Distinguished Conduct Medal.

Mr. Pine won the D.C.M. in 1918, at Merville with the 12th Glosters, when all the officers were killed and he took command of the company.

WOUNDED

Mr. Pine, who joined the Glosters in 1908 as a bugle boy, was honourably discharged in 1919 with the rank of company sergeant major.

He was wounded three times—the last one a head wound serious enough to bring to an end his Army career.

Mr. Pine and his wife Edith (72) were married in 1916, when he was on leave from France.

They have just moved from 89, Bellevue Road, Easton, which had been their home all their married life.

They have four sons, "all of whom have worn the Queen's uniform," one daughter and 10 grandchildren.

Mr. Pine retired from Bristol Omnibus Company 10 years ago after 36 years' service.

George in Frenchay Hospital in the early 1970's – enjoying a visit by a caring neighbour. *(Ken Pine)*

George enjoying a toast with two of his lady friends at Greystoke Elderly Persons' Home, Southmead. *(Andy Pine)*

continued to manage their ageing years as best they could. However, Violet's health continued to deteriorate and at the age of 73, she passed away at Frenchay Hospital on 29th November 1967. With the assistance of a Home Help, George managed to stay on his own until August 1968, but eventually moved from Nuthatch Drive to live with his daughter Joan Pymm at Robertson Road, Eastville for two years. He also spent a while living with his son Ken and daughter-in-law, Shirley at their home in Whitehall.

George continued to suffer from the effects of his First World War injuries and he was a regular at Frenchay Hospital where he often needed a procedure carried out on his back. His last visit was in early 1972 where he was given a spinal injection. It brought back memories of the lumber punch he endured at the Wheatley Military Hospital that specialised in head injuries – an experience he didn't wish to be reminded of.

To become a little more independent George moved into Greystoke Elderly Persons' Home in Southmead on 17th November 1970. According to the family, his time in the Nursing Home 'was the making of him'. He enjoyed organising things and even set up and ran the library. He was very popular with the residents – particularly the female ones!

Seven months after starting to write his memoirs George passed away suddenly at the Elderly Persons' Home on 1st October 1972.

He was extremely meticulous in managing his domestic affairs and in a notebook he set out precisely what was to happen when he died. He rarely threw documents away and he stored over 100 items in an old trunk that used to belong to his sister, Edith. Other treasured objects like his War Medals, were squirreled away in his Contents Box.

Without his 44,000 word manuscript, his notebook, the contents of Edith's Trunk and the objects contained in his Contents Box the story of George Pine, DCM could not have been told.

It has been an honour to help tell it.

Clive Burlton

Sister & Brothers
The Pines of Easton

Frederick Thomas Pine MM
born 1888, died 1918

In around 1903 and in an apparent effort to escape family hardship, Fred Pine left Charles Street, Easton, Bristol to stay with relatives in South Wales. According to George's memoirs he went to work in the South Wales Coal Mines, but in 1906, aged 18, he enlisted with the South Wales Borderers Regiment at Pontypool Barracks. He was the first of the Pine brothers to become a regular soldier.

He was posted to the 2nd Battalion and between 1906 and 1910 he was stationed at Tidworth, Aldershot and Chatham Barracks.

Between January 1911 and October 1912, Fred went overseas for the first time and was stationed in the Battalion's Artillery Barracks at Pretoria in South Africa. In November 1912, the Battalion left South Africa for a two-year tour of Tientsin, in Northern China. This was initially a peace station but the outbreak of the First World War was to change the relationships in this part of Asia.

In 1898, China granted Germany a 99-year lease over its colony on the Shantung Peninsula on its North East coast. The colony was a parcel of land of around 50 square miles that contained the Port of Tsingtao and the town of Kiaochau with its strategic rail links to Peking. The Germans converted the Port into a naval base as well as a popular resort city. At the time, German controlled territory also extended to a series of islands in the Pacific. Japan felt threatened by the presence of German forces and Britain was keen to curtail the German naval forces in the Pacific. So, when war broke out in Europe, Japan issued an ultimatum to Germany on 15th August 1914, demanding she turn over Tsingtao to Japanese control and calling for the removal of German warships from Chinese and Japanese waters.

With the ultimatum ignored, Japanese forces landed to the north of the Peninsula on 23rd August 1914 and began advancing on the town of Kiaochau on 2nd September 1914 – capturing it a few days later. The eight British Battalions in China at the time – including five from India – were on standby to help and on 17th September 1914 orders were given to assist the Japanese forces.

Around 1,500 British troops including Fred and the rest of the 2nd South Wales Borderers were transported by ship from Tientsin and landed to the north of the Shantung Peninsula on 23rd September 1914. In support of 23,000 Japanese troops, they arrived on the outskirts of the heavily

Postcard of himself sent to his father from Brecon on 21st June 1907. The reverse contains a simple plea… "Just a postcard to see how it gets through to you. Dear Father please let me know." *(Robin Pine)*

THE UNRIVALLED PICTURE-RECORD OF THE WORLD-WAR

The War Illustrated 2ᵈ Weekly

Tsing-tau: Allies of the East and West crush the "Mailed Fist"   No. 14

Front cover of *The War Illustrated* **from November 1914. The scene depicts the allied victory at the Port of Tsingtao in China – Fred Pine's first action in the War.** *(Author's own collection)*

defended Port of Tsingtao five days later. As George recalled, Fred was about to have his 'first bash at the Germans'. The German garrison contained only 4,000 men and although the defenders held out for around 10 weeks, Tsingtao was captured on 7th November 1914, at a cost to Fred's Battalion of 14 men killed or died of wounds or disease and two officers and 34 men wounded.

Back home, with war on the Western Front gathering momentum, there was a growing need for the return of the Regular Battalions that were on Foreign Service throughout the British Colonies. So, not long after the capture of Tsingtao, the 2nd South Wales Borderers were on their way home. The Battalion initially went to Hong Kong from where it left on the SS Delta on 4th December 1914 – arriving in Plymouth on 12th January 1915.

The next three months were spent in billets and barracks in Coventry and Rugby where the Battalion joined the 87th Brigade of the 29th Division. The other Battalions in the Brigade were the 1st King's Own Scottish Borderers, the 1st Royal Inniskilling Fusiliers and the 1st Border Battalion. These English, Scottish, Welsh and Irish Battalions formed the 'Union Brigade' as it became known. Coincidently, Tom Pine was in the same Brigade and Fred was to see his brother a few months later at Gallipoli.

Following an inspection by the King on 12th March 1915, the 29th Division made final preparations for departure for Gallipoli. On 17th March, Fred's

Battalion left Avonmouth on the SS Canada and reached Malta on the 24th March. They then arrived in Alexandria in Egypt on 29th March with the rest of the 'Mediterranean Expeditionary Force' as the troops allotted to the Gallipoli Campaign were known.

As historians have noted in hundreds of manuscripts, the Gallipoli Campaign was a disaster. A British naval bombardment of the peninsula in November 1914 – repeated in February 1915 – gave early notice to the Turks and their German allies to prepare their defences. By the time Fred Pine and the 2nd South Wales Borderers landed at 'S' Beach on 25th April 1915 there was little surprise to the attack and solid fortifications had been prepared. Consequently, progress was limited and the ground gained was minimal. In a letter home to his sister Edith, Fred mentioned that he had seen their brother Tom being transported to a hospital ship – this would have been on around 16th May 1916. In the eight months Fred's Battalion was ashore, it suffered around 430 casualties. Fred was lucky to have survived and he took part in the final evacuation of the Peninsula on 8th January 1916, from where he was sent to Egypt with the remains of the Battalion.

In March 1916 the Battalion arrived in France and its first big action was on 1st July 1916 – the opening day of the Battle of the Somme. The Battalion was involved in the attack on Beaumont Hamel and whilst advancing south of the village its leading line was mown down by machine guns in the first few minutes of the attack. The Battalion lost 66 per cent of its men with 246 killed or missing and 153 wounded. Again, Fred was lucky to have survived.

The Battalion was reformed and after periods in various parts of the line it fought at Monchy Le Preux during April and May 1917. It was quite possibly here that Fred's bravery in battle was recognised with the award of the Military Medal. Notification of his award was made in the *London Gazette* on 9th

The group wedding photograph on 15th December 1917. *(Robin Pine)*

July 1917. However, the entry does not include a citation; nor does the Battalion war diary refer to Fred by name – so the circumstances surrounding his bravery award will probably never be known.

During the summer and autumn of 1917 the Battalion fought in the Third Battle of Ypres – Passchendaele – and in November and December, it was heavily engaged near Cambrai where losses were again heavy.

Away from the Western Front, the end of December 1917 was a far happier occasion for Fred Pine and his family. Back in Bristol on leave, Fred married Amy Dinah Andrews on 15th December 1917.

However, it wasn't long before Fred was back in the thick of things. He returned to his Battalion in early January in the Boesinghe and Steenbeek areas of Belgium and on 18th January 1918, the Battalion, along with the rest of the 29th Division took over the Passchendaele sector. The recent losses were made good with new drafts of men with around 80 per cent of the Battalion being made up of inexperienced recruits. The Passchendaele sector was hardly an encouraging first experience of life in the trenches.

February 1918 was relatively quiet but things got warmer during March 1918 and Fred was witness to

an act of bravery that led to the award of a Military Cross to Second Lieutenant Seager – Fred's company commander. At around 7am on 11th March 1918 and following a heavy barrage, the Battalion was attacked by a German force estimated at 400-strong. The German barrage was not very accurate with the shells falling mostly behind the line held by Fred's company. When German troops started their advance, Second Lieutenant Seager helped to organise the defence

Fred Pine's handwritten note. *(South Wales Borderers Museum)*

by effectively directing the company's rifle and Lewis gunfire so that the attack was repelled.

When searching through the archives at the Regimental Museum in Brecon, Fred Pine's handwritten note about the attack and Second Lieutenant Seager's bravery was discovered.

Following the success in repelling the attack of 11th March, the Battalion had another week in the line and then it spent 12 days in reserve during which the men 'bathed and deloused' as the War Diary put it. On 2nd April 1918 the Battalion went back into the line again with an almost full complement of 29 officers and 887 men. It held a series of posts covering the ruins of Passchendaele – described in the history of the Battalion as 'a horrid piece of line, the ground was waterlogged, several posts were so shallow that by day it was impossible to stand up in them and the wire was very bad'. The only comfort was that the enemy was relatively quiet.

However, this was about to change for the worse. The Battalion left Passchendaele in a rush to help stem a major German offensive along the Lys Valley. Generally regarded as a 'quiet' portion of the British front line the area was used for recuperation purposes by Battalions who were thinned and exhausted by offensive operations. The depleted ranks here were full of young and inexperienced drafts that had not had the time to prepare for what was to follow. The defenders also included two Portuguese divisions, which were undermanned, lacked almost half of their officers, had very low morale and were set to be replaced the day of the German attack. Following a two-day artillery bombardment, on 9th April 1918 German forces launched their Spring Offensive. Known as the Battle of the Lys, the Fourth Battle of Ypres or the Third Battle of Flanders this was the last major German offensive of the war. With US forces arriving, the German command knew it had one last chance to

Map showing the retreat of Fred's Battalion between the 9th to 13th April 1918. From studying the Battalion's War Diary and other accounts, it appears that Fred fell somewhere between Le Petit Mortier and Le Verrier on 11th April 1918. He has no known grave. (*The History of the South Wales Borderers 1914 – 1918*)

make a decisive blow along the Western Front.

At the start of the attack, the 2nd Portuguese Division comprising 20,000 soldiers was completely overrun by the 50,000 German troops facing them. Retreating five miles and suffering around 7,000 casualties, the Portuguese withdrawal gave enormous encouragement to the advancing German forces. British troops were forced to pull back to help plug the gap and reinforcements were urgently requested.

At 1.40am on 9th April 1918, Fred Pine and the rest of his Battalion left the village of Passchendaele and were transported by train to Poperinghe. They then marched to St Janter Biezen and arrived at 6.30am. Accommodated in huts, they had little time

SPECIAL ORDER OF THE DAY
By FIELD-MARSHAL SIR DOUGLAS HAIG
K.T., G.C.B., G.C.V.O., K.C.I.E
Commander-in-Chief, British Armies in France.

D.Haig, 7.14,

To ALL RANKS OF THE BRITISH ARMY IN FRANCE AND FLANDERS.

Three weeks ago to-day the enemy began his terrific attacks against us on a fifty-mile front. His objects are to separate us from the French, to take the Channel Ports and destroy the British Army.

In spite of throwing already 106 Divisions into the battle and enduring the most reckless sacrifice of human life, he has as yet made little progress towards his goals.

We owe this to the determined fighting and self-sacrifice of our troops. Words fail me to express the admiration which I feel for the splendid resistance offered by all ranks of our Army under the most trying circumstances.

Many amongst us now are tired. To those I would say that Victory will belong to the side which holds out the longest. The French Army is moving rapidly and in great force to our support.

There is no other course open to us but to fight it out. Every position must be held to the last man: there must be no retirement. With our backs to the wall and believing in the justice of our cause each one of us must fight on to the end. The safety of our homes and the Freedom of mankind alike depend upon the conduct of each one of us at this critical moment.

D.Haig. 7.14.

General Headquarters,
Thursday, April 11th, 1918.

Commander-in-Chief,
British Armies in France.

Haig's Special Order of the Day urging British Forces to fight it out until the end. Fred obliged with his life – dying on the same day as the order was written. *(www.firstworldwar.com)*

for rest. At 2am on 10th April they were on the move again – this time by bus to Neuf Berquin to help prop up the front line that was being held very thinly by exhausted soldiers from the 40th and 50th Divisions. During the day, and now with 20 Officers and 704 ordinary ranks, including Fred, the Battalion dug-in as best it could along an unfamiliar line in front of Le Doulieu and between Le Petit Mortier and Le Trou Bayard. Its orders were to retake the town of Estaires if at all possible.

However, there was no time or opportunity to prepare for any offensive operation as at daybreak on 11th April 1918, the Germans attacked the line held by the Battalion. The very same morning, Field Marshall Sir Douglas Haig issued his famous 'Backs to the Wall' Special Order to all ranks in the British Army. For Fred and for hundreds of others, Haig's words of urging and encouragement were to fall on

dead as well as deaf ears. The German attack opened with a heavy trench mortar barrage on the line held by the exhausted troops of the depleted 40th and 50th Divisions who were just in front of Fred and his Battalion. As the German forces advanced in large numbers, the soldiers of the 40th and 50th Divisions were either overrun or by 9am, were retreating through the line held by Fred's Battalion. They retreated around 900 yards and this uncovered the flank of the 2nd South Wales Borderers.

Despite efforts to bridge the gap and resist the frontal attack on the line, the Germans could not be held up for very long. The situation was changing too fast for the Divisional Commanders or even the Brigadiers to keep abreast of it and the orders they issued were usually out of date almost before they had been given. After nearly two hours of fighting, the Germans managed to work around the Battalion's left-hand side and it was rushed from behind. The Battalion headquarters put up a desperate fight and Major Somerville, the Commanding Officer, and his men were last seen defending a trench with the Germans right round their flank and on top of them.

Quite when Fred Pine was killed on 11th April 1918 is impossible to know.

The Ploegsteert Memorial in Belgium where Fred is remembered. *(In Flanders Fields Museum, Belgium)*

Ploegsteert Mémorial Anglais (Vue de côté).

MISSING.

SERGEANT F. PINE, 2ND S.W.B.

Mr C. Pine, of 16, Charles Street, Lower Easton, writes that he has had four sons serving in the war. The youngest was killed in the Dardanelles affair. The eldest, Sergt. F. Pine, No. 9570, 2nd South Wales Borderers, has been missing since April 11, 1918, and a notification to that effect was received from the War Office. Sergt. Pine was familiarly known as "Tich"

by the men of the regiment. He won the Military Medal.

Any news concerning him will be greatly appreciated.

It is interesting to note that the other two sons, Sergeant H. Pine, Royal Engineers, was awarded the Croix de Guerre; and Company Sergt.-Major G. Pine, 12th Gloucesters, won the D.C.M., and is at present in Beaufort Hospital recovering from wounds in the head and shoulder.

Article from the Bristol Times and Mirror in January 1919 appealing for information about Fred's whereabouts. *(Ken Pine)*

Remnants of his B Company did manage to get away, though their casualties were heavy and it was only in small and disorganised groups that they managed to extricate themselves. They appear to have mostly joined up with other units and fought alongside them in a stubborn rear-guard action that was maintained for the rest of the day. By the evening, all that could be collected of Fred's Battalion was barely 150 men

and three officers – three quarters of the 2nd South Wales Borderers, including Fred, had been lost.

Reinforcements, including those from the Italian Front, arrived in time to help stop the German advance but too late to save Fred. On 12th April 1918, George Pine and the 12th Gloucesters were thrust into the defences around Nieppe Forest – just three or four miles away from where Fred died the previous day. George never knew that the area he would be fighting in for the next few months was so close to where his brother fell.

Fred was officially classed as 'missing' for some considerable time and the family even made a desperate plea through the *Bristol Times and Mirror* in January 1919 for any information about his whereabouts.

Fred has no known grave and is among 11,000 others commemorated at the Ploegsteert Memorial in Belgium. He is also remembered in Brecon Cathedral where his name and those of the 5,777 Officers and Men of the South Wales Borderers Regiment who died in the First World War are remembered.

Sadly, Fred never returned home after his wedding to Amy in December 1917 and when he died, he probably didn't know that his wife was pregnant with their child. Eleanor (Nora) Pine was born in September 1918.

In 1924, Amy married Albert Hunt who ran a grocery business in Chaplin Road in Easton, Bristol.

The daughter Fred never saw. Eleanor Pine, born five months after Fred died. *(Wendy Cross)*

Thomas Silvester Pine
born 1893, died 1915

Tom Pine had a pretty tough life – even by Victorian and Edwardian standards.

His relatively short life couldn't have got off to a worse start, with his mother dying whilst giving birth to him. George Pine thought a lot of Tom and used to look out for him as 'he could not rough it like me and I used to shield him when any trouble occurred'.

As young boys Tom and George did a lot together and George recalled many occasions where they tried to raise a few coppers to help put food on the table. When he left school in 1904, Tom worked as an assistant in the local butchers. With George in a grocery shop and Harry working in a bakery, there were always a few food treats to be brought home.

Life at home got tougher when Tom's stepmother died in 1910. From George's recollections, this appears to have been the catalyst for a good deal of family upheaval that prompted Tom and his sister Edith to leave home for good. In 1911 when he was just 17, Tom moved out, and for a while he was a boarder at the Army Recruitment Office at No. 8 Colston Street, Bristol. He lived with Army Pensioner George Cook and his wife Mary and their five children.

It was from here that Tom enlisted with the 1st Battalion Border Regiment in Carlisle in 1912 – the second of the Pine brothers to join the regular army.

He completed his training at the Regimental Depot at The Castle in Carlisle before being posted on garrison duty overseas. From George's memoirs, before he could go overseas he had to recover from a broken leg that occurred when he fell down whilst carrying a side of beef – the Regiment appears to have utilised Tom's butchery skills in his early days in the Army.

Initially posted to India, Tom arrived with the rest of the 1st Battalion in Maymyo in Burma in 1912, where he stayed until the start of the First World War.

With the war on the Western Front gathering momentum, the Battalion was recalled to England and left Maymyo on 19th November 1914. The following morning the Battalion reached the Port of Rangoon from where it boarded the P&O liner Novara bound for Calcutta. With several stops and changes of ships, Avonmouth was finally reached on 9th January 1915 – the closest Tom had been to home in Bristol in nearly four years.

On arrival, the Battalion disembarked and left by train for Rugby where the men were billeted with local people. There was little scope for training in the Midlands and so the time was taken up in receiving mobilisation equipment. Like Fred, Tom would have been inspected by King George V near Rugby on 12th March 1915. Shortly afterwards, the 1st Battalion left Avonmouth for Gallipoli on the SS Andania on 17th

March 1915. Both Tom and Fred Pine left their home Port of Avonmouth with their respective Regiments on the same day, but on different ships.

Tom's passage to Gallipoli was pretty much the same as Fred's given they were in the same 'Union Division' – the main difference was in the location of the eventual landing on the Helles Peninsula. At dusk on 24th April 1915, and from its base at Mudros Harbour on the Island of Lemnos, the 1st Battalion Border Regiment again boarded the SS Andania – this time en-route to the mainland. They were under orders to leave the ship by 6am and for those who wanted it, breakfast was served at 5am.

At daylight on 25th April 1915, a naval bombardment of the Helles Peninsula began in order to pave the way for the landings. At around 8am, Tom and the whole Battalion (about 950 strong) squeezed aboard Mine Sweeper No 6 and prepared to land. A few hundred yards from the beach they were transferred to small pinnaces and cutters and landed on 'X' Beach.

By the end of a full day of fighting, 'X' Beach was tolerably secure, but the Battalion had lost 26 officers and men killed and 85 wounded during the advance.

A few days later, the Battalion was ordered to take part in what became known as the First Battle of Krithia. Fierce fighting took place all day on 28th April 1915 with very little ground gained. There had been no reconnaissance over the ground, no

The 1st Battalion Border Regiment and their families about to leave Maymyo by train on 19th November 1914. Some of the soldiers looking in good spirits.

His Majesty King George V inspects Tom's and Fred's Regiments on 12th March 1915 near Rugby prior to them leaving for Gallipoli.

The 1st Battalion Border Regiment on board Mine Sweeper No. 6, heading for 'X' Beach on 25th April 1915. Tom Pine was somewhere among this mass of soldiers. The men are carrying full marching order equipment and extra ammunition. Many have removed their cap badges to be less of a target. *(All pictures from The Border Regiment and King's Own Royal Border Regiment Museum)*

The 1st Battalion on 'X' Beach sorting stores and equipment between 25th-28th April 1915. The firing line was at the top of the cliff. *(The Border Regiment and King's Own Royal Border Regiment Museum)*

accurate maps and no intelligence as to the strength or positions of the enemy. The attack was carried out by men who had not slept for three days or nights; had little food and no hot meal. No wonder then that by the end of the day, a further 30 officers and men had been killed and 131 wounded.

The Second Battle of Krithia took place on the 6th-8th May 1915 and was again a disastrous failure. Only 500 yards had been gained with heavy casualties. Krithia and Achi Baba, the objectives, were still in Turkish hands and remained so for the rest of the campaign. By the time Capt Le Measurier, the Commanding Officer, rejoined the Battalion from injury on 9th May 1915 it numbered just 6 officers and 350 men, compared to the 26 officers and 924 men that had landed exactly two weeks earlier.

With nearly 600 Battalion casualties in the first fortnight, Tom Pine was one of the lucky ones – but his luck wasn't to last. On 16th May 1915, whilst the Battalion's first reinforcements were coming ashore, Tom was wounded and evacuated to England. He was reported as wounded in *The Times* casualty list published on 18th May 1915.

Tom was admitted to the 1st Southern General Hospital in Birmingham and according to George's memoirs, he had been shot in the neck. It seems that Tom spent some time back home in Bristol as his father was concerned at his condition and took him to the Bristol Royal Infirmary where a bullet was removed.

Tom spent four months recovering from his wounds but was ordered to return to Gallipoli and he rejoined his Battalion in a draft of new and returning soldiers on 14th September 1915. The pressure to get him back fighting again must have been immense given the losses that were being incurred. Tom's father was not happy at his son's return as he felt he was still not fit enough as he had difficulty swallowing food.

When Tom did return, he didn't last long. Although George believed Tom was shot through the eye and killed, the Battalion War Diary is less clear. According to the official notification to his family, Tom 'died of wounds' on 20th November 1915. However, it appears that the only casualties during the week ending 20th November were caused by a catapult bomb accident at dawn on 17th November when one person was killed and two were injured. When the statistics were compiled on 20th November, casualties

Notice received by the family informing them of Tom's death. *(Ken Pine)*

HM Dongola taking on supplies and soldiers at Malta during the early stages of the War. The vessel doubled as a Hospital Ship and during the evacuation of Gallipoli, Tom was buried at sea from it. *(Author's own collection)*

for the week were listed as one killed, two died of wounds. Was Tom a victim of an allied accident? We shall never know for sure…

After visiting the Helles Peninsula himself and on receiving a gloomy report on the state of the troops, the strength of the Turkish positions and their dominance of the battlefield, Lord Kitchener finally decided on 21st November 1915 – the day after Tom's reported death – that evacuation was the only course of action. This was too late for Tom and for many others. During the evacuation Tom was buried at sea from the troopship Dongola which also doubled as a hospital ship during the Gallipoli Campaign.

Following Tom's death, the Padre of the Regiment returned his personal effects to the family. These included a Bible that Tom shared with Private J Cross who was also in 11 Platoon of 'C' Company. Both

Tom's and Private Cross's signatures are written on the inside cover. They must have been close friends and had he lived, no doubt Tom would have been pleased that despite all the odds, Private Cross survived not only the disaster on Gallipoli, but the rest of the war.

Among the pages of Tom's Bible and cut to fit within, was found the photograph of Fred Pine that appears at the top of page 177. Edith Pine is believed to have treasured both as mementos to the memory of her fallen brothers. Tom Pine and 21,000 other names are remembered at the Helles Memorial which stands on the tip of the Gallipoli Peninsula. Tom's name is also recorded in the Memorial Book in the Border Regiment's Chapel in Carlisle Cathedral.

Henry (Harry) Charles Pine Croix de Guerre
born 1889, died 1961

Like his elder brother Fred, Harry spent some time in South Wales staying with relatives. It's not clear whether he too worked in the pits, but he was certainly home in Bristol by 1910 – probably to offer support to his father, following the death of his stepmother. For a while he worked in the bakery near to his home in Bellevue Road. He left the bakery and on 21st January 1910 he signed on as a Reservist in H Company of the 3rd Reserve Battalion the Gloucestershire Regiment at Horfield Barracks where he completed six months training. His initial period of engagement as a Reservist was for six years, expiring on 20th January 1916.

In around 1911 Harry went to work for H J Packer's Chocolate Factory in Greenbank. In later years George's daughter Joan Pymm also worked for the company. The chocolate factory was an important employer in the Easton, Whitehall and surrounding areas and developed a reputation for looking after the welfare of its employees.

In 1881 Edward Packer left his job at J S Fry & Co to establish his own chocolate and cocoa manufacturing business. He set up Packer & Co at 47 Armoury Square, Stapleton Road and in 1884 he went into partnership with H J Burrows who had also worked for J S Fry – the company then changed its name to H J Packer.

The company moved its operations to Greenbank in early 1903 and continued to add manufacturing capacity at the site during the early 1900s. Although the Greenbank factory concentrated on the cheap end of the market, in 1912 Packer's formed a subsidiary company, Charles Bond Ltd, to manufacture and supply a variety of higher quality products. Also in 1912, Packer's acquired a controlling interest in Carson's Ltd, a Glasgow chocolate manufacturer which also specialised in the high-quality end of the market. In 1913 its production was moved from Scotland to a new factory built on land

Entrance to Horfield Barracks, 26th January 1906 and the register entry for 21st January 1910 when Harry signed on as a Reservist. *(Soldiers of Gloucestershire Museum)*

BRUCE COLE HOSPITAL, BRISTOL.

The Recreation Centre that was used to house The Bruce Cole Hospital for wounded soldiers during the First World War. *(Bristol Record Office)*

Harry in his Royal Engineers uniform about September 1915. This is the photograph that was attached to Harry's pigeon house in the back garden at Bellevue Road. *(Ken Pine)*

Harry looking longingly at a bottle of the amber nectar in New South Wales, Australia in the 1930s. *(Robin Pine)*

Packer's already owned at Shortwood in Mangotsfield. As George recalled, Packer's had a lovely sports ground and a good football team. In fact, Packer's won the Gloucestershire Football Association's Senior Amateur Challenge Cup in 1913/14 – the last season before the First World War.

At the outbreak of the First World War, Packer's, Charles Bond and Carson's were between them employing more then 3,000 people, and they immediately began encouraging their staff to join the armed forces – readily releasing any men of military age, including Harry Pine.

During the First World War, Packer's supplied large quantities of chocolates to the Navy & Army Canteen Board and equipped and ran the Bruce Cole Hospital for wounded soldiers – the 100 beds they provided being installed in the recreation centre in the corner of the sports field.

Being a Reservist, Harry was called up at the start of the First World War. He went across to France with the 1st Battalion Gloucestershire Regiment as part of the Expeditionary Force on 11th September 1914.

He was wounded near Le Preol on 1st February 1915 and his name was listed as wounded in the *Cheltenham Echo* on 2nd March 1915.

His injuries are not known but following his recovery, he was discharged from the 1st Gloucesters but re-enlisted with the Royal Engineers later in 1915. He was almost certainly attached to the 1st Gloucesters whom he was with when George met him on George's 'best day in France' during the war.

Harry was awarded the French Croix de Guerre and although the bravery award was notified in the London Gazette on 10th October 1918, there was no citation for why it was given. Family legend suggests that Harry fought off some Germans armed only with a shovel. Little is known about Harry's war service although he did attend with George the Reception at the Colston Hall on 15th February 1919 to honour Bristol men who had received military decorations during the war. In around 1920, Harry left Bristol for good and he

Harry (seated far left) with his Australian mates on an apparent rabbit shoot in New South Wales. *(Robin Pine)*

sought a new life in Australia. He was engaged to Lil Watkins and it is understood that she was going to join him once he got settled. She never did and it is believed that neither Lil Watkins nor Harry Pine ever married or had children.

It seems that Harry spent most of his time in the Crookwell area of New South Wales. His sister, Edith, used to write to him and a number of photographs were sent home by Harry.

According to George's recollections, Harry 'got mixed up in the war against the Japs' during the Second World War – probably in the South Pacific. The details are not known but a little more information about Harry's life down under has emerged.

For much of his time he lived in a little hut on property owned by the Storrier family at 'Loughrea', Cotta Walla – around five miles from Crookwell. He worked there digging potatoes, ring-barking trees and clearing scrub.

Terry Storrier recalls ....

"I can remember Harry, I was a young boy and he worked for my father and uncle. I was 11 when he died. He was picking up potatoes and living on our property. I remember he was slightly deaf and when *he could not understand what we said he would put his hand to his ear and say 'pep on'. I'm not really sure what this meant, but we always repeated ourselves. He often visited our house to telephone for a taxi to come and pick him up and take him to Crookwell."*

Harry was probably a 'soldier drifter' and would have been well looked after and respected by the people of Crookwell. He died on 6th January 1961 at the Royal Hotel in Crookwell. As there were stables at the back of the Hotel that the old soldiers used to sleep in when they had nowhere else to go, it's possible that old Harry Pine used to live there too from time to time.

In conveying much of this information, Julienne Belford from the Crookwell and District Historical Society said…" This information sounds a little depressing I know, but the fact is a lot of these old soldiers ended up this way and the hospitality of the Crookwell people even then and now is unbelievable… I can assure you that if Harry was a 'drifter', Crookwell would have been the place to be."

Edith Adelaide Pine
born 1885, died 1947

Edith Pine appeared to be the rock that her father and brothers relied upon to help them through troubled times. She was eight years old when her mother died and this must have had an enormous effect on her. She left school as a 14-year-old in 1899 and went straight into service.

When she returned home to help her father run the house following the death of her step-mother in 1910, she was not well treated by her half-sisters. Family relationships took a turn for the worse and she left home for good and continued her work as a general domestic servant. George was upset about how her half-sisters treated Edith and both he and Harry rued the day she left because Edith probably fussed over them and ensured they were generally looked-after.

By 1911 Edith was working for Florence and Charles Bowman (a Surgical Instrument Maker) and lived in their house at 17 Julius Road, Bishopston. An ever present in family photos she was always writing to the press about the exploits of her brothers and she remained friends with Fred's widow Amy for many years.

Little is known about where else Edith worked and she retired from service in around 1945. In a trunk, Edith kept many mementos of her brothers including Tom's Bible that was returned from Gallipoli after he was killed. In the Bible, Edith also kept a photo of Fred – the other brother killed during the First World War. Unfortunately, she didn't enjoy a long retirement as she passed away in 1947 aged 62.

The same trunk used by Edith to store family objects and photos was acquired by George for the same purpose. George never threw things away and 'Edith's Trunk' was crammed full of documents and ephemera – over 100 items in total. When George died in 1972, the trunk passed to his eldest son, 'George Jnr', who lived in Henbury, Bristol.

The trunk remained undisturbed for 30 years until 2002 when Eileen Pine 'rediscovered' it in a bedroom wardrobe. The contents of 'Edith's Trunk' have been invaluable in helping to fill in many gaps and to accurately date the various threads to George's story.

Edith (standing) with Fred's wife, Amy. *(Ken Pine)*

Edith's Trunk. *Photograph by David Emeney*